P9-CCI-476

COMPARATIVE ECONOMIC
TRANSFORMATIONS

COMPARATIVE ECONOMIC TRANSFORMATIONS

Mainland China,

Hungary,

the Soviet Union,

and Taiwan

Yu-Shan Wu

Stanford University Press
Stanford California

Stanford University Press
Stanford, California
© 1994 by the Board of Trustees of the
Leland Stanford Junior University
Printed in the United States of America

CIP data appear at the end of the book

Stanford University Press publications are
distributed exclusively by Stanford University Press
within the United States, Canada, Mexico, and Central
America; they are distributed exclusively by
Cambridge University Press throughout
the rest of the world.

Original printing 1994
Last figure below indicates year of this printing:
04 03 02 01 00 99 98 97 96 95

To my father,
Dr. Chen-Tsai Wu

Preface

T his book is a study of the industrial reform that took place in mainland China from 1984 to 1991. It employs a unique methodology. First, it uses a property rights approach to re-conceptualize the reform process. Second, it visits three historical cases for comparison with the experience of the People's Republic of China (PRC): Hungary in the 1960's and 1970's, the Soviet Union in the 1920's, and Taiwan in the 1950's and 1960's. It attempts to grasp the main features of the Chinese reform, to explain them through comparisons with historical cases, and to make predictions for the future. As such, it is a bold attempt.

The property rights approach has a focus: it differentiates between ownership and control. Only if we make this distinction do hybrid concepts such as market socialism make sense. In an attempt to reap the benefits of market while maintaining socialism, post-Mao Chinese reformers try to maintain public ownership while delegating control power—the power to make production and exchange decisions—to property users. Their strategy is one of marketization but not privatization. In practice, the Chinese reform does not always adhere to this strategy, but market socialism is indeed its main thrust. In 1982, the Twelfth Party Congress of the Chinese Communist Party (CCP) stressed the auxiliary but necessary role of market vis-à-vis plan. Five years later, the Thirteenth Party Congress adopted the formula of "the state regulates the market, the market guides the enterprises," relegating plan to a secondary position. In 1992, "socialist market economy" became the catchword at the Fourteenth Party Congress. Market was formally enshrined. However, throughout this decade of reform, socialism, understood as the dominance of public ownership, was upheld unswervingly.

This phenomenon shows that market and private property do not have to go hand in hand, a fact that leads me to investigate other economic systems based on the ownership/control dichotomy: laissez-faire capitalism (private ownership and private control), state capitalism (private ownership and state control), and command economy (state ownership and state control). How do these economic systems come about? In view of the PRC's reform experience in particular, what factors prompt a strong authoritarian regime to launch an economic transformation that leads to this or that economic system? I believe that only through a comparative and general understanding of property rights reform under a strong authoritarian regime can the mainland Chinese case be fully explored.

In undertaking such an exploration, this book offers not a detailed account of the reform process in the PRC, but a reconceptualization of it and comparisons with three historical cases. It is thus more a work in comparative institutional study than in area studies. My interest is not in uncovering new facts, but in analyzing and comparing facts that have already been presented by area specialists and economists. This book aims not only at reconceptualization, but at explanation and prediction. It includes three historical cases and one contemporary case. It is not intended as an exhaustive study of these cases, and it may not fully satisfy area specialists already familiar with them. But its emphasis is on comparativeness, not exclusiveness. I strongly believe that the Chinese experience can be best understood through comparative analysis, and that methodological exclusionism (an overemphasis on Chinese uniqueness) is a major obstacle to academic inquires in area studies. The more I learn about economic reform in comparable historical cases, the stronger this belief becomes.

This book is based on my Ph.D. dissertation for the University of California at Berkeley. It was substantially modified as it went through the review process and when the second-wave industrial reform was launched in mainland China at the end of 1991. I would like to express my most sincere gratitude to Chalmers Johnson for leading me to the field of political economy and giving me unreserved support and constant encouragement. I also thank Lowell Dittmer, who guided me in the field of Chinese politics throughout my studies at Berkeley, and who offered me valuable comments on my dissertation. I am grateful too to Laura D'Andrea Tyson, who introduced me to the literature of comparative economics and property rights and inspired me to find interesting cases for comparison across time and space. This committee allowed me to explore uncharted territory.

I would like to thank Ken Jowitt for guiding me to the field of comparative communism, Richard Buxbaum for introducing me to the legal aspects of property rights, and Harry Harding at the Brookings Institution for carefully reading two draft chapters and offering me detailed comments on them. I am also grateful to the two anonymous readers for Stanford University Press, who offered valuable comments on the first draft of the book. The bulk of the work was done while I was a research fellow at the Brookings Institution from September 1989 to August 1990. I would like to thank Brookings for the funding and other resources they generously offered.

My father, Dr. Chen-Tsai Wu, has always inspired me as an academic model and encouraged me to pursue advanced studies in my areas of interest. I am glad that I can finally show him the result of seven years of work. I also thank my wife, Hui-Chun, who made it possible for me to concentrate on my work by taking good care of her husband and our lovely and energetic daughter, Angela. Without the strong support of my family, this work would not have been completed.

Finally, the American Political Science Association gave me the greatest encouragement by granting me the 1992 Harold D. Lasswell Award for the best doctoral dissertation in the field of policy studies for the dissertation on which this book is based. I would like to thank the selection committee and the APSA for their encouragement.

An earlier version of Chapter 2 of this book, titled "Reforming the Revolution: Industrial Policy in China," was published in 1991 by Routledge in *The Pacific Review* (vol. 3, no. 3). A version of Chapter 3 was published in 1991 by the Political Science Department of National Taiwan University in *Political Science Review* (no. 3, December) under the title "Hungary and Mainland China (PRC): A Comparison of Industrial Reform." I am grateful that these two journals permitted the reproduction of the articles in this book.

Y.S.W.

Contents

Tables and Figures

A Note to the Reader

In this book, I use pinyin spellings for the Chinese names and terms associated with the PRC (for example, Deng Xiaoping) and the Wade-Giles system for those associated with the ROC (for example, Ch'en Ch'eng). In doing so, I am following the established pattern in each place.

COMPARATIVE ECONOMIC
TRANSFORMATIONS

-■-●-■-●-■-●-■-●-■-●-■-●-■-●-■-●-■-●-■-●-■-●-■-●-■-

Chapter One

Introduction

A t the time of this writing, we have witnessed the collapse of state socialism throughout Eastern Europe
and the former Soviet Union. One after another Communist party
lost power, and the nascent democratic regimes that replaced the
old party states struggled to make transformative economic reforms. Societies underwent tremendous strain as they adjusted to
the unprecedented changes brought about by the reform. As the initial exultation over political liberalization gradually evaporated and
gave way to frustration and discontent, the reform path taken by the
Chinese Communist Party (CCP), one in which economic reform
takes precedence over political reform, was hailed by some as a
more rewarding way to transform state socialism. It is appropriate,
then, for us to take a careful look at Chinese economic reform.

This can be done in two ways: by concentrating on the details of
the Chinese reform, or by putting it in perspective through comparative studies. The first approach has produced a huge literature by
able economists, political scientists, and area specialists. This
study, however, opts for the second, the comparative, approach.
Though relatively few works have compared the PRC's reform path
with other cases (Stark and Nee 1989; Van Ness 1989), the potential
for conducting in-depth analysis in this area is enormous.

Of the Leninist regimes that have existed in the world, the People's Republic of China has undergone the most radical shifts in basic policy orientation, shifts that have always startled outside observers. Ultraleftist Maoism and ultrareformist Dengism are diametrically opposite poles that verge on the definitional borders of a

Leninist system.[1] At first glance, the PRC seems to be so unique and unpredictable as to defy any general comparative or developmental statements. However, since the post-Mao reform started, more and more striking parallels can be found between the PRC and other countries. Thus, for example, comparative economists, drawing on their experience with similar reforms in Eastern Europe, are quick to point out the consequences of Deng Xiaoping's economic policies (Balassa 1987; Hare 1988). Historians, on the other hand, cannot help making a comparison between "Socialism with Chinese Characteristics" and the Soviet New Economic Policy (NEP), or between Dengism and Bukharinism (Chevrier 1988). Finally, East Asian studies scholars point to the heavy institutional borrowing so evident in this area, citing the PRC's Special Economic Zones, "golden coast," and "outward economy" as examples of latecomers' imitations of their predecessors (Goodman 1988). The East European experience, Soviet history, and the track records of the newly industrialized countries (NICs) of East Asia—South Korea, Taiwan, Hong Kong, and Singapore—appear to constitute the three major reference areas rich in comparative resources that should be exploited in a study of post-Mao reform in the PRC.

The aim of this study is to take advantage of these new opportunities for comparison and to challenge the ostensible uniqueness and unpredictability of mainland China. The objective is to put the politically motivated economic reform under Deng Xiaoping[2] in a genuinely comparative perspective, so that we can better understand it. The core questions asked are, What causes an authoritarian regime that fully controls a society to restructure its economy? and What is the relationship between these causes and the types of economic restructuring undertaken? This study focuses on post-Mao reform in the PRC, but comparable historical cases are also investigated and compared with that of the Chinese mainland in an attempt to answer these questions. At the core of the analysis, because of its intrinsic importance, is Chinese industrial reform, but agricultural reform will be brought into the picture whenever necessary. It deals with the period between 1984, when the first urban industrial reform was introduced, and 1991, when three years of retrenchment finally gave way to the second-wave reform.

An analytical framework is needed to conduct this comparative study, and there are two requirements for the framework. First, it should grasp the essence of the reform as a dramatic change of economic structure brought about by a highly autonomous and penetrating state.[3] Second, it must be capable of characterizing comparable political economies and facilitating comparisons with the PRC.[4] Based on these considerations, I use the property rights approach to analyze the process of economic reform.

Property Rights

Property rights, as enforced by the state, are a set of legal relations between people with regard to some means of production.[5] There are four aspects of this definition that need to be clarified. First, property rights are not about legal relations between the rights holder and the property, but about legal relations among people with regard to the property, because our rights of property depend fundamentally on prohibiting others from interfering with our use of the object of property (Bhalla 1984: 3). Second, property rights holders can be private persons or public institutions, such as the state. In the former case, the rights are private; in the latter, the rights are public. The notion that property rights are always private rights is unwarranted.[6] Third, the object of property in this definition is the means of production, which excludes objects such as personal possessions that cannot generate income. This is the case because in virtually all societies that we know of, one can find personal possessions that can be called private,[7] whereas it is the rights pertaining to the means of production that differentiate the economic structure of one society from another. It thus makes sense to adopt a definition that is sensitive to the major difference among property rights structures around the world. Fourth, property rights are positive rights and are enforced by the state. This is the case whether the rights are private or public. Private property rights are as dependent on the power of the state to prevent incursions by non–rights holders as are public property rights. To think of a private property rights structure as totally devoid of any role for the state is contradictory to the nature of property rights as positive rights.

The various property rights with respect to an asset (e.g., the right to use, to manage, to bequeath or transmit an asset, the right to any income generated by it, and the absence of term) are dividable, even though in particular historical contexts they coalesced into an absolute whole. In the West, the coalescent notion of property rights has its origins in Roman law, which assigned the *usus* (the right to use a thing), the *fructus* (the right to the proceeds of a thing), and the *abusus* (the right to dispose of a thing) to a single property rights holder who was allowed complete freedom in the exercise of his rights (Piettre 1973: 75). Feudal law replaced the unitary rights of Roman law with a fragmented rights structure, in effect adopting a "bundle of rights" notion of property rights. Thus, for example, the rights to a piece of land could be sliced up into various interests called estates, each of which might be held by a different person, a tradition still evident in common-law legal systems today (Simonton 1926: 285).

A revival of the Roman-law concept of absolute and coalescent property rights occurred in the seventeenth century. It accompanied the rise of a full market economy and the replacement of limited rights in land and other valuable assets by virtually unlimited rights (Macpherson 1973; Reeve 1986). The reason for this replacement is that in order to maximize the utility of an object as a property, it has to be treated as unified and cannot tolerate a variegated rights structure (Rariden 1983). Early capitalism was characterized by a large number of proprietorships, which combined the various property rights with respect to an asset in the hands of a single rights holder. Contemporary capitalism, on the other hand, has witnessed the growth of corporations, which typically separate management from ownership. Marxist socialism adopted the capitalist concept of absolute and coalescent property rights while proposing socialization of the rights structure, that is, changing the rights holders from private persons to public institutions without debundling the rights. Market socialism, as practiced in the former Yugoslavia, in Hungary, and in the PRC, decouples the *usus* from the *fructus* and the *abusus*, delegating the former to property users.

Ownership

The absolute and coalescent notion of property rights gave rise to the concept of ownership. An owner is usually understood to be the person with the most complete control possible over a thing, the *plena in re potestas*. Since property rights pertaining to an asset are often divided among different rights holders, and for certain social purposes are always limited by the state (in the United States, for example, by eminent domain), the actual content of ownership depends on its specific definitions in a given jurisprudence (Olsen 1983). It is difficult to find a common denominator for all definitions of ownership, even though certain attributes seem to stand out as the core of the concept. The right to income generated by an asset; exclusion; lack of circumscription (i.e., the embracive and residuary character); an absence of limits on the term of ownership; and transmissibility are the most prominent among these attributes.

In this study, the income definition of ownership—ownership as the right to the income from an asset—will be adopted, primarily for two reasons. First, in any commodity economy, the major purpose of owning the means of production is to generate income, which means the right to income is the essence of ownership of this type.[8] Since we will concentrate on the property rights of the means of production, the income definition of ownership serves our purpose here. Second, the income definition of ownership is the one adopted by Marxism in its criticism of all pre-socialist (except primitive communist) societies and in its concept of how a socialist system is superior to those it tries to replace. In short, Marxism proposes to abolish private property because the private owners of the means of production have the exclusive right to its income, which leads to an expropriation of the surplus value produced by laborers.[9] Socialism is superior to capitalism (or any other system plagued by private property) not only because it is an inevitable step forward in human historical development, but also because it eliminates such expropriation by placing the right to this income in the hands of the proletariat. The income definition has been built into the economic structures and official ideologies of socialist countries, and hence carries particular significance in the study of how these systems work and how they differ from other systems around the world.

As a result of this choice of definition, the terms *ownership* and *income power* will be used interchangeably. Obviously, to operationalize the definition of ownership runs the risk of deviating from the official use of the term; that is, ownership in terms of income power may not be conterminous with ownership as legally defined in a particular case. This should not deter us from adopting a fixed definition of ownership, since we cannot change our definition across case and time. There is a need, however, to point out the difference between the definition adopted for this study and the official usage when it arises. In these cases, I designate the income power holder as the de facto owner, and the natural or legal person holding the ownership title as the de jure owner.

Income Power Versus Control Power

With the divisibility of property rights in mind, we can construct a useful framework for the discussion of the distribution of property rights pertaining to the means of production. The two most important categories of property rights are *income power* (or ownership) and *control power*. Income power refers to the power to appropriate income accruing to the means of production and to dispose of it. Control power refers to the power to make production and exchange decisions, such as what to produce, how and in what quantity and quality to produce it, and with whom and on what terms to make transactions. Both income power and control power are subaggregates of property rights that can be further disintegrated and assigned to different property holders. Each of these powers has two critical variables: tenure and transmissibility. Tenure refers to the length of time for which the right is assigned to the holder. Transmissibility refers to whether the right can be transmitted to another person (natural or legal), and if so, under what conditions.

Given the various possible combinations of income power, control power, tenure, and transmissibility, there are unlimited ways in which the property rights with regard to an asset can be assigned. For example, an ordinary worker employed by a typical joint-stock company in a capitalist society does not have any property rights over the means of production he or she happens to use. The general manager of the company may have full control power and limited income power over the company assets (e.g., when he makes decisions on profit distribution), both of which are nontransmissible and subject to withdrawal by the owners of the company, the shareholders. Finally, the shareholders appropriate income accruing to the company but assign control power and limited income power to management while maintaining the power to withdraw the dele-

TABLE I

The Role of the State in Various Economic Systems

	State ownership	
State control	Yes	No
Yes	Command economy	State capitalism
No	Market socialism	Laissez-faire capitalism

gated rights. They can also transmit their property rights in different ways (e.g., on the stock market).

The codetermination laws in the former West Germany provide another example of how property rights can be divided. These raised the employees' position by putting their representatives on the board of directors, in effect granting limited property rights (both income and control power) to ordinary workers.[10] Workers in the former Yugoslavia are granted even greater property rights over enterprises because there are no shareholders' representatives on their councils. In both cases, however, the workers' property rights are fractionalized (they can exercise them only as a collective), nontransmissible, and limited to the period of employment.

The State's Role in the Economy: A Typology

Throughout the world, states have taken on the job of engineering their economies, in various blunt or subtle ways, and have been held responsible for the social as well as economic outcomes. One fruitful way of looking at the state's role in the economy is property rights analysis. Ownership and control are the two most important categories of property rights. Ideally, the state can assign property rights in four different ways. State ownership combined with state control is known as a command economy. State ownership without state control is the ideal type of market socialism. Private ownership with state control can be called state capitalism. And private ownership without state control is laissez-faire capitalism (see Table 1).

The prototype of a command economy is the Soviet Union from the 1930's to the 1980's. This model was reproduced in other socialist countries, including the People's Republic of China, which during its First Five-Year Plan period (1953–57) created an economy

patterned after that of the Soviet Union.[11] Market socialism as an
ideal-type economy was first proposed and debated during the "socialist controversy" of the 1930's.[12] With Yugoslavia making decentralized market arrangements in the early 1950's while maintaining
public ownership, market socialism was put into practice. The idea
spread through Eastern Europe as reform-minded Communist leaders and their economic advisors tried to improve the efficiency of
their economies without touching on the issue of private property.[13]
Czechoslovakia and Hungary underwent similar socialist market
reforms in the late 1960's, though the former's was undone after the
Prague Spring of 1968. Finally, the PRC joined Yugoslavia and Hungary in the late 1970's by adopting a marketizing strategy and preserving the state as dominant owner of the means of production.

State capitalism[14] refers to an economy in which private ownership is controlled by meticulous state regulation. A good example
is wartime Japan after the passage of the 1938 National Mobilization Law. As a result of the law, which put Japan's economy on a
wartime footing, company ownership rights turned out to be virtually the only civilian rights that were respected throughout the
war (C. Johnson 1982: 139). Even though it toned down the state's
administrative regulation of the market after World War II, Japan
still stands out as a singular case of strong government control combined with near absence of state ownership (Samuels 1987: 2).
Among the NICs, Taiwan and South Korea have economic institutions resembling Japan's, making them good examples of state capitalism (C. Johnson 1985).

In laissez-faire capitalism, the state restricts itself to providing
public goods and services that the economy cannot generate by itself and to safeguarding private ownership and the smooth operation of the self-regulating market. Great Britain in the nineteenth
century and the United States before the New Deal are good models
of laissez-faire capitalism. The British colony of Hong Kong, however, may serve as the best example of this economic libertarian tradition in the late twentieth century.

These four ideal types—command economy, market socialism,
state capitalism, and laissez-faire capitalism—are mutually exclusive and jointly exhaustive. They are also capable of identifying important characteristics of an economic system based on highly visi-
ble and elemental information. Thus they provide good typological

characterizations of the phenomena of interest in this study (Sartori 1976: 291; Lange and Meadwell 1985: 84).

Property Rights Theories and the Synthetic Framework

There are four important groups of property rights theories. *Normative theories* apply value judgments to manifestations of property and focus on the "ought" or the "should." Many of the great political philosophers in history expressed opinions on the "just" form of property.[15] The focus of normative theory literature is to arrive at a guiding principle or principles for assigning property rights so that justice is served. Self-preservation, a decent life for everyone, personal contribution to the market economy, acquisition of the fruits of one's own labor, conduciveness to maximum utilization of resources, and political liberty have all been proposed as such principles.

Descriptive theories are primarily legal discussions of the institution of property in a positive (i.e., nonnormative) manner. The purpose of these discussions is not to come up with certain prescriptions for assigning property rights, nor to look behind the institution of property for its social or historical origins, nor to look beyond it to ascertain its impact on society, but simply to analyze the institution as such. The issues dealt with include whether property is a single right or a bundle of rights, whether ownership is equivalent to property, and whether property refers to the legal relation between a person and a thing or between a person and other persons with regard to a thing.[16]

Developmental theories concern the factors explaining the emergence, distribution, and pattern of property relations. The most famous of these are Karl Marx's *Critique of Political Economy* and Friedrich Engels's *The Origin of the Family, Private Property, and the State*. In their theories, the institution of property is directly related to a society's stage of economic development. Thus, for Marx, property relations are but a legal expression of the relations of production that correspond to a definite stage in the development of a society's material productive forces. Developmental theories literature is usually sociological or ethnological.[17]

Finally, *impact theories* focus on the effects of particular types and patterns of property rights on individual or group behavior. The

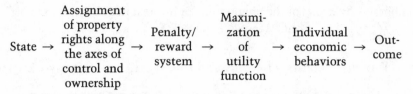

Fig. 1. The state and the impact of property rights distribution I.

literature is mainly economic. The property rights approach in comparative economics provides the most important studies in this area. The central issue of the property rights approach is to ascertain the causal connections between different property rights assignments and the performance of the system (D. North 1981). It is argued that individuals respond to economic incentives and disincentives provided by the penalty/reward system, which in turn is defined by the scope and content of property rights assignments (Furubotn and Pejovich 1973). Individual economic behaviors are characterized by rational maximization of the utility function under the property rights structure, and the interactions of these individual behaviors produce various economic outcomes. With certain aims in mind, the ruling elite can and do direct individual behaviors toward elite goals. Even though it is not always assumed that the state possesses a high degree of economic rationality (D. North 1981), the function of the state in assigning property rights and manipulating the economy is widely emphasized (Furubotn and Pejovich 1973; Pryor 1973; D. North 1981).

Because this study is primarily concerned with empirical and institutional investigation, the normative approach is of little relevance here. The insights provided by the legal analysis used in the descriptive theories approach have been incorporated into the conceptual framework of this study (the definition of property rights, their divisibility, the ownership issue, income power versus control power, etc.). Developmental theories mainly take a bottom-up approach, emphasizing social factors in explaining property structure and neglecting the role played by the state. Impact theories, however, particularly the property rights approach in comparative economics, provide a valuable tool for comprehending the outcomes of property rights assignments. By connecting the typology of the state's role in the economy with the property rights approach, we arrive at the chain of relations in Figure 1.

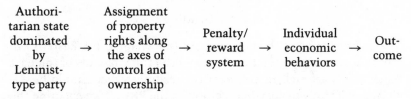

Fig. 2. The state and the impact of property rights distribution II.

After constructing an analytical framework, we are in a position to look for empirical cases that render meaningful comparisons with the PRC. We must first decide on a basis for comparison. What political economies are appropriate subjects for the kind of comparative study we are interested in? What is the common thread that runs through all the cases in our comparative scheme? These questions are methodologically important, because if we can hold certain characteristics constant across cases, variations among the cases can then be linked with other, variable characteristics (Lijphart 1971: 687).

In this study, I will compare the PRC only to political economies with a centralized authoritarian political system[18] dominated by a highly disciplined Leninist-type party. Thus Yugoslavia, a good case for market socialism, does not qualify for this discussion because of its federal structure and that structure's impact on the League of Yugoslav Communists. Japan, a democracy, does not meet the criteria of state capitalism; nor does South Korea, a country dominated by military regimes. Also eliminated from the list is Hong Kong, because even though it has been under Britain's authoritarian rule, that rule is not characterized by the domination of a Leninist-type party (a situation that may change after 1997). By focusing on authoritarian states dominated by Leninist-type parties, we arrive at the chain of relationships illustrated in Figure 2.

This analytical framework satisfies the requirements set at the beginning of this chapter. It emphasizes the role of a highly autonomous and penetrating state in deciding the economic structure of a society. It is also genuinely comparative and facilitates intersystem comparisons with the PRC (witness the separation between ownership and control and the typology of the state's role in the economy). Equipped with this analytical framework, we can start looking for empirical cases that shed light on the economic reform in mainland China.

Case Studies

As mentioned at the beginning of this chapter, the Eastern European experience, Soviet history, and the track records of the East Asian NICs are rich in comparative resources that should be exploited in a study of post-Mao reform in the PRC. If we examine the histories of these areas within the analytical framework we have constructed, three historical cases stand out as offering the greatest potential for making comparisons with the PRC in the area of restructuring industrial property rights: Hungary in the late 1960's and the 1970's, the Soviet Union in the late 1920's, and the Republic of China (ROC) in Taiwan in the 1950's and early 1960's.

There are four major reasons for making these choices. First, these three and the mainland Chinese case were all characterized by an authoritarian political system exclusively controlled by a Leninist-type party: the Hungarian Socialist Workers' Party (HSWP) under Janos Kadar, the Communist Party of the Soviet Union (CPSU) under Joseph Stalin, the Kuomintang (KMT) under Chiang Kai-shek, and the CCP under Deng Xiaoping. This meant that maximum state autonomy and state capacity were assured, and the political elite enjoyed great leeway in assigning property rights.[19]

Second, each had experienced a major liberal institutional change in agriculture before making the critical decision to reform its property rights structure. In Hungary, it was a marketizing reform in agriculture that followed the completion of the recollectivization drive of the 1960's. In the Soviet Union, it was the shift from requisitioning under War Communism (*voennyi kommunizm*) to a single tax in kind under the New Economic Policy. In Taiwan, it was the "land-to-the-tiller" reform of the 1950's. In the PRC, similar changes were made in agriculture under the household responsibility system. The causes of these agricultural reforms are similar: the desperate desire of the elite to boost regime legitimacy by radically changing property rights structures in order to motivate peasants to increase food production in the aftermath of a major national disaster. The suppression of the 1956 popular uprising and the recollectivization campaign in Hungary, the catastrophic civil war and War Communism in the Soviet Union, and the effects of land reform in mainland China and the quashing of a serious local rebellion in Taiwan forced the ruling elite in each country to take

TABLE 2
The Role of the State: Case Studies

State control	State ownership	
	Yes	No
Yes	Soviet Union	ROC
No	Hungary	—

drastic measures to assure that the most basic needs of the population were met. This was also the case in the PRC, which introduced agricultural reform in the aftermath of the disastrous Cultural Revolution decade.

Third, in all three cases—as in the PRC—the industrial sector was dominated by the state. The highly concentrated state enterprises in Hungary, the "commanding heights" in the Soviet Union, and the corporations established by the Japanese and taken over by the KMT state in Taiwan all dwarfed the private elements in those countries.

Fourth, despite their structural similarities, these countries opted for entirely different paths of development at critical historical junctures. Hungary moved into market socialism (state ownership and marketization) under the New Economic Mechanism (NEM) and remained in this property rights structure, with some fluctuations, during the 1970's. The Soviet Union launched an industrialization cum collectivization drive at the end of the 1920's and installed a command economy (state ownership and state control). Taiwan initiated and deepened state capitalism (privatization and state control) in the 1950's and early 1960's, as the island economy went through primary import substitution and export expansion.[20]

If we array the three comparison cases according to whether or not they feature state ownership and state control, the result is Table 2. The lower right position—no state ownership and no state control—remains empty, because in the empirical world, there is no historical or current case of a state combining laissez-faire capitalism with an authoritarian political system dominated by a Leninist-type party. There is a possibility we will see one in the future—Hong Kong after 1997—but even that is highly questionable.

To treat Hungary, the Soviet Union, and Taiwan as representa-

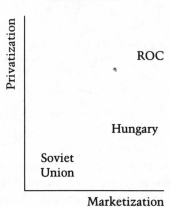

Fig. 3. Privatization and marketization: relative post-reform positions of the Soviet Union, ROC, and Hungary.

tive cases of market socialism, command economy, and state capitalism does not mean these empirical cases are perfect reflections of the three ideal types. There will inevitably be some distance between real-world cases and ideal forms. In Hungary during the late 1960's and the 1970's, there was still some state control, and state ownership was not complete; in Taiwan, state enterprises were not insignificant, and state control was by no means complete. In fact, in order to create a more realistic picture, we can treat state ownership and state control as continuous, instead of dichotomous, variables. In Figure 3, the privatization axis shows decreasing state ownership, and the marketization axis represents diminishing state control.

Clearly, when we talk about property rights restructuring, we mean the *direction* of economic reform: is marketization much more pronounced than privatization (a trend toward market socialism), privatization more pronounced than marketization (a trend toward state capitalism), or are the two of roughly equal importance (a trend toward capitalism)? Since it is the direction of reform that concerns us most, rather than the exact positional points of the system in question at any particular time, we may find, for example, that a socialist economy that has experienced market reform (see Hungary's position in Fig. 3) is still less marketized than a state capitalist economy whose reform path was mainly along the axis of privatization (see Taiwan's position in Fig. 3).

That said, and knowing full well that one should treat with caution the possible deviation of the cases from the ideal concepts, in the following discussion I will stick to the original typology and treat the three cases as representative of the ideal types. I adopt this methodological strategy because the typology is powerful in identifying the characterizing attributes and dominant features of the political economies dealt with, and its analytical benefits more than offset the possible costs, which can always be minimized by pointing out specific differences between the cases and the ideal types as they arise in the discussion.

The original structural similarities among the three cases and the subsequent divergence of their development lead us to the crucial factors underlying each regime's decisions at the critical juncture. The authoritarian nature of the regime and the state's role in the economy at the time the critical decisions were made were clearly not among the crucial factors, since these structural traits were common to all three cases. The relation between the property rights structure created as a result of the regime's critical decisions and its underlying factors is illuminating in the case of the PRC, which shares the same original similarities with the three cases and has thus far opted for a property rights structure that is closest to Hungary's, but nevertheless has the potential to develop into a structure like that of the Soviet Union or Taiwan. For the PRC, the Hungarian road leads to sustained market socialism, the Soviet model stands for restoration of the command economy, and the Taiwan experience suggests privatizing industry by encouraging the emergence of private enterprise. The factors that were critical in the three historical cases will be identified and examined in the context of recent economic reform in mainland China, both to gain insight into the reform process and to provide a comparative perspective for the discussion of the future of the reform.

Chapter 2 analyzes industrial reform in the PRC from 1984 to 1991 as an independent case, drawing on the concepts of property rights without making comparisons. The purpose of the chapter is to establish empirical and analytical bases for the comparisons that follow; therefore, no detailed account of the reform is provided, but the main features of the stages in the reform process are captured through property rights analysis. The Chinese case is then presented in a format readily comparable with the three historical cases. It is the assumption of this study that the configuration of the Chinese reform will be thrown into relief when compared with structurally similar cases with different outcomes (i.e., when studied through controlled comparisons). Hence the burden of analyzing the Chinese reform is shared by the single-case study in Chapter 2 and the three comparison studies in the chapters that follow it.

In Chapters 3 through 5, the Hungarian, Soviet, and ROC experiences are juxtaposed with that of the PRC, with the crucial factors underlying the regimes' historical decisions to restructure their economies both identified and examined in the context of the PRC reform. Emphasis is placed on the values and perceptions of the elite, and the role these values and perceptions played in property rights assignment. The comparison between Hungary and the PRC concentrates on the developmental trajectory the two countries have shared thus far, whereas the chapters on the Soviet Union and Taiwan focus on the critical decisions themselves, emphasizing explanations for the divergence between the two cases and the PRC, but also exploring the possibility of convergence under certain conditions.

Chapter 6 provides a general framework linking the conclusions of the foregoing chapters. Here the similarities and differences among the four cases are summarized in terms of property rights, and the explanations for their divergence presented. An authoritarian political system, prior upheaval or a traumatic event, economy in command, liberal agricultural reform, and state dominance in industry are the outstanding similarities across the four cases. Their later divergence into market socialism (Hungary and the PRC), command economy (the Soviet Union) and state capitalism (Taiwan) is then attributed to the impact of agricultural reform, ideological constraints, a security threat and/or preparation for war, and international economic pressure. Finally, the future of PRC economic reform in the 1990's is discussed in terms of the variables that prove historically significant in all four cases.

Chapter Two

Industrial Reform in the PRC

E conomic reform in the People's Republic of China has
entered its second decade. After an initially successful
agricultural reform and a promising open-door policy, the regime introduced industrial reform to urban areas in 1984, with mixed results.[1] Four years after its introduction, the industrial reform was
halted in a major retreat announced in late 1988. The political regimentation following the Tiananmen incident in June 1989 imposed
further constraints on the reformers, who had to deal with both
thorny economic issues and political survival. After three years of
retrenchment (1988–91), economic reform was relaunched at the
end of 1991, with the regime under great financial pressure because
of its subsidizing of inefficient state enterprises. These enterprises
thus became the major target of the PRC's second-wave industrial
reform.

   In this chapter the property rights approach is applied to Chinese industrial reform from 1984 to 1991. Property rights are a set
of legal relations between people with regard to some means of production (e.g., the right to use, bequeath, or transmit it, and the right
to any income from it, without term limitations). There are two important categories of property rights that deserve particular attention: ownership and control. Ownership refers to the power to appropriate and dispose of income generated by a means of production.[2] In this chapter, the terms "ownership" and "income power"
are used interchangeably. Control refers to the power to make decisions regarding production (e.g., what to produce, in what quality
and quantity, and how to produce it) and exchange (e.g., with whom
to make transactions, and on what terms).

TABLE 3
Economic Efficiency and Property Rights

	Category A	Category B	Category C	Category D
Requirement for maximizing economic efficiency	Sufficient linkage between users' personal rewards and the retained profits of economic units	Sufficient linkage between retained profits and net profits realized through units' behavior on the market	Economic units capable of gearing production and exchange decisions to price signals from the market	Perfect competition with prices reflective of relative scarcities
Cumulative outcome	Users act as retained profit maximizers	Users act as net profit maximizers	Users act as net profit maximizers by responding dynamically to price signals from the market	Users act as net profit maximizers by responding dynamically to price signals from the market that reflect relative scarcities
Prescription for assigning property rights	Privatization: transfer to users the (income) power to distribute retained profit	Privatization: transfer to users the (income) power to retain net profits; harden budget constraint	Marketization: transfer to users the (control) power to make production and exchange decisions	Marketization: transfer to users the (control) power to make decisions on prices

In socialist economic reforms, the transfer of income power to property users is called privatization, while the transfer of control power to users is called marketization. Privatization has two distinctive goals: to link personal rewards of property users (promotions, wage increases, bonuses, etc.) with the retained profit of the economic unit, and to link the retained profit with the net profit realized through the unit's behavior in the market. Two policy goals are also discernible in marketization: to make economic units capable of making autonomous decisions on production and exchange in response to price signals, and to make prices reflective of relative scarcities. (In Table 3, the four policy goals are designated as categories A, B, C, and D, and they are referred to as such in the following discussion.) The purpose of privatization is to increase motivational efficiency, and the purpose of marketization is to increase allocative efficiency, both of which are conspicuously lacking in, a command economy.

Unlike agricultural reform, which culminated in a unitary household responsibility system, post-Mao industrial reform has resulted in a variegated property rights structure. Phenomena of both marketization and privatization can be found in the reform, which has emphasized these two directions alternately since 1984. Although the fundamental principle of the economic reform— namely, decentralization of property rights—was established at the very beginning, the actual forms that this principle had to take evolved only as the reform experiments went on. This phenomenon is called "groping for stones to step on while wading across the river" (*mozhe shitou guohe*), and it has injected a heavy dose of uncertainty and volatility into the reform process (Tang 1988).

The October 1984 Decision on Reform of the Economic Structure ushered in a whole package of urban-industrial reforms built on the momentum of the hitherto successful agricultural transformation. The initial thrust was toward establishing a socialist market with only marginal privatization. An overheated economy ensued in 1985. In 1986, the regime adopted contractive policies and shifted its focus to the reform of ownership (*suoyouzhi gaige*). The year 1987 witnessed the downfall of Secretary-General Hu Yaobang, the campaign against bourgeois liberalization, and the ultimate triumph of the reformers at the Thirteenth Party Congress in November. "The primary stage of socialism" was put forward as an ideological justification for unorthodox reform measures. At the beginning of 1988, Premier Zhao Ziyang introduced with much fanfare the strategy of the "outward economy" (*waixiangxing jingji*), aimed at enlarging the capitalist enclaves on China's east coast and plunging these areas into the "grand international circulation."[3] In May, the reform pendulum swung back to marketization and an urban price reform was announced. Inflation accelerated at an unprecedented rate. The reformers were forced to give in to pressure from urban residents and conservatives. The Beidaihe meeting and the following Third Plenum of the Thirteenth Central Committee in September registered a major retreat from the four-year urban reform by shifting national attention to countering inflation and combating profiteering (*zhili zhengdun*).

From that time on, and especially after the Tiananmen incident in June 1989, the PRC entered a period of retrenchment, though openness to the outside world was still emphasized. This retrenchment-cum-openness policy helped the PRC survive the post-Tiananmen economic recession and international sanctions. However, the strain of financing government subsidies to state enterprises forced the regime back on the track of economic reform in late 1991. An end was put to *zhili zhengdun*. The September working conference and the following Eighth Plenum of the Thirteenth Central Committee ushered in the second-wave industrial reform, which concentrated on improving the performance of state enterprises. The aim was to perfect market socialism.

Though both marketization and privatization trends existed in the industrial reform of 1984–91, the underlying principle was clearly one of market socialism, that is, introducing market mechanism while retaining socialist ownership (Ye 1991). It was hoped that market could bring about competition and efficiency, while socialist ownership would maintain the basic identity and positive features of socialism (White 1993: 10). The basic premise of market socialism was the decoupling of ownership and management, or of income power and control power, and the transfer of management and control power to the users of the means of production. This principle worked differently for enterprises of different scales and in different locations. In general, small economic units and firms located in the capitalist enclaves enjoyed a higher degree of privatization than their large and inland counterparts. However, the fundamental features of market socialism remained intact. Chinese industry today can be best characterized as consisting of predominantly socialist enterprises acting on partially liberalized markets. The retrenchment policies following the Third Plenum in September 1989 did not change this basic structure, nor did the market-perfecting measures proposed in the second-wave reform launched at the end of 1991. What follows is a property rights analysis of the economic reforms in industry from 1984 to 1991.

Marketization I: 1984–85

It is clear from the October 1984 Decision on Reform and other measures of that year[4] that reformers were trying to make a major shift from mandatory planning to guidance planning. The primary difference between the two is the instruments used by the state to direct production and exchange: while mandatory planning relies on administrative orders, guidance planning depends on economic levers. Privatization or transformation of the public ownership structure was not in the minds of the reformers.

The 1984 reform affected all four of the policy goals—A, B, C, and D in Table 3—but the most dramatic changes were in category C, where there was a serious curtailment of the system of physical allocation. The purpose of this curtailment was to grant enterprises the power to make decisions on production and exchange, so that they would have the capacity to compete on the market and increase efficiency. The emphasis was on delegating control power to enterprises (*fang quan*) and treating them as constituent units of the economy, not just appendixes to the state bureaucracy (*qiye benwei lun*). There were exceptions to the general rule, however; strategic materials and products continued to be controlled by the plan. Where market was introduced, the state did not hesitate to distort it through the various economic levers at its disposal. There was also a lack of specific tenure: managers could be removed from their positions, and property rights could be rescinded by the central bureaucracy at any time. There was no contract safeguarding the interests of the new property rights holders.

In a command economy, physical allocation was paired with fulfillment of the plan as the success indicator. With market partially replacing physical allocation, a new criterion was required to judge the performance of managers. Profit was the natural choice, since the essence of the reform was to simulate a dynamic capitalist market (category A). But the replacement of gross output with profit as the primary success indicator did not represent a transfer of income power, or privatization. The central bureaucracy simply linked managerial rewards with a different aspect of the performance of the enterprise. Whereas administrative supervisors had previously told managers to maximize output, after the reform they were asked to maximize profit. The relationship between enterprise profitability and managerial incentives was just as indirect, and just as dependent on the formulas designed by the central supervisors, as the relationship between fulfillment of the plan and rewards for managers had been under the old system (Solinger 1993: chap. 4). Managers still had to focus on dealing with their bureaucratic supervisors for a better formula. It is true that some measures aimed at transferring limited income power to the enterprises had been implemented. The retained profit ratio had been rising steadily, due to the profit retention system introduced in 1979–80, the profit contract system of 1980–81, and the two "tax for profit" (li gai shui) moves of 1983–84 (Naughton 1985: 244). The latitude with which an enterprise could dispose of its retained profit according to its own needs had also increased (category A) (Perkins 1988: 616). As with the transfer of control power, however, enterprises were not protected against revocation of the income power they had acquired. In fact, profit retention and disposition were the subjects of perennial individual bargaining between enterprises and bureaucrats, even after the introduction of the new tax system, as witness the enterprise-specific "adjustment tax" (tiaojieshui) (Hua, Zhang, and Luo 1988: 26).

After providing enterprises with the capacity and motive to pursue profit in the market, the state, still interested in guiding the economy, proceeded to use "economic levers" to guide enterprise behavior. It simply changed its strategy from one of direct, administrative, physical allocation to one of indirect, economic, fiscal guidance, an approach succinctly described as "the state regulates the market, the market guides the enterprises" (guojia tiaojie shichang, shichang yindao qiye) (R. Zhao 1988). Taxes, grants, credits, and prices were the four major levers in the state armory. They could be applied either administratively, as taxes were, or through the monopolistic position of the state in the market, as were the prices of state-monopolized production factors. Taxes and grants disrupt the linkage between enterprise profit and retained profit, thereby reducing motivational efficiency (category B); price and credit levers dislocate resources and increase the opportunity costs of production, hence reducing allocative efficiency (category D). But by utilizing these economic levers, the state kept for itself pertinent instruments with which to guide profit-maximizing enterprises in a socialist market.

The shift from mandatory planning to guidance planning intensified the problem of the "soft budget constraint," that is, the paternalistic state's automatic bailout of enterprises operating at a loss. Under the old system, the enterprise budget was of little significance, because both inputs and outputs were cast in physical terms and prices mainly served an accounting purpose (Prybyla 1986). Money allocation was centrally controlled through a monetary plan that corresponded to a real plan. With the shift to the new system, money began to matter for the first time in the PRC (Holz 1992: 1). Enterprises were sensitized to their budgets, but financial discipline was weak. Since bureaucrats had the discretionary power to manipulate various economic levers in the pursuit of goals other than efficiency, profit-conscious managers were necessarily interested in bargaining with the state for favorable treatment. They negotiated for subsidies, tax exemptions, increases in centrally fixed prices, generous credit terms, and extensions on credit payments already due, using initial advantages, bias toward equal treatment, employment size, sector priority, and personal connections as bargaining chips. The result was the soft budget constraint. This lack of financial discipline, coupled with the increasing profit retention ratio, meant that enterprises enjoyed the benefits of their profits without taking responsibility for their losses (Naughton 1985: 248). Investment risk was minimized, and demand for inputs became insatiable. Extravagant bonuses were awarded because managers were not sensitive to cost. Much attention was devoted to bargaining, making enterprise adjustments to the market insufficient (Kornai 1986a; Perkins 1988). The economic levers were finally twisted into compromises and undermined the bureaucrats' original intentions.

On the side of government, there was a serious lack of credit and

wage control. Local officials and local banks were eager to boost local industrial growth (Shirk 1988: 351), and they were not effectively checked by the center. Decontrolling enterprises thus led to
expansion of macro demand. State investment increased by 25 percent in 1984 and by another 43 percent in 1985. The wage bill rose
by more than 20 percent during each of the same two years (Y. Li
1989: 657). In the aftermath of the 1984 urban reform, increases in
investment and consumption were accompanied by a hike in food
prices, a measure taken by the party to rationalize the pricing system, which had been distorted by heavy government subsidies. Artificially low food prices surged when the state relaxed its price controls. The average retail price of produce rose by 9 percent in 1985—
a very steep increase for a society accustomed to price stability, and
one in which food already accounted for 59 percent of household expenditures (Harding 1987; Zhou 1988: 1). A consumption surge
caused by decontrolled wages, an investment boom precipitated by
the newfound freedom of enterprises and the state's soft budget constraint, plus an ill-timed price reform, pushed the inflation rate to
8.8 percent, the highest rate since the disastrous Three Red Flags period of 1961 (when it reached a record 16.2 percent). Measures were
taken to cool down the overheated economy. Credit was contracted,
the money supply was tightened, imports were cut, and investments were slashed. In adopting the contractive policies, Premier
Zhao Ziyang relied mainly on the advice of economist Wu Jinglian
of the State Council's Research Center for Economic, Technological, and Social Development, but he was dissatisfied with the slackened growth rate of the economy. Clearly new measures were
needed to move the reform forward, measures that went beyond the
marketization policies under guidance planning. Since it was enterprise behavior that fueled the 1985 inflation, attention naturally
fell on the internal mechanisms of the enterprises. Decontrolling
state firms was clearly not the solution to this problem. In fact, it
was the cause of it. Some form of enterprise reform was thus in order (Hua, Zhang, and Luo 1988: 28).

Privatization I: 1986–87

The new solution was ownership reform (*suoyouzhi gaige*), and
its leading proponent was Li Yining, professor of economics at Bei-

jing University. Li and Wu were at each other's throats, the former stressing the importance of ownership reform (privatization), the latter the need for price reform (marketization).[5] In 1985, the atmosphere clearly favored Li's position. Li attributed the 1984 investment surge to the soft budget constraint and called for ownership reform to make enterprises responsible for the management of their funds. He juxtaposed ownership reform and price reform and asserted that price reform was primarily directed at creating an environment suitable to the development of the commodity economy, but reform of the ownership structure truly touched on the questions of interest, responsibility, stimulation, and motivation. Only when ownership issues were straightened out would the enterprises respond efficiently to price signals. Therefore, ownership reform had to precede price reform (*Beijing Ribao*, May 19, 1986; *Global Views*, July 1988, pp. 89–92).

The proposal put forth by the "Beijing University school" (Beida Xuepai) headed by Li called for a shareholding system and conglomeration for large and medium-sized enterprises, complete privatization or leasing for small enterprises, specialized household farming on optimally sized plots of land, and multifunctional corporations that combined agriculture with marketing, transportation, manufacturing, and construction (*World Journal Weekly*, Sept. 25, 1988, p. 236). The same proposal called for moderate price reform while the ownership structure was being transformed, and thorough price reform only after the transformation was complete.

Li's proposal was of course too radical for the reforming elite to accept. After all, "socialism with Chinese characteristics" at its primary stage (Chinese market socialism) was still based on public ownership.[6] Nevertheless, the responsibility system found in agriculture seemed to have the potential for being transferred to the urban economy (Hua, Zhang, and Luo 1988).

Throughout the summer and fall of 1986, ownership reform built momentum through highly publicized discussions. Scattered practices in the past were evaluated, proposals were put forward, and experiments were conducted on a large scale. In December, the State Council issued its Decision on Deepening Enterprise Reform and Energizing Enterprises, which suggested the adoption of various forms of a management responsibility system for medium-sized and large state enterprises. It also suggested a leasing system

TABLE 4
Property Rights Transferred to Users Under Various Industrial Reform Programs in the PRC, 1984–87

Property rights dimensions	Getihu and private enterprises[a]	Leasing system[b]	Contract responsibility system[c]	Director responsibility system[d]	Pre-reform system
Control power	Full	Full	Limited: quota to be delivered, full discretion above quota	Limited: quota to be delivered, full discretion above quota	Minimal
Income power	Full (except for precarious taxing); hard budget constraint	Full (except for rent and precarious taxing); hard budget constraint	Full (except for precarious taxing); hard budget constraint	Limited: profit retention and distribution subject to bargaining with supervisors	Minimal
Tenure	Unlimited	Fixed by lease	Fixed by contract	Not guaranteed	Not guaranteed
Scale	Small	Small to medium	Medium to large	Large	Small to large
Example	Wenzhou model	Guan Guangmei phenomenon	—	—	Daqing model

[a] Emphasized after 1986.
[b] Emphasized after 1986; similar to the post-1985 household responsibility system in agriculture.
[c] Emphasized after 1986; similar to the 1983–85 household responsibility system in agriculture.
[d] Main emphasis of the 1984–85 urban reform under guidance planning.

(*zurenzhi*) for small and medium enterprises running at a loss or with slim profits (Sah 1991: 211). The emerging models usually combined the traits of the officially sanctioned principle of market socialism, that is, the decoupling of ownership and management (*liangquan fenli*) and the transfer of the latter to property users, with the new feature of guaranteed income power for a specific time period as stipulated in a contract. The idea was that agricultural reform had fared successfully because it aimed at both marketization and privatization, and urban reform was lagging behind owing to its one-sided emphasis on transferring only control power. Therefore, privatization measures were required.

Table 4 shows the various property rights forms found in industry as of 1987. As can be clearly seen, the larger the economic unit, the smaller the degree of property rights transfer from state to users (Naughton 1985: 238). One can also observe a temporal trend toward more liberal forms of property rights as the pre-reform Daqing model gave way to the director responsibility system, which was in turn replaced by an emphasis on the contract responsibility system, leasing, *getihu*, and *siying qiye*.[7] The same trend can be observed in the shift from the 1983–85 household responsibility system, which resembled the contract responsibility system in industry, to the post-1985 household responsibility system, which resembles the leasing system. Finally, the major property rights reform of 1987 was to put the relations between the state and medium and large enterprises on a contractual basis in the new "contract management responsibility system" (*qiye chengbao jingying zerenzhi*, QCJZ), which was the industrial equivalent of the responsibility system in agriculture. This was a significant move toward property rights reform. However, it was actually a concession made by reform leaders to enterprise managers when the more radical shareholding system turned out to be politically infeasible.[8]

Following the State Council's Decision of December 1986 and a research report by the State Economic Commission of March 1987, Premier Zhao gave his personal endorsement of QCJZ on April 6. In May, a national campaign was launched to promote the new system in medium and large state enterprises. Toward the end of 1987, QCJZ had been implemented in 82 percent of medium and large in-budget (*yusuannei*) enterprises. Its coverage reached 92 percent in 1988.

Under QCJZ, both control power and income power were partially transferred from the state to the enterprises, though the emphasis was on income power. In this sense, it was a continuation of the profit retention, profit contracting, and tax for profit reforms of the early 1980's. Most enterprises were governed by contracts lasting three to five years. In most cases, the enterprise manager was required to satisfy specific tax/profit quotas and production obligations, beyond which he then had great discretionary power (*quebao shangjiao, chaoshou duoliu*).[9] The new system had some positive impact on the motivational efficiency of state industry, but it did not remove the basic defects of the old profit sharing system: enterprise-specific treatment, vertical bargaining, and the soft budget constraint. Hence, state industry continued to lag behind the nonstate sector in terms of growth, and it gradually went from being a major source of state revenue to a great drain on the government budget.

Economic reforms are embedded in the political structure, and when there are great changes in that underlying structure, reforms are bound to be affected.[10] Ownership reform was given a boost in the liberal atmosphere of 1986, as China celebrated the 30th anniversary of the policy of "letting a hundred flowers bloom and a hundred schools of thought contend." Deng's call for political structural reform also provided favorable conditions for discussing bold economic liberalization. But the political pendulum soon swung the other way. The December 1986 student protests for democracy and better living conditions touched off a series of political repercussions that culminated in the deposition of Secretary-General Hu Yaobang. The early months of 1987 witnessed the campaign against "bourgeois liberalization." Reformers and conservatives found themselves in a tug of war over defining the parameters of that campaign. Zhao Ziyang and his colleagues were busy confining the movement to the political and cultural domains and keeping it from spilling over into the economic realm.

In May, the tide changed direction as Deng threw his weight on the side of the reformers. At the Thirteenth Party Congress in November, Zhao was named general secretary of the party. Li Peng, a Soviet-trained technocrat and moderate reformer, succeeded Zhao as acting prime minister. Powerful conservatives, including Hu Qiaomu, Deng Liqun, Peng Zhen, and Yu Chiuli, retired from the

Central Committee (Fang Shue-ch'uen 1987: 27). The theory of the "primary stage of socialism" was officially endorsed by the party, providing ideological justification for whatever unorthodox policies the political elite considered desirable. The reformers thus consolidated their positions, and Zhao resumed the initiative in pushing forward the economic reform that had been brought to a halt by the political turbulence preceding the party congress.

Outward Economy: Early 1988

Zhao's first major move after assuming leadership of the party was to emphasize the "location" element of the reform. Reformers have used two criteria to determine the degree of marketization and privatization appropriate for different parts of the economy: scale and location. The general rules are: the smaller the economic unit, the greater the degree of property rights transfer (scale); and the closer the unit to the world market, the higher the degree of economic liberalization (location). The scale rule is pretty clear when one takes a look at the whole array of property rights forms emerging from ownership reform (see Table 4). The location rule particularly applies to the five Special Economic Zones (SEZs), fourteen open cities, and three delta areas. The enterprises situated in these capitalist enclaves enjoy a much higher degree of economic liberalization than their inland counterparts. In sum, Zhao's idea was to enlarge the capitalist enclaves to include the whole east coast of China, an area of 320,000 square kilometers with a population of 160 million (*People's Daily*, June 16, 1988). The major goal of this strategy was to promote exports. In fact, this was a replica of the export expansion policy so successfully pursued by the East Asian NICs.

Zhao's strategy of an "outward economy" took shape against the backdrop of PRC socialist market reform and the country's ensuing balance-of-payments problems. The soft budget constraint that accompanied the 1984–85 marketization reform gave rise to investment hunger. The state would, of course, periodically slash investments when they grew to ridiculous proportions and when many projects failed. But after a while, the need to maintain economic growth to validate the whole enterprise of economic reform would force the state to loosen controls again, leading to a resurgence of investment. Thus, investment rose and fell in cycles. Since the major purpose of the open-door policy was to introduce advanced Western technology and raise productivity, the investment hunger of Chinese enterprises was easily translated into an insatiable demand for imported producer goods. Investment cycles then turned into import cycles, as imports surged to satisfy investment demand and then fell as the regime took austerity measures in response to the pressure of balance-of-payments problems. There have been at least three such discernible cycles since the late 1970's (Lin 1991). Imports first went up in 1978 under Premier Hua Guofeng's Ten-Year Plan. This surge had more to do with the "great leap Westward" mentality of the time than with a changed economic structure. After Deng Xiaoping and Chen Yun consolidated power in their hands, they slashed imports in 1982–83, which resulted in trade surpluses during those two years. In 1984, serious industrial reform began, and imports, together with the trade deficit, surged again. In 1986, dramatic measures were taken to curb investment and imports. The third cycle began in 1987. As a result, the trade deficit doubled in 1988 from US$3.8 billion to US$7.7 billion, while foreign debt jumped 36 percent.

At this time, Beijing began to endorse the strategy of export expansion based on cheap labor. This meant a decisive shift in the emphasis of the PRC's open-door policy. When that policy was first adopted toward the end of the 1970's, the reformers' goal was to absorb Western capital and technology, first in a massive way, as under Hua's Ten-Year Plan, then at a pace more commensurate with the country's export capacity. Thus, for example, the original idea of the SEZs was to introduce advanced technology to upgrade the mainland's industrial capacity, not to promote export based on labor-intensive products. This was in sharp contrast with Taiwan's Export Processing Zones (EPZs) (Fitting 1982). However, the worsening balance-of-payments problems of the mainland in the latter half of the 1980's forced the leaders in Beijing to adopt an export expansion strategy. This strategy was first proposed by Wang Jian of the Planning Commission of the State Council in June 1987, and was adopted by the CCP at a politburo meeting in February 1988. Wang's idea was to expand labor-intensive exports in order to import more capital and technology. The same strategy can be used to solve the problem of increased unemployment caused by newly released rural labor. In the long run, industry, with its increased capacity and higher productivity, can support agriculture. An economic circle is created that links the industrial and agricultural sectors of the economy through the international market (Sah 1991: 101–2). This is the "grand international circulation," later known as the "outward economy," designed primarily for the development of mainland China's "golden coast."

Zhao Ziyang, the premier turned general secretary, and Deng Xiaoping, the PRC's senior leader, swiftly endorsed Wang's proposal and put it into practice. Besides foreign exchange considerations, they were also sensitive to the unique timing of the strategy: the international division of labor was experiencing fundamental change, with the PRC in a favorable position to succeed the East Asian NICs as a major manufacturing and export center of labor-intensive goods. Thanks to the endorsement of Deng and Zhao, the strategy of an outward economy was implemented quickly. The areas open to the outside world now included not only the original SEZs, open cities, and deltas, but the entire east coast of China. The province of Hainan was designated the fifth SEZ, the largest and most autonomous one. The east coast of China was to become the world's largest export zone based on cheap labor. Beijing was willing to waive its previous insistence on joint ventures and to allow other property rights arrangements (including completely foreign-owned enterprises) as long as direct foreign investment was attracted to the mainland. The conditions for using domestically manufactured parts and introducing advanced foreign technology were also relaxed. Zhao put emphasis on rural industry, treating it as the backbone of the outward economy. Even agriculture was emphasized as long as it could generate foreign exchange (Sah 1991: 107). In short, in early 1988 there was a decisive shift in the emphasis of the open-door policy, from importing technology and raising productivity to exporting labor-intensive products and accumulating foreign exchange.

The choice of the new strategy is interesting in that Zhao's first move after the 1987 interregnum of the reform was neither to perfect the market mechanism nor to straighten out ownership relations. These two thorny issues were set aside while a less controversial one was put in the limelight. Unlike marketization or privatization, the export-led growth strategy was merely an improvement on the old open-door policy. Unlike marketization, it did not pose an immediate threat to any material interests; unlike privatization, it was not ideologically or politically risky. Though the strategy certainly had implications for transfers of control power and income power, it was not directly about assigning property rights. It was, in this sense, a policy change, not a structural reform.[11] As such, the new strategy was no substitute for fundamental economic reform. This point was obviously stressed by the Chinese economists who urged Zhao to put property rights reform back on the agenda.

Marketization II: Late 1988

Those Chinese economists who consider price reform the central piece of the reconstruction of the economic system have long been frustrated by the actual reform process begun in the late 1970's. The household responsibility system did not put much emphasis on freeing agricultural prices. The 1984–85 urban reform was aimed at abolishing the system of physical allocation and shifting the planning mode from command to guidance. Here prices were treated as a major economic lever at the bureaucrats' disposal, not as an independent equilibrating mechanism to balance supply and demand. The partial lifting of urban price controls on agricultural products in 1985 created the highest inflation rate since 1961. The resulting urban unrest not only blunted the momentum for further guidance planning reform, but also thwarted any preliminary attempt at comprehensive price reform. The 1986–87 ownership reform had as its major purpose the transfer of income power to the enterprises and the establishment of full financial accountability (categories A and B). Price reform (category D) was again neglected. The new developmental strategy of the outward economy advocated by Zhao in early 1988 once more bypassed price reform and opted for a low-risk substitute.

Members of the price reform school (which included Wu Jinglian, Zhou Xiaochuan of the State Commission on Restructuring the Economic System, and others) did not hesitate to point out the defects of the guidance planning cum quasi-privatization system as of early 1988.[12] Zhou called the right to set prices for one's own products an integral part of enterprise autonomy that should not be singled out, externalized from the package of property rights transferred to the enterprises, and preserved by the state as an economic lever. Manager-bureaucrat price bargaining, corruption, the soft budget constraint, and investment hunger were all considered to be linked with the price lever (Zhou 1988). Wu, on the other hand, criticized irrational relative prices, the absence of a competitive market, and the lack of allocative efficiency under the current system (Wu and Reynolds 1987). He attacked Li Yining's ownership reform as an appropriation of state property and an atomization of the economy. For both Wu and Zhou, it was absurd to expect healthy enterprises to emerge from a distorted pricing system, and price reform, the single most important aspect of China's economic reconstruction, had been postponed because of a lack of political will.

In May 1988, the price school finally convinced top leaders to see things its way. But the timing was bad. In 1986, the inflation rate had dropped to 6 percent from the 8.8 percent of the previous year. But in 1987 it had risen to 7.3 percent, and officials admitted that 21 percent of the urban population had suffered a decline in living standards that year. By the end of 1987, pork, sugar, and eggs were being rationed in the major cities, and official figures showed an 11 percent rise in prices during the first quarter of 1988. And yet the reformers seemed determined to rationalize the pricing system at whatever cost (*chuang wujia guan*).

Deng Xiaoping, Zhao Ziyang, and State Chairman Yang Shangkun all vigorously embraced the cause of price reform, characterizing it as the key to the success or failure of the whole reform enterprise. The complete package of arguments by the price school was accepted in the editorials in the *People's Daily*, which called all reforms of the past nine years shallow and easy, and only the price reform fundamental and critical. The limited ability of urban residents to absorb the price shocks was acknowledged, but it was claimed that economic reform had created favorable conditions for liberalizing prices, and further postponement of such liberalization would result in even higher costs (*People's Daily*, May 30 and June 10, 1988).

The new round of price reform basically repeated the 1985 scenario, only on a larger scale. On May 15, the prices of pork, vegetables, eggs, and sugar rose by 30 to 60 percent. On July 28, cigarette and liquor prices rose by 15 to 290 percent. Workers and students received ten renminbi (rmb) to partially offset the price shocks, and CCP leaders began to link price reform and wage reform, with the latter acting as a compensating measure for the price increases. But inflation had already been touched off. Between January and September, retail prices rose 16 percent. Urban residents rushed to withdraw their money from the nation's banks and engaged in panic buying. On September 1, commercial banks raised the interest rates of their time deposits, and the People's Bank of China raised the reserve ratio by 1 percent. Measures were taken to slash investment, tighten credit, and check indiscriminate bonuses. The inflation took its political toll at the August Beidaihe meeting, where Zhao was heavily criticized by moderate reformers and saw his power migrate to Premier Li Peng and Vice Premier Yao Yilin, both conservatives on the politburo's standing commission. In September, the Third Plenum of the Thirteenth Central Committee made an all-out retreat from price reform, and shifted national attention to improving the economic environment and rectifying the economic order, that is, curbing inflation and combating profiteering (*zhili zhengdun*).[13]

The fate of the 1988 price reform was predictable. Three structural factors clearly contributed to its failure.[14] The first was the fact that the soft budget constraint had not been overcome by the proliferation of ownership forms and the shift from the director responsibility system to the new contract management system. The lack of financial discipline minimized managers' cost considerations and paved the way for investment hunger and extravagant use of wage increases and bonuses. The insatiable demand for inputs raised price levels on the factor markets, while the increase in disposable income at the hands of workers drove up prices on the product markets.

The second prime reason for the inflation was economic regionalism. Ever since the 1958 administrative decentralization, China's local governments have had more power vis-à-vis the center than have their counterparts in other command economies (Wu and Reynolds 1987). The repeated cycles of centralization and decentralization that followed did not change this basic feature. The profit contract system adopted among smaller enterprises in 1981 had local officials bargain with enterprise managers on the base profit figures each enterprise undertook to deliver to the state (Naughton 1985:

234). This system intensified local governments' control over enterprises under their supervision. In 1984, the move to delegate state-owned enterprises to the key cities (*jianzheng fangquan*) further enhanced local autonomy and gave rise to provincial protectionism, market monopoly, and regional blockade. The major cause of regionalism is the substitution of administrative decentralization for genuine marketization (Naughton 1985). It was estimated that only 40 percent of the control power delegated by the state had actually been transferred to enterprises by the end of 1987, with the rest falling into the hands of local governments (R. Zhao 1988). Beijing made all kinds of contracts of responsibility with provinces and municipalities on investment, materials, credits, and foreign trade and foreign exchange (*difang baogan*). The results were local administrative intervention into enterprise behavior and fragmented markets across the country. Without a free flow of factors and products, one cannot expect pricing that reflects relative scarcities, only monopolistic pricing that contributes to inflation. Local governments were also interested in promoting local industry, and they put pressure on the local branches of the People's Bank to extend easy credit to enterprises. Redundant and excessive investment was the natural result.

The failure of the 1988 price reform can also be attributed to the unique two-tier pricing system that came into being in 1984.[15] Dual prices (different plan prices and market prices for the same products) were considered necessary to reduce shocks as the urban economy shifted from mandatory planning to guidance planning, and when four price categories were created: state-fixed prices, floating prices, negotiated prices, and free prices. They were but a part of the coexistence of the old and new systems. But because managers had been turned into profit maximizers, it was hard for them not to take advantage of the price differences between the control realm and the market realm, especially when the two realms existed side by side in the same enterprise. The natural tendency was for products and materials to flow from the plan to the market, trespassing the border between the two. Often this was done after the bureaucrats-turned-entrepreneurs had already effectively raised the market price by their administrative authority or through hoarding. This phenomenon is called *guan dao* (official profiteering) and has been widely considered a major culprit in urban inflation. Thus the Third

Plenum of the Thirteenth Central Committee set as one of the party's two major tasks in 1989 and 1990 rectification of the economic order, aimed at suppressing profiteering activities on the market.

Retrenchment with Outward Openness I: 1989

Two phases are discernible in the 1989–91 period that share the feature of the retrenchment-cum-openness strategy but differ significantly in economic performance, especially on the trade front. The first phase (1989) was characterized by austerity, economic downturn, a trade deficit, and international isolation. The second phase (1990–91), on the other hand, witnessed an increasingly expansionary policy, a corresponding revival of the economy, a more favorable trade balance, and a gradual improvement of the country's international status.

Suffering from a whole range of economic problems associated with the socialist market reform, including structural inflation, rampant corruption, trade deficits, and income differentiation, the PRC headed toward an extended period of austerity and retrenchment (*zhili zhengdun*) after September 1988. If there was any hope that this setback of the reform was merely temporary, like the 1987 antibourgeois liberalization interregnum, and the reform process would be resumed after a few months of recuperation, that hope was smashed after the political upheavals touched off by the death of Hu Yaobang on April 15, 1989. The June Fourth Incident and subsequent suppression led directly to Zhao's political demise and the arrests of his liberal advisors, while strengthening the conservatives' grip on economic decisions.

Cooling the overheated economy was more difficult this time than it had been in 1985, when the state had more control and the inflation rate was 8.8 percent, compared with 18.5 percent for 1988 and 25.5 percent for the first half of 1989. After the Third Plenum of the Thirteenth Central Committee, the strategy of the regime was to tighten direct control over the public sector and restrict the private sector that lay beyond state command. Although reform as a principle was still stressed, greater emphasis was put on rectifying its side effects. To bring them within the party line, serious encroachments were made on the control power and income power of managers and private owners.

For the medium and large enterprises, the state ordered a price squeeze, a slash in investment, and a scheme of compulsory savings that forced workers to spend 30 percent of their wages on government bonds. The banking system indexed long-term interest rates to encourage savings, and it squeezed credit. The purpose of these measures was to check excessive demand in investment and consumption. As a result, there were loan defaults, delayed payments, the emergence of a large financial market outside the banking system, and the sale of shares by enterprises to their employees to raise capital (do Rosario 1989: 47). Because the state was unwilling to allow bankruptcies, it provided price subsidies to enterprises, which increased budget deficits. State enterprises also had top priority in receiving credit, raw materials, and energy supplies. The result of this squeeze-and-release approach was an extended time lag before the inflation rate began to decline slowly in 1989, from 25.8 percent in April to 13 percent in September. The economy finally responded to the austerity measures, but not without serious costs. The month of September registered an industrial output growth rate of only 0.9 percent, the lowest in 10 years, and light industry even recorded negative growth. The unemployment rate doubled from 2 percent in February to 4 percent at the end of the year. Finally, the regime had indicated since June that party officials should resume the major role they had played in business affairs before economic reform started, meaning that ideological cadres would join state bureaucrats in interfering with managerial decisions, a move clearly against the essence of the 1988 law on state enterprises that established full authority for enterprise directors, and one that represented a great leap backward to the pre-1984 situation (*Financial Times*, Oct. 17, 1989).

Private businesses found themselves in a much more difficult situation than their public counterparts. They were subject to two kinds of attack from the regime: one was economically motivated, the other was based on political accusations. After the austerity program began in September 1988, the private sector found credit, raw materials, and energy supplies squeezed by the regime in order to contract the economy and support state enterprises. As budget deficits grew, governments on all levels imposed punitive taxes on the private sector, charging its members with tax evasion and illicit activities. The second kind of attack came after the Tiananmen incident. Conservatives in the party had always been hypersensitive to the potential of economic reform, particularly privatization, to spill over into the political realm and create a demand for democracy, and it was reformers who denied this linkage (Pye 1988b). With the reformers in dismay after June, official discrimination against private businesses intensified as the regime drew a link between private ownership and the "counterrevolutionary riots" throughout China. Although lip service was paid to the importance of the private sector as a complement to the socialist public economy (as stipulated in the 1988 constitutional amendment), harsh measures were taken to suppress private entrepreneurs. The central planners now could decide which private businesses should be shut down because they were unable to meet public needs. The party also decided to exclude private business owners from its 47,000-strong membership in order to preserve its unity. As a result of these economic and political pressures, in the first half of 1989 the number of private enterprises and people employed by them dropped by 15 percent and 15.7 percent, respectively, the first such decline in recent years.[16] Some prominent businessmen fled the country.[17]

Even with all of these demarketization and deprivatization measures, a line was carefully drawn between the domestic economy and the outward economy. Austerity was to be accompanied by continued openness to the outside world in terms of an invigorated export drive. By this time, the decade-old open-door policy had been redefined by Zhao Ziyang to give it an export thrust. This strategy of an outward economy survived the price reform of May 1988, the inflation that followed, the adoption of a retrenchment and austerity policy, the Tiananmen crisis, and the subsequent political suppression and economic recession. This was the case not only because the PRC still needed foreign capital and technology to modernize its economy, but also because the domestic credit squeeze had forced many enterprises to seek loans from foreign creditors. The Tiananmen incident and subsequent economic sanctions imposed by the West (particularly Japan and the World Bank) only made Beijing more dependent on external economic relations. In the first half of 1989, the PRC's trade deficit increased nearly fivefold over the level of a year earlier, to US$5.79 billion. Foreign debt had reached US$40 billion at the end of 1988, and the debt-servicing peak would come in 1992. Unless the PRC could boost its exports and get its creditors to roll over some debts and invest new money, servicing the debt would require an even greater domestic squeeze. Thus authorities continuously stressed that the door to the outside remain open.

Retrenchment with Outward Openness II: 1990–91

Mainland China's balance-of-payments problems loomed large at the end of 1989 and the beginning of 1990. The PRC had accumulated trade deficits for the six consecutive years from 1984 to 1989. Foreign indebtedness reached US$41.3 billion at the end of 1989. The contractive policy adopted in late 1988 did not bring about any significant change in the overheated economy until after the Tiananmen incident, when recession struck with a vengeance. The first quarter of 1990 registered an unprecedented zero growth for industry. Post-Tiananmen international sanctions were in full swing. A large number of foreign companies withdrew their investments on the mainland. Many others refrained from investing or reconsidered their projects. Approved direct foreign investment dropped by half from the third quarter of 1989 to the first quarter of 1990. An investment vacuum was created that had a direct impact on the mainland's ability to service its foreign debt (the annual payment obligation for the 1990's was estimated at US$7–10 billion). Foreign exchange reserves dropped to the 1987 level. The need to attract foreign investment and expand exports became more acute than ever.

The response of the regime to its worst economic crisis was slow, but it eventually proved effective. Though shunned by Western investors, mainland China was able to attract direct foreign investment from across the Taiwan Strait. Many labor-intensive industries that had formed the backbone of Taiwan's successful export drive in the early years of the island's economic development were uprooted from Taiwan and moved to the mainland. Investment-related exports of raw materials and unfinished goods from Taiwan also surged, constituting the bulk of cross-Strait trade. By the end of 1991, Taiwan's accumulated investment on the mainland had reached US$3.6 billion, and trade between the two through Hong Kong hit the US$5.7 billion mark. Most significant is the fact that this new wave of investment was aimed squarely at exports.

Around 70 percent of all products manufactured by mainland firms receiving Taiwan investment were exported. Thanks to this development and other measures taken to boost exports and slash imports, including a 26.3 percent devaluation of the rmb in December 1989 and another 9.57 percent devaluation in November 1990, the mainland was able to achieve a trade surplus of US$8.71 billion in 1990, its first since 1983. The trend continued in 1991, when the trade surplus soared to US$12 billion. Foreign exchange reserves increased from US$17.02 billion at the end of 1989 to US$28.59 billion one year later, and to US$39.96 billion by September 1991. The lifting of international sanctions against Beijing in the latter half of 1990 (first by Japan, then the West) added to the momentum of economic recovery by pumping new international financial resources into the country.

Favorable trade expansion coincided with overall improvement of the economy. The turning point came around the third quarter of 1990, when several expansionary moves adopted by the government earlier in the year (such as lowering interest rates) halted the recession (Kao and Wang 1991). Industry grew by 7.6 percent in 1990 and 13.2 percent in 1991. The economy recovered from the recession by growing 5.0 percent in 1990 and 7.0 percent in 1991. The recovery did not come at the expense of macro stability: inflation declined from 17.8 percent in 1989 to 2.1 percent in 1990 and 2.9 percent in 1991 (Ch'en Te-Sheng 1993: 38). Obviously, the economy had resumed its high-growth pattern and improved significantly on macro balances (low inflation, favorable trade balance, etc.).

The export expansion strategy was so successfully pursued by the PRC that Beijing immediately faced strong protectionist reaction from its trading partners, especially the United States. The PRC's 1991 trade surplus with the U.S. was US$12 billion, exceeding the ROC's US$9.9 billion and placing the Chinese mainland after Japan as the second largest source of the U.S. trade deficit. Products made in the PRC captured a market share of 3.23 percent in the U.S. for the first half of 1991, up from 1.73 percent in 1988. This export surge soon invited great pressure from the U.S., particularly as post-Tiananmen sentiment against the Chinese Communist regime was still very strong in the Congress. A familiar scenario then unfolded, one reminiscent of U.S.-Taiwan relations: Beijing sent a "buy America" mission to the U.S. while the latter resorted to Section 301 of the 1988 Omnibus Trade and Competitiveness Act to force the PRC to protect intellectual property rights. Mainland China is indeed in the process of becoming a super NIC. The only question is whether the world market is large enough to absorb all the labor-intensive goods it produces (Perkins 1988: 29).

Second-Wave Industrial Reform: 1992

Despite its remarkable performance on the trade front, the PRC faced a very serious financial crisis toward the end of the retrenchment period, which compelled the regime back to the reform track in late 1991. This second-wave industrial reform focuses on large and medium-sized state enterprises. Its major goal is perfecting the market, not privatizing the state sector.

The reason behind the second-wave reform is quite clear. During the period of *zhili zhengdun*, emphasis was put on export promotion, and as a result, the export sector grew rapidly. On the other hand, though *getihu, siying qiye*, and rural industry were squeezed at the initial phase of retrenchment in order to free up raw materials and capital for the state sector, they bounced back with a vengeance when the government began relaxing its restrictions on the economy in early 1990. Foreign trade and the non-state sector thus provided the momentum for economic growth. At the same time, state enterprises suffered from rigidities and inefficiencies while being protected from real competition by the soft budget constraint. The encroachment of non-state enterprises (especially rural industries) severely damaged their economic position (Naughton 1992).[18] Their profits dropped by 18.8 percent in 1989 and 58 percent in 1990. Since medium and large state enterprises constituted the bulk of the mainland's industrial sector (accounting for two-thirds of fixed assets, more than half of total output, and 60 percent of realized profits and tax revenues), their lagging behind dragged down the national economy, wasted resources, and put tremendous pressure on the government budget. In 1990, PRC subsidies to state enterprises rose to 57.85 billion rmb and its budget deficit grew to 15.04 billion rmb (50.9 billion rmb if debts are deducted from income), a 57.7 percent increase over the previous year.

The loss in government revenues from the drop in state enterprise profits could not be compensated for by taxes imposed on fast-growing sectors such as rural industry. Whereas in the past it could rely on its ability to directly tap the monopoly profits of state-owned industry, the government lacked a competent tax administration with which to tap the revenues of the non-state sector (Naughton 1992). It was quite clear that something had to be done to fix the state sector lest it bankrupt the regime.

Here one finds that the issue of state financial solvency looms large in the considerations of the political elite. This issue becomes even more urgent for those sensitive to the ownership structure of the economy (White 1993: 128). The miserable performance of the state enterprises compared with the non-state sector signifies the decline of socialist production vis-à-vis the emerging capitalist or quasi-capitalist order on the Chinese mainland. In 1990, the state sector grew by a meager 2.9 percent, compared with 9.1 percent for collectives, 21.6 percent for private enterprises, and 56 percent for the three kinds of firms with foreign investment (sanzi qiye). The state enterprise share of gross industrial output fell from 76 percent in 1980 to 64 percent in 1985 and 54.5 percent in 1990. If left alone, mainland industry may become more private than public, more capitalist than socialist. It is indeed a critical juncture for the regime.

At a working conference held in September 1991 in Beijing, the three-year retrenchment was ended and a renewed industrial reform was launched in the state sector. Reformers enjoyed an additional boost when Deng Xiaoping, on his southern inspection tours to Shenzhen, Zhuhai, and Shanghai before the Chinese New Year in 1992, stated that reform was the only way out for the country and anyone resisting it should resign.[19] This public gesture removed any political constraints on the reform remaining after the Tiananmen incident. Deng's urge was related to his desire to keep reform alive in order to forestall the kind of political turbulence Eastern Europe and the former Soviet Union were experiencing. Since zhili zhengdun had outlived its usefulness, Deng's logic required launching the second-wave reform.

The reform measures promised by Prime Minister Li Peng and Zhu Rongji (deputy prime minister and head of the State Council's Production Office) and Gao Shangquan (deputy director of the State Commission for Restructuring the Economy) included further reducing mandatory planning, shifting from administrative interference to market regulation, enhancing enterprise autonomy (category C), imposing financial discipline, closing down unprofitable firms in accordance with the bankruptcy law (category B), and reforming the price structure (category D). None of these—including the bold moves to smash "iron rice bowls" (job security) and "iron armchairs" (cadre tenure)—goes beyond the confines of market socialism. At the same time, accompanying these reform policies were auxiliary measures aimed at easing pressure on state enterprises, for example, by lowering their income tax rate. This means the thrust of the reform is to save the state sector, the material base of socialism, through whatever means necessary, and not to improve economic efficiency at the risk of decimating state enterprises. Since the goal is to preserve and strengthen the state sector, there is every reason to expect that the policies granting power to the state firms will be implemented, while the painful, disciplinary measures will be thwarted, especially when there seems to be macro stability and decent growth in the overall economy (thanks to the non-state sector), and the regime is not driven by the kind of desperation that would motivate it to overhaul the economy. The initial phase of the second-wave industrial reform thus remained one of perfecting the market, while large-scale privatization would have to wait until macro stability was seriously disturbed.

Conclusion

The property rights analysis in the previous discussion suggests that industrial reform in China has brought about a socialist market system in which marketization is more prominent than privatization. However, marketization and privatization did compete for supremacy during the reform process. The alternating emphasis on the two principles in the industrial reform after 1984 suggests the relevance of both to reforming the economy. It also suggests the cautious, tentative, and yet tenacious attitude of reformers, who always try the easy approach first, retreat when the costs appear too high, and then, after a recess, return with a new approach. The top reformers have shown themselves willing to make compromises but determined to sustain the momentum of reform (Shirk 1988: 351). They may retreat because of macro instability caused by particular economic reform measures, such as the inflation that followed the 1985 price reform; or they may retreat because of a political crisis that the conservatives can blame on them, such as the student demonstrations in the winter of 1986–87. The most serious setback for the reformers, the 1988–91 retrenchment (*zhili zhengdun*), was initially caused by economic instability (the inflation that followed the 1988 price reform), which was then reinforced by a political crisis (the June Fourth Incident) and forced reformers to retreat. This protracted interregnum, however, did not prevent them from recuperating and launching the second-wave reform at the end of 1991. The cyclical pattern of the PRC's economic reform is thus sustained.[20]

The thrust of the new reform is toward marketization, not privatization. However, the debate is still being waged between the price school and the ownership school on which of the two reforms should take precedence. There is contention over the relative importance of allocative versus motivational efficiency, the opportunity cost associated with each approach, the ability of one to create a favorable environment for the other, and the right sequence. Even though there are economists who have taken the position that the two reforms are but two sides of the same coin and should be pursued simultaneously, as long as reformers are wary of taking on both tasks at the same time, the debate on priority and sequence will doubtless continue (R. Zhao 1988).

This debate is about economic efficiency. But efficiency is only one of the many variables that enter into the calculations of the political elite.[21] The broader context is one in which all policy alternatives are evaluated in terms of their political impact. The economic reform process was started when it became obvious to the elite that the regime's major legitimacy base had shifted from revolutionary ideology to material well-being. Economic efficiency was singled out as the most important goal in the reform because it was recognized as the key to raising living standards. However, there are other important variables that affect the quality of life of the population, such as job security, price stability, and equitable income distribution, that compete with economic efficiency on the reform agenda. Furthermore, indispensable legitimacy bases other than material well-being, such as socialist ideology and international prestige, must be taken into account. Finally, there are power resources other than legitimacy that the regime is interested in preserving, such as state financial solvency and an ownership monopoly in strategic sectors of the economy. These considerations constitute a multitiered value framework that a Leninist state has to deal with. Consciously or unconsciously, the elite assign different weights to different value considerations, try to locate the trade-off ratios between the values, and manage to maximize the power of the regime. In order to understand the political context of industrial reform and the interaction of politics and economy in the PRC, one needs to look at comparable historical cases in which strong party-states authoritatively redefined property rights in order to achieve elite goals. For this purpose we now turn to Hungary, the Soviet Union, and the Republic of China in Taiwan.

Chapter Three

Hungary and the PRC

B etween 1984 and 1991, by making its industrial reform
stress marketization much more than privatization,
the PRC transformed its industry on the pattern of market socialism. This strategy brings its industrial property rights structure
closer to Hungary's than to that of any other country in the world.
In addition to the similarities in the concrete measures of the two
countries' industrial reforms, one can find resemblances between
their overall developmental trajectories, basic orientations, the
origins of their reforms, the preceding changes in agriculture, the
limits on their reform policies, the costs of and resistance to their
respective reforms, the retrenchment each underwent, and the pressure for a second wave of reform. To be sure, there are also differences between the two countries, such as size, degree of economic
development, and the international environment in which each
finds itself. However, the overall patterns of reform are so strikingly
similar that one is inclined to explore the causes of their similarities.[1]

This chapter will compare the prominent aspects of the Hungarian and Chinese reforms and discuss their underlying political and
economic causes. As will become clear in the discussion that follows, a unique set of elite values and perceptions, interacting with
politico-economic institutions that were similar in both countries,
led to a common reform pattern. Since the Hungarians were the predecessors in this development, the Chinese were under pressure to
conform to the pattern that they established. However, there are
several interesting differences between the two that may lead the

Chinese into alternative property rights structures. We will explore these alternatives in Chapters 4 and 5.

Developmental Trajectories

Many Leninist regimes start out as people's democracies that tolerate leftist parties as junior partners, then shift to the high gear of totalitarianism and five-year plans, and finally settle for some version of postrevolutionary authoritarianism. However, there are great differences between them once these regimes reach the post-revolutionary stage.[2] Here the most important differentiae are the pattern of economic reform, the way in which the reform is introduced, and whether there is spillover from the economic to the political realm. When the trajectories of different Leninist regimes in the postrevolutionary stage are compared with an eye to these issues, commonalities are replaced by differences in most cases. The Hungary-PRC case is an interesting exception.

Both Hungary and the PRC had a united front period before moving into high totalitarianism. The adoption of a constitution (in 1949 in Hungary and in 1954 in the PRC) marked the beginning of Stalinist politics and socialist transformation. Matyas Rakosi and Mao Zedong were charismatic despots who enjoyed personality cults and ran their respective party-states in a dictatorial way. The First Five-Year plans (1949–53 in Hungary, 1953–57 in the PRC) were characterized by agricultural collectivization and heavy industrialization. Bottlenecks developed in industry and agriculture toward the end of this period. In the case of Hungary, the death of Stalin and the emergence of a new leadership in the Soviet Union forced Rakosi to step down from the premiership and let Imre Nagy adopt a "new course." In the PRC, Mao Zedong pushed the already strained economy even further by raising the "Three Red Flags," plunging the whole country into communistic economic campaigns. The disastrous results then forced Mao to retreat to the "second line," although he maintained his party chairmanship. Like Nagy in Hungary, State Chairman Liu Shaoqi and Secretary-General Deng Xiaoping took power and adopted "revisionist" policies to salvage the national economy, emphasizing agriculture and light industry. The country enjoyed temporary economic relief.

In both countries, the revisionist policies were in effect for only a short period of time. Rakosi made a comeback in 1955. Though Nikita Khrushchev's denunciation of Stalin at the Twentieth Congress of the CPSU in 1956 tilted the balance of power in Hungary, forced out Rakosi, and resulted in the second Nagy regime, the Hungarian revolution that followed was swiftly put down by Soviet troops. Janos Kadar became first secretary of the party and had Nagy and his entourage executed. Not until the Eighth Congress of the Hungarian Socialist Workers' Party (HSWP) convened in November 1962 was there any sign of political relaxation. In the PRC, the second wave of totalitarianism occurred when Mao launched the Great Proletarian Cultural Revolution at the end of 1965. Liu was tortured to death and his policies were abolished. Class struggle dominated the political scene until after Mao's death in 1976 and Deng's ascendancy at the Third Plenum of the Eleventh Central Committee at the end of 1978.

Political and economic pragmatism finally dominated both countries after the second wave of totalitarianism. Class struggle was put to rest and economy was in command. The paramount leaders who directed this transformation were Kadar in Hungary and Deng in the PRC. Kadar was one of Rakosi's most important lieutenants. He headed the Ministry of the Interior and took charge of the show trials that were held in the heyday of totalitarian rule. He was then victimized by Rakosi and jailed and tortured from 1951 to 1954. Deng, as secretary-general of the CCP, was instrumental in Mao's purge of the nation's intellectuals in the Anti-Rightist Campaign of 1957.[3] Deng was later accused of being a "capitalist roader" and was subjected to much humiliation during the Cultural Revolution. Both Kadar and Deng were totally disillusioned with party ideology, but each remained authoritarian in terms of his party's political control of the country. Under their "enlightened authoritarian" rule, political campaigns subsided, the economic realm was depoliticized, and major economic reforms were launched. The legitimacy base of both party-states shifted from ideological claims to material benefits for the people.

The economic reforms in both Hungary and the PRC began in agriculture. The purpose of agricultural reform was to satisfy the most basic needs of the population. The Hungarian approach was distinctively market socialist, whereas the Chinese reform verged on quasi-privatization, but in neither case was there a transfer of ownership. The agricultural successes prompted reformers to introduce a similar set of measures in the cities. On January 1, 1968, the New Economic Mechanism (NEM) was put into effect in Hungary, and in October 1984, the Third Plenum of the Twelfth Central Committee of the CCP passed the Decision on Reform of the Economic Structure. Both industrial reforms created a limited and guided market with socialist ownership of the means of production basically intact. The Hungarian NEM ran smoothly for five years before blue-collar workers began to strongly protest their deteriorating position with regard to income distribution. Kadar sided with the workers and reversed the reform trend in November 1972. Hungary thus moved into retrenchment until seven years later, when trade imbalances and mounting foreign debt forced the country back on the reform track. In the case of the PRC, it was unprecedented inflation and an ill-timed price reform that forced the regime to start retrenchment in September 1988. Three years later, the financial burden of subsidizing state enterprises compelled the Chinese regime to launch its second-wave industrial reform. The new Hungarian reform gradually evolved from market perfection to small-scale privatization as the country's economy continued to deteriorate in the 1980's. Even before the political demise of the HSWP in 1989, the party had contemplated a scheme of full privatization. On the Chinese side, the initial thrust of its second-wave reform was clearly aimed at perfecting market socialism. Whether this new reform will follow the Hungarian pattern and evolve into full privatization remains to be seen.

When we juxtapose the trajectories of Hungary and the PRC since the founding of the two people's republics, we see striking parallels between them not only during the stage of high totalitarianism, but also in their postrevolutionary development. These are not simply superficial resemblances. They are rooted in a common set of elite values and perceptions, which interacts with politico-economic institutions that are similar in both countries. In order to look into the dynamics of these developments, we need to examine specific aspects of the two reforms.

Political Background

The industrial reforms in Hungary and the PRC were embedded in "socialist enlightened absolutism."[4] This is the ruling philosophy of postrevolutionary regimes that seek on the one hand to restore their legitimacy by improving the living standards of the population, and on the other to retain monopolistic political control. People are no longer required to participate fervently in political campaigns, as in the heyday of totalitarianism. Their major responsibility is now to accept the enlightened rule of the reforming elite. Radical economic reforms are undertaken, most of them flying in the face of Marxism-Leninism. Economic and political realms are carefully separated, so that no reform dynamism will spill over into politics. The only political changes made are to purge conservatives within the regime who are against the economic reform, and to reduce the role of the party in managing the economy. These measures are intended to facilitate the reform, not to democratize the political process. The essence of socialist enlightened absolutism is to retreat on the economic front so as to better safeguard the political core; to thoroughly reform the economy, so that politics does not have to be reformed; or to substitute economic liberalization and a higher living standard for political democratization.

In Hungary, socialist enlightened absolutism first took the form of Kadar's "alliance policy," announced in June 1957, at the first conference of the newly organized HSWP, but not implemented until after the Eighth Congress in 1962. This policy changed the pre-1956 party slogan representing the concept of class struggle—"Whoever is not with us is against us"—to "Whoever is not against us is with us." Any public office could be held by a non–party member without regard to family background, past activity, or personal philosophy, as long as he or she had the necessary qualifications and was willing to contribute to socialist construction (Toma and Volgyes 1977: 15). After the announcement of the alliance policy, Kadar nevertheless had to battle the dogmatists in the party, and he was able to impose his will only after Khrushchev's victory over the Soviet hardliners at the 22nd Congress of the CPSU in October 1961. With the consolidation of his power at the Eighth Congress of the HSWP in 1962, Kadar was able to set in motion a trend of political relaxation that reduced the number of forced labor camps, released political prisoners, abolished the system of internal exile and internment without trial, purged the political police, relaxed travel restrictions, and put an end to the jamming of Western radio stations (Gati 1974: 24; Toma and Volgyes 1977: 14). The Eighth Congress signified the end of class struggle and shifted national attention to economic construction. From this time on, economic reform became the centerpiece, the *ultima ratio*, of the alliance policy (Kovrig 1987: 118).

The signs of political relaxation under the alliance policy should not be confused with pluralism and democracy. Even though there were limited electoral reforms after 1966, the leading role of the party was never to be questioned.[5] What one saw here was a clear case of "one-party pluralism" (Y. S. Wu 1990). The persecution of intellectuals and writers whose views differed from those of the party testified to the authoritarian nature of Kadar's rule.[6] The New Economic Mechanism was contemplated and implemented by the regime on the advice of a group of reform economists, without consultation with the public. It was a "reform from above" (Kornai 1989: 100). The economic liberalization was carefully prevented from spreading to the political realm (Volgyes 1976: 107). There were reform measures aimed at removing enterprise management from the purview of party hacks, but these policy changes were administrative in nature and really only served to boost managerial authority vis-à-vis the workers. The regime followed a deliberate policy of depoliticization of its citizens, not only in the sense of discontinuing political campaigns, but also in the sense of discouraging genuine political participation. What Kadarism cultivated was a "subject culture" (Almond and Powell 1978: 35) that neither forced nor allowed the population to participate in the political process, but instead encouraged passive acceptance of the enlightened rule of the reforming elite.

Deng's political dominance was assured at the Third Plenum of the Eleventh Central Committee in December 1978, but his victory over the leftist remnants of the Cultural Revolution (as represented by Hua Guofeng) was not complete until 1981.[7] At the Sixth Plenum of the Eleventh Central Committee in June 1981, a historic document on party history was approved that proclaimed the end of class struggle, recognized the need to free the mind, pledged support to CCP leadership, and reinforced the paramount goal of economic construction.[8] These statements translated into political relaxation, authoritarian rule by the party, and economic reform, the defining features of socialist enlightened absolutism. The 1981 plenum of the CCP was comparable to the Eighth Congress of the HSWP in that a powerful statement was made in favor of political relaxation and economic reform, as signified by the document and the elimination of Hua Guofeng. Under the liberal policies of Deng and CCP Secretary-General Hu Yaobang, the Chinese alliance policy took the form of measures removing political labels (such as "rightist," "counterrevolutionary," "bad element," and the like) and rehabilitating millions of political pariahs, establishing a rudimentary legal framework, holding multi-candidate elections (*chae xuanju*), allowing more intellectual freedom, and relaxing travel restrictions (Harding 1984c).

As in the Hungarian case, this political relaxation in the PRC should not be confused with democratization. Whenever there were signs of a political challenge to the party's absolute rule, Deng sided with conservatives in carrying out crackdowns. This was the case in the CCP condemnation of writer Bai Hua in 1981, the Anti–Spiritual Pollution Campaign in 1983, the Anti–Bourgeois Liberalization Movement in 1987, and the bloody suppression of the student demonstrators in Tiananmen Square in 1989. In the last two cases, Deng showed a strong revulsion toward mass politics and a marked preference for "subject culture" that partially reflected his experience with the Red Guards during the Cultural Revolution. Deng went so far as to remove two of his successors—Hu Yaobang (in 1987) and Zhao Ziyang (in 1989)—as he tightened political control, but he never failed to stress the importance of economic reform at the same time. This painstaking separation of politics and economics, and the insistence on applying different principles to the two realms, suggests the duality of Deng's approach, a duality that is the essence of socialist enlightened absolutism (Chang 1989). There were times when the regime talked about making political reforms, but these were mainly administrative measures aimed at reshuffling personnel and restricting the party's role in the economy (Luo 1986). The major purpose of these measures was to provide a political environment amicable to the economic reform. Democracy as an idea was emphasized by Deng on several occasions. What he meant, however, was democracy as an instrument of mobilization, to strengthen the link between the citizens and the state (Nathan 1990: 175). In practice, political mobilization was initiated by reformers on rare occasions when the need to defeat their conservative opponents justified such moves (Y. S. Wu 1990). Institutionalized democracy that restricts state power and holds the government responsible to the population was never a goal of even the most ardent reformers, such as Hu Yaobang.

Origins of the Industrial Reform

Socialist enlightened absolutism ended class struggle and shifted the regime's attention to economic construction. In order to understand how this basic orientation was translated into concrete reform measures in Hungarian and Chinese industry, we need to take a look at the common factors that led to the two industrial reforms: the traumatic imprinting event, the victimized leader, the requirements of consumption-oriented and intensive growth, and the success of the preceding agricultural reform.

Both Hungary and the PRC experienced a traumatic imprinting event after the Communists took power: the suppression of the 1956 uprising in Hungary and the Cultural Revolution in China. These events destroyed the ideological righteousness of the regime and totally disillusioned the population, a fact the ruling elite were keenly aware of. Unable to claim regime legitimacy in the old way, the leaders were forced to rely on the universal legitimating mechanism: improvement of the people's living standards. To a certain extent this shift of the legitimacy base from ideology to economic performance was true of all postrevolutionary regimes in socialist countries, but the frank acknowledgment of the attenuated regime legitimacy and the single-minded pursuit of consumption-oriented development were nowhere more obvious than in Kadar's Hungary and Deng's China (Kovrig 1987; Deng 1984). Historical trauma thus created fertile ground for radical economic reform.

Not only was the population traumatized by the past, the leaders were also victimized. Kadar was responsible for the show trials of high-level cadres Jozsef Mindszenty and Laszlo Rajk, among others. Kadar's internment between 1951 and 1954, however, changed his political beliefs and turned him into a pragmatic politician keenly aware of the excesses of charismatic despotism (Gati 1974). Even though he deserted Nagy and joined the Soviet-supported Revolutionary Workers' and Peasants' Government in 1956, before the Soviet intervention, and was chosen by Moscow as the HSWP's leader after the suppression, his disillusionment with Communist dogma and his pragmatic attitude toward economic reform gradually became obvious as he announced the alliance policy, purged hardliners from the party, and implemented the New Economic Mechanism. Deng's experience was similar in that he started out as Mao's major lieutenant but then was purged and humiliated (together with Liu Shaoqi) during the Cultural Revolution. Even though Deng chanted revolutionary slogans after his rehabilitation in 1973, his major goal was to help Premier Zhou Enlai promote the Four Modernizations (in agriculture, industry, science and technology, and national defense), an act that caused his rift with the Gang of Four and resulted in his purge after the 1976 Tiananmen incident. Deng's second rehabilitation in 1977 and his political ascendance after the end of 1978 gave him the best opportunity to implement his reformist policies. The dramatic fluctuations of Deng's political career turned him into a pragmatist par excellence and made him capable of defying dogma and promoting economic reform. As with Kadar, his past experience thoroughly removed the ideological constraints on this first-generation Communist leader, who was then in a position to contemplate and implement radical economic reform.

With the improvement of the people's living standards perceived as the only way to rebuild legitimacy, and given maximum flexibility on the part of the elite to change the economic structure, the regime is nevertheless left with the question of what kind of economic reform is needed to achieve its objectives. The pre-reform economic structure in Hungary was a typically Stalinist command system with its priorities set on high investment and heavy industrialization. The old Maoist system in the PRC was also built on a command hierarchy with similar priorities and was infused with a strong dose of egalitarianism, a disdain for material incentives, and an obsession with provincial self-sufficiency (Harding 1987: chap. 2). As far as the postrevolutionary elite of the two countries were concerned, the major defects of the old system were stagnant consumption and sluggish growth.[9] The primary tasks, then, would be to shift national resources from accumulation and heavy industry to consumption-oriented development, and to improve efficiency at a time when easy sources of growth had been exhausted and increased productivity would have to be tapped if growth were to continue (Hewett 1980: 520).

The two reform tasks could be tackled using two strategies. The first strategy would command a shift of resources from investment and heavy industry to agriculture, light industry, and services. It would also make administrative and technical reforms within the command system in order to improve its efficiency. The second strategy would introduce market as the main resource allocator so that profit-maximizing enterprises would produce more consumer goods to satisfy popular demand. It would also rely on market to generate competition among enterprises and force them to be more efficient. The first strategy is one of perfecting the planning system, whereas the second is one of replacing plan with market.[10] All post-revolutionary regimes in the socialist countries had tried the first strategy to some extent, but Hungary and the PRC (together with Yugoslavia) were distinct in adopting a marketization program. However, marketization, or delegation of control power, is not to be confused with privatization, or delegation of income power. The marketizing strategy, however radical it may appear in comparison to plan perfection, is still short of a transformation of the ownership structure. What the elite were aiming at was a version of market socialism, with public enterprises competing in liberated, though not totally free, markets. It was assumed that this hybrid model would improve living standards by shifting national resources to satisfy consumer needs, and by increasing productivity while maintaining the party-state's ultimate claim on the means of production.

In 1965, Hungarian reformers began to decentralize the newly recollectivized agricultural sector by dropping obligatory plan targets except in grain production.[11] Further marketization reforms, heavy investment, and subsidies led to success in terms of abundant self-sufficiency, prominent export of farm products, introduction of new technology, acceptable income distribution, and high labor and land productivity. There was a small efficient private sector in symbiosis with the dominant socialist realm. In general, the Hungarian socialist market reform proved capable of meeting the elite's objectives of improving living standards while preserving the socialist character of the ownership structure (Marrese 1983; Csaki 1983).

In the PRC, measures to transfer both control and income power to households had been implemented since 1979. The "household responsibility system" gradually gained dominance as a result of spontaneous actions at the local level and subsequent approval and encouragement from Beijing. The new system allotted a certain amount of land to an individual household on a long-term basis, with the household to receive all income from the land after meeting certain obligations to the collective and the state. In June 1982, the household responsibility system had spread to 86.7 percent of all agricultural production teams, and in January 1983, a uniform policy was announced to officially install the new system at the national level. In 1985, a decision was made to abolish the three-decade-old compulsory procurement system and transfer full control power to households. The only remaining restriction on households' property rights was their limited tenure. The PRC's rural reforms thus brought about a decollectivization and quasi-privatization of its agriculture (Perkins 1988; Harding 1987).

As in the Hungarian case, the successful agricultural reform created pressure to introduce reform measures in industry (Hare 1988: 57; Marshall Goldman 1987: 244–45; Shirk 1988: 360).[12] But while Hungary's collective agriculture thrived on the principle of market socialism, the PRC's household responsibility system was from the very beginning a move toward both marketization and privatization (Yan 1989).[13] Indeed, the thorough transfer of income power to households was the earmark of the Chinese agricultural reform. Thus, the Hungarians and Chinese had different referent experiences in agriculture. As a result, when they shifted the focus of reform to the cities, the Hungarians tended to stick to the principle of market socialism, that is, marketization without privatization, to a greater extent than the Chinese, who tinkered with privatization proposals and various ownership forms shortly after marketization measures proved unable to solve their economic problems in industry.[14]

Content of the Industrial Reform

The basic principles of the Hungarian NEM of 1968 were the same as those embodied in the CCP's October 1984 Decision on Reform of the Economic Structure. Both introduced market as the major allocator of materials and products, replacing the traditional system of central planning (Bauer 1983). Managers were granted the control power to make production and exchange decisions. Still, there were four sets of constraints on enterprises that prevented them from behaving like their counterparts in a capitalist economy. These were state ownership, circumscribed markets, monopolies, and economic regulators or levers.[15]

In general, reformers in both countries stuck to the principle of market socialism, that is, marketization without privatization. Both were interested in preserving the state's role as the dominant owner in the national economy. Since privatization was excluded as a means of providing a penalty/reward system for enterprises, the state was forced to simulate its effect by linking enterprise profits, retained profits, and personal rewards through complicated formulas.[16] These formulas were designed and implemented by economic bureaucrats and were subject to change. Goals other than that of improving motivational efficiency, such as equitable distribution of enterprise profits, worker job security, and control of inflation, were simultaneously pursued using the same formulas. The soft and multifunctional nature of the incentive structure led on the one hand to vertical bargaining between managers and bureaucrats, and on the other to reduced attention to market signals. Finally, the state still wielded great power over managers, which subordinated them to their bureaucratic superiors (Kornai 1989: 80).

In both Hungary and the PRC, bureaucratic manipulation of the incentive formulas created two distortions: "whipping the fast ox" (*bianda kuainiu*), wherein profits were skimmed from efficient enterprises through adjustment taxes; and the soft budget constraint, whereby the state bailed out loss-making enterprises. At the root of these two distortions was state ownership of enterprises. Since the state was interested in actively using its ownership rights to influence the distribution of profits and losses, the treasured principle of "taking responsibility for one's own profits and losses" (*zifu ying-kui*) could not be honored.

The major difference between the Hungarian NEM and the Chinese economic structural reform resides in their different attitudes toward marginal privatization. This difference, as stated, has to do with the preceding reform program in agriculture. Another important reason for this divergence was the difference in relative resource endowments between the two countries. The PRC is labor abundant and its industry had difficulty absorbing the surplus labor released from agriculture as the reform improved its efficiency (Hare 1988: 61). *Getihu* (small private businesses) and, later, *siying qiye* (larger private enterprises) were tolerated, legalized, and ultimately protected by the 1982 constitution and a 1988 constitutional amendment partly because they provided employment for displaced peasants. The situation in Hungary was entirely different. Even though reformers were initially worried that the NEM might create unemployment problems as enterprises tried to lay off unnecessary workers, full employment was achieved in Hungary and the country actually faced a labor shortage, not unemployment (Portes 1970; Kornai 1986b). Because they had no need to tolerate unorthodox ownership forms in order to absorb displaced labor, Hungarian reformers did not touch on the issue of privatization in their first wave of industrial reform (from 1968 to 1972). In stark contrast, ownership reform was in vogue in the PRC shortly after the guidance planning of 1984–85 created an overheated economy (the toleration of *getihu* began much earlier, in 1982), and the reform pendulum basically swung between marketization and privatization in the first wave of the Chinese industrial reform (from 1984 to 1988). In Hungary, even though the second economy and the black market were prominent phenomena, the regime did not begin to incorporate them into the formal sector until 1982, fourteen years after the NEM was introduced, and not without a retrenchment interlude between 1972 and 1978 (including a 1975 campaign against private businesses) (Kovrig 1987). Finally, only *getihu*-sized private businesses (those with no more than seven employees) were allowed after the reform (Kornai 1989: 89). In short, compared with the Chinese, the Hungarians had a more conservative attitude toward privatization.[17]

Although industrial reform brought about marketization in both Hungary and the PRC, the markets that emerged were carefully circumscribed. Reformers preserved large territories for plan, where the state commanded enterprises in the old way. In Hungary, this market circumscription was necessitated by the country's role in the Council for Mutual Economic Assistance. In order to trade with socialist countries that remained faithful to central planning, Hungary had to retain direct control over the sectors that fulfilled the council's delivery obligations. This control then extended into areas supposedly covered by market principles. In the PRC, a two-tier system was created that carefully separated the market and plan realms. The purpose of this system was to reduce the shock of transition as the economy shifted from the old to the new structure, to "change a big earthquake into several small tremors" (Wu and Zhao 1987: 314). Because the plan and market realms were not divided on the basis of product (i.e., certain products would be governed by plan, others by market) or enterprise (i.e., specific enterprises would produce goods under plan directives, others would follow market signals), but instead on the basis of *quantity* (i.e., fixed quotas had to be delivered to the state, and any above-quota output was at the disposal of the enterprises), enterprises ended up producing the same goods for different realms. Since price differences always exist between the plan and market sectors, an irresistible temptation was created for managers (who had been turned into profit-maximizers) to take advantage of the situation by shifting materials and products from the plan realm to the market realm. As a result, the plan was thrown off balance, the market was distorted, and a hotbed was created for official profiteering that caused such a public outrage as had never been seen in Hungary.

Both Hungary and the PRC introduced price reform as they began to reconstruct their industry. But the emerging pricing system in both countries was a distorted one, prone to inflation as a result of its monopolistic structure. Chinese enterprises gained monopolies mainly through regionalism, as local governments protected their markets against the incursion of outside enterprises. The Hungarian functional equivalent of Chinese regionalism was its industrial structure. If we look at the record of the Hungarian price reform, it is clear that the monopolistic structure of the market constituted a major block to competitive pricing once administrative control had been lifted. Hungary had one of the most highly concentrated industrial structures in the world as a result of decades of conglomeration. In fact, in order to retain control over individual enterprises, the state effected a series of mergers in 1967, right before the reform started, which drastically reduced the number of enterprises. The result was an industrial structure shaped like an upside-down pyramid: it was characterized by a preponderance of big enterprises and a significant lack of small and medium-sized ones (Ehrlich 1985). The first wave of industrial reform witnessed a partial liberalization of the pricing system that created three categories: state-fixed prices, maxima (roof) prices, and free market prices. Monopolistic enterprises then took advantage of their market positions by raising prices to maximize profits. As the NEM liberated producer prices more than consumer prices, a strong inflationary trend was generated throughout industry.[18] With producer prices rising, the state subsidized consumer industries in order to prevent inflationary prices from being passed on to the general populace (Buky 1972: 34). Wage control was also strengthened to suppress demand. The common lesson learned from the two countries is that price liberalization does not automatically lead to a competitive market, because enterprises holding monopolistic positions try to maximize their profits by raising prices, not improving efficiency (Hua, Zhang, and Luo 1988: 21).

The final set of constraints imposed on the enterprises operating on the Hungarian and Chinese socialist markets were the economic regulators or levers. These were the financial instruments bearing on the profit prospects of the enterprises that the state manipulated to guide the profit-maximizing behavior of managers. They included prices, taxes, credits, grants, interest rates, and so forth.[19] The state manipulated these instruments to guide enterprise behavior in an indirect way. Since economic bureaucrats had the discretionary power to apply these regulators or levers on an enterprise-specific basis, it is no wonder managers bargained with them to seek favorable treatment. Instead of maximizing profits "in the real sphere," enterprises devoted much effort to maximizing concessions from their bureaucratic supervisors "in the control sphere" (Kornai 1986a).

The existence of the economic regulators or levers was the most serious challenge to the ideal principle of market socialism. This was the case because whereas circumscribed markets and monopolies were either measures necessary to stabilize external economic relations, transitional policies to reduce shocks created by the reform, or the unintended result of delegating decision-making power, the strategy of "the state regulates the market, the market guides the enterprises" was an enshrined reform philosophy that conflicted with the very notion of true marketization. The idea was to create autonomous firms that would respond vigorously to market signals and to put into the hands of central policymakers all the instruments of indirect control. The state then pulls the strings and the profit-maximizing agents respond like obedient puppets. In this way, central planners can make sure that enterprises conform to the requirements of the plan. The reformed economy is thus still a planned economy, only the planners now have a new set of instruments at their hands. In this respect, there was no difference between the NEM reformers in Hungary and their Chinese counterparts in the early 1980's. Based on this observation, Janos Kornai refutes Richard Portes's claim that the Hungarian reforms "do make the basic change from a command economy to a socialist market economy" (Portes 1970: 307), and insists that the reforms simply shifted the Hungarian system from one under direct bureaucratic control to one under indirect bureaucratic control (Kornai 1986b: 1701). That said, one cannot deny the fact that the thrust of reform in the two cases was toward market socialism, even though what emerged was a limited and guided socialist market.

On the basis of the preceding discussion, we can actually differentiate between two types of marketization reform. One is a shift from mandatory to guidance planning, following the principle of "the state regulates the market, the market guides the enterprises," that is, indirect bureaucratic control. The other, and the more thorough one, is to introduce a self-regulating market, that is, to let supply and demand reach equilibrium without state intervention. Both types of reform aim at creating a market as the main allocator in the economy. The major difference lies in the state's relation to the market: does the state manage it or respect it? The Hungarian NEM and the PRC's first-wave industrial reform of 1984–88 are clearly of the managing type. Thus market socialism is still a proper description of the reform process in these two countries, but we have to bear in mind that the market that emerged was governed by the state.[20]

Suspension of the Reform

In Hungary and the PRC, with the major legitimacy base of the regime shifting from ideology to the material well-being of the populace, pragmatic leaders adopted a marketizing strategy to channel national resources to consumer goods and create a competitive environment to improve efficiency. However, socialist marketization had serious trade-offs in terms of the material benefits that the regimes had provided under the old system.

The most palpable benefits that socialist central planning

brought to Hungary and the PRC were stable prices for consumer goods (and subsidized prices for necessities), a relatively flat income distribution, and guaranteed full employment. These were the major principles in socialist ethics (Kornai 1986a). The policies based on these principles always had their costs in terms of lost efficiency (in the utilization of productive factors and waste of many products) (Hewett 1980). Consumer prices frozen at low levels were based on government subsidies and failed to send the right signals to the market. A flat income distribution dampened worker incentive. Job security, especially in the version in which everyone was locked into his or her current job, excluded the possibilities of bankruptcy and a shift of labor to more productive activities. As a result, the penalty/reward system was weakened and price signals were rendered meaningless. Both motivational efficiency and allocative efficiency were sacrificed.

After the industrial reform, each regime's marketizing strategy emphasized efficiency, inevitably at the expense of socialist ethics. To be sure, not all the principles of those ethics were challenged to the same degree by the reform. Job security, the most fundamental aspect of the socialist welfare network, was the target of verbal threats but was not actually undermined. In Hungary, the closing of plants was not contemplated when the NEM was introduced (Balassa 1978: 260). Although toward the end of the first-wave reform, in 1971 and 1972, Jeno Fock (the prime minister) and Rezso Nyers (the party secretary in charge of economic affairs) made repeated arguments for "eliminating unprofitable production" and "regrouping labor" (Portes 1977: 786–87), these threats never materialized because the November plenum of 1972 registered a major retreat from market reform. In the PRC, the Bankruptcy Law was removed from the agenda of the National People's Congress several times, mainly owing to the strong opposition of conservatives led by Peng Zhen, the chairman of the Standing Committee of the Congress. When the law was finally put into effect on November 1, 1988, the regime had already made the decision to halt the reform at the September plenum of that year. It was true that in both countries one could find individual cases of bankruptcy, but these were rare exceptions. In short, bankruptcy was not put on the agenda until toward the end of the first-wave reform, and then it was swiftly brushed aside.

The remaining two issues of socialist ethics, price stability and egalitarian distribution, were tackled by the reformers in both countries, though in very different ways. The Hungarians were highly sensitive to the inflationary pressure the reform could create and were successful in controlling consumer prices, mainly through tight wage controls. At the same time, they were keenly aware of the incompatibility between efficiency and equality, and therefore adopted a distributional policy that strongly favored the managerial class vis-à-vis the workers. However, they failed to correctly gauge the discontent of blue-collar workers. The trade unions allied themselves with conservatives to stall the reform. In the PRC, on the other hand, reformers failed to put into their package any serious measures for wage control. The result was less working-class discontent but stronger inflationary pressure generated by extravagant wage increases and bonuses. Then came the ill-timed price reform that touched off unprecedented inflation. The conservatives gained the upper hand in the power struggle and put an end to the first-wave reform. In short, the major issue that touched off retrenchment in Hungary in 1972 was increasing income dispersion, while the prime reason for the retrenchment in the PRC after 1988 was inflation.[21]

The experiences of the two countries show that there is a trade-off between controlling income dispersion and stabilizing consumer prices in a socialist market economy: successfully controlling inflation by suppressing wages leads directly to the deterioration of manual labor's income position. A reforming socialist regime could postpone ownership reform and put aside the bankruptcy issue. It could further control the degree of income dispersion or inflation, but not both. In the Hungarian and Chinese cases, the contradictions between economic and social values strengthened the position of conservatives and put an end to the first drive of industrial reform.

Hungary: Wage Control cum Stratification

Hungarian reformers introduced the NEM in a unique manner. In 1957, a number of economic committees, made up of both party and nonparty specialists, proposed the adoption of indirect methods of economic guidance. These proposals were first published, then rejected, and finally rediscussed and implemented after Kadar ousted his dogmatic opponents: Karoly Kiss, Imre Dogei, Gyorgy Marosan, and others. The Central Committee decided in December 1964 to initiate full discussions of the decentralizing reform. A dozen working panels of experts were formed to deliberate on reform proposals in planning, prices, wages, investment, trade, agriculture, finance, and so on. A consensus emerged and a comprehensive plan was drawn up. However, no significant changes were made until January 1968 (Portes 1970). The reformers tried to construct a complete and coherent model and introduced the reform en bloc in 1968, having taken only limited transitional measures in 1966–67.[22] The long gestation period and the en bloc, coherent introduction of the NEM enabled reformers to carefully think through its possible side effects and to add preventive measures to the reform package. As it turned out, the regime created relatively favorable macroeconomic conditions for decentralized decision making.

Wage control was the technical secret of Hungary's success (Wiles 1974). From the very beginning, reformers were aware of the destabilizing effect inflation would have once the pricing system was liberated. Macro stability was considered necessary if structural reforms were to succeed. Thus reformers put into the policy package a tight wage control that linked managerial income with a "sharing fund," which would be reduced if there was an increase in the average wage.[23] The average wage control pitted managers directly against workers, since their incomes were inversely related. It aroused great resentment and was modified at the end of 1969. However, the new formula (there had been numerous versions of it since 1970) still linked specific aspects of wages (wages paid to newly hired workers, total wage bills, levels of individual employee earnings, wage increases exceeding the increases in value added, etc.) to managerial rewards. It accomplished this in a number of ways (direct deduction of wage increases from the sharing fund, levies on the sharing fund, wage taxes, progressive taxation of individual earnings, etc.).[24] Some form of wage control was always in place, forcing managers to restrict wage increases that they were inclined to make under the soft budget constraint.

The Hungarian wage control served the dual purpose of checking both cost and demand inflation. With labor cost under tight control, the enterprises were not forced to raise product prices. The limits on wage increases also stabilized the level of consumption. Although the regime had difficulty controlling investment hunger under its soft budget constraint (witness the unexpected investment boom of 1970–71), the control over consumption still brought about a manageable aggregate demand. With both cost and demand inflation suppressed, the average inflation rate between 1967 and 1973 was only 1.6 percent (Kornai 1986b: 1770).[25]

Consumer price stability brought about by harsh wage control had its costs. Low productivity and income dispersion were the two major problems. Managers' widespread practice of hiring a large number of unskilled, low-paid workers so that the base wages of more established employees could be increased while the wage level was kept under control resulted in low labor productivity.[26] This problem, however, could be solved by shifting enterprises from wage-level regulation to wage-bill regulation, under which any decrease in staff translated into a greater opportunity for higher wages for remaining workers. The new regulation system gave enterprises strong incentives for rational utilization of labor, without undermining the basic goals of wage control and the suppression of inflation.

The other major problem associated with tight wage control was income dispersion. The income group that bore the brunt of wage control was manual labor. Between 1967 and 1972, these workers lost ground slightly to all social strata except pensioners. Their real wages showed a sharp deceleration in 1971–72 (Portes 1977: 786). They became the have-nots, for whom life seemed to have been better under the old system, when there were no striking differences in income across the populace (Volgyes 1976). They resented the new "middle class": the managers, shopkeepers, scientists, medical doctors, plumbers, and prosperous peasants. This problem was exacerbated by the deliberate actions taken by reformers to differentiate incomes across enterprises and industries. The architects of the NEM, Rezso Nyers in particular, believed that there was a conflict between efficiency and equality, that an increase in equality was associated with no increase in productivity, and that the material incentive system could stimulate work effort and productivity only if it was used for differentiation purposes on quite a large scale (Flakierski 1979: 17). These propositions then translated into a distributional policy strongly favoring the managers and workers in more profitable, not necessarily more productive, enterprises and industries.

Worker frustration with income differentiation on the interenterprise, interindustrial, and intersectoral levels found an outlet in the newly liberated trade unions. In 1967, when the regime decided to legitimate interest group activities, it enacted a new labor code that granted trade unions the right of consent, the right of decision, the right of control, the right of veto, and the right of opinion. Since then the union had evolved into the strongest interest group in Hungary. Although still not comparable to its Western counterparts, the Hungarian union stood in stark contrast to the utilitarian and subservient role played by all other East European unions except those in Yugoslavia. Under the NEM, the union gradually transformed itself from a "transmission belt" to a genuine representative of the workers' interest. The National Trade Union Council took an active role in the decision-making process and often came up with criticisms of the party's policies concerning labor (Robinson 1973: 329). Union leaders insisted on wage equalization and limits on the distribution of income according to skill or ability, on general wage increases, and on reaping for the dispossessed the same benefits enjoyed by the new "middle class." At the HSWP's Tenth Congress in 1970, the 22nd Trade Union Congress in 1971, and the Central Committee plenum in 1972, union leaders exerted great pressure on the regime to change its wage policy. This "workers' opposition" to the NEM and its antiegalitarian tendencies also found support in the Soviet Union and other socialist countries (Gati 1974: 30). The leveling impulse in the ideology of Marxism-Leninism, the long years of repetitious propaganda slogans about the workers' favored position and "leading role," the obvious fact that it was the regime, and not some impersonal forces, that determined wage levels, and the correct understanding that the flawed markets and enterprise-specific treatments were not just distributors of rewards further contributed to the resentment of the working class. High tensions between the state and labor were created that could not be released through the minor compromises promised by the reformers (Robinson 1973: 332).

The first-wave reform in Hungary faced the greatest worker opposition, though other factors also contributed to its reversal in 1972. In order to assure bureaucrats and managers that the reform would not undermine their interests, the institutional hierarchy remained essentially unchanged under the NEM. The individualism and materialism encouraged by the reform were deplored by conservatives in the party. The enterprises and ministries were reluctant and ill prepared to accept the risks of decentralized decision making. Soviet criticism encouraged conservatives to launch an antireform campaign. The 1970–71 investment boom and subsequent austerity measures hampered the reformers' efforts to release the "brakes." Finally, the oil crises and worldwide recession created unfavorable conditions for liberalizing reforms. Despite all of these factors, the fundamental issue determining policy changes after November 1972 remained income distribution and the discontent of the urban working class. The reform simply left out the proletariat (Portes 1977: 784).

At the November 1972 plenum, Kadar sided with the "workers' opposition." He stressed the relative drop in the position of industrial workers, argued that equality had to take precedence over efficiency, and criticized petit bourgeois excesses. As a result, the plenum increased wages for manual workers in state industry by 8 percent, ordered ministries to look into problems in the 50 largest industrial enterprises (which resulted in the restructuring of six of them by direct central intervention), and increased the powers of the planning and price control bodies. By 1973, central allocation planning was restored to 50 percent of the country's larger industrial enterprises (Gati 1974: 30). Price control regulations were tightened and a new interministerial State Planning Committee was set up with the National Planning Office acting as its working arm. In 1976, this committee became the administrative vehicle for the reintroduction of direct administrative control in input allocation and import and export quotas. A campaign against private business was launched in 1975, directed against the auxiliary activities of cooperatives and the second economy in general (Bauer 1983: 314). A system shielding large industrial enterprises against external economic shocks was established (Haberstroh 1978; Bognar 1984: 48). Retrenchment took a political toll, too. Nyers was removed from the Central Committee's Secretariat in March 1974, together with Gyorgy Aczel, the party's leading advocate of cultural tolerance. Then in May 1975, Jeno Fock was replaced as prime minister, and in July 1975 Deputy Prime Minister Matyas Timar was removed from his position. The three major architects of the NEM were no longer in positions of power. Because the Hungarian first-wave industrial reform had hardly touched on the issue of privatization, retrenchment mainly took the form of demarketization. The reform thus ended with the reformers removed from power and the system devolving back in the direction of the old administrative model. The political costs of economic efficiency proved too high for the regime to bear, and the country moved into a period of extended retrenchment for the bulk of the 1970's.

The PRC: Excess Demand and Inflation

The PRC's reform was primarily characterized by trial-and-error experimentation. For example, the household responsibility system was the product of local initiatives and the regime's flexibility in adjusting to new environments and taking advantage of the status quo to achieve its own economic goals (Tang 1988). The industrial reform launched in 1984 was characterized by the same approach, which meant maximum flexibility and a lack of coherent planning, in stark contrast with the Hungarian NEM. Even though a PRC delegation visited Budapest in 1979 specifically to study reform procedures (Hare 1988: 60), and the 1984 Decision on Reform of the Economic Structure reflected a consultative decision-making process involving scholars and experts both inside and outside government (Harding 1987: 212), the lack of a coherent and comprehensive platform put the Chinese reformers in an unfavorable position compared with their Hungarian counterparts. It also prevented them from anticipating possible side effects and taking measures to prevent them.

The crux of the problem was a lack of demand control (both in investment and in wages). Any marketizing reform entails liberating the pricing system. That in itself inevitably creates a one-time price hike, as previously suppressed prices jump to reflect supply and demand, but not sustained price increases that constitute inflation. However, price reform can trigger inflation by activating the full potential of excess demand. It is thus imperative that market reformers take preventive measures to control aggregate demand when the prices are set free.[27] Though not immune from the investment cycle, the Hungarians managed to suppress inflation in consumer prices by tightening wage controls and using state subsidies to prevent the inflationary pressure in industry from spilling over to the consumer goods market. Their Chinese counterparts, however, failed to institute any effective regulation of either investment or wages.

In the PRC, as in Hungary, excess demand was mainly created by a soft budget constraint. The industrial reform had transformed enterprises from output maximizers to profit maximizers, but they still enjoyed a secure position even when making losses. Immune from bankruptcy and buttressed by government subsidies, these enterprises tended to play down cost considerations and jump into risky investments and extravagant use of wage increases and bonuses to stimulate production. In the PRC, the contracts between the center and the provinces that set up the financial responsibility system (*caizheng baogan*) gave provincial governments a strong incentive to expand the enterprises within their jurisdictions.[28] Furthermore, growth in production was still used as a major criterion for evaluating the performance of local leaders (Y. Li 1989: 659). These factors, together with the innate drive of managers and their bureaucratic supervisors to seek expansion for the purpose of gaining prestige and influence, fueled the enterprises' insatiable demand for inputs. With the contraction of the central allocation system, state enterprises could purchase factors of production directly from the market. Since there was no effective wage or investment control, the demand on the factor markets rose sharply after the reform.[29]

The most politically sensitive issue, however, was not producer prices on the factor markets, but consumer prices on the product markets. Neither the PRC nor Hungary was capable of fully controlling its producer prices, though the Hungarians did not have to worry about rising labor costs. It was the lack of effective wage regulation in the PRC[30] and its impact on consumer prices that made a great difference between the two countries (see Table 5). A rapidly expanding wage bill in China directly raised the level of demand on the consumer product markets through workers' marginal propensity to consume. Rising wage levels also contributed to cost increases by raising the price of labor. Unable to control this critical aspect of the economy while pursuing market reform, Chinese reformers conjured up the specter of both demand-pull and cost-push inflation on the consumer product markets.

TABLE 5
Inflation in Hungary and the PRC as
Measured by the Rate of Increase in
the Annual Consumer Price Index

Hungary		PRC	
1968	0.0%	1984	2.7%
1969	1.4	1985	8.8
1970	1.3	1986	6.0
1971	2.0	1987	7.3
1972	2.9	1988	18.5
Avg.	1.5%	Avg.	8.6%

SOURCES: Hare 1977: 322; Y. Li 1989: 685.

The loose wage control can be attributed to the regime's unwillingness to suppress worker income when the reform significantly
improved the living standards of the peasants, the getihu, and those
involved in emerging private businesses, and later on, when inflationary pressures built up in the economy. In 1976, the real wage
reached its lowest point since the mid-1960's. After declining
steadily through the Cultural Revolution decade, it sunk to around
10 percent below the 1965 level. Over the period from 1977 through
1980, it increased by an amazing 20.9 percent. From 1980 through
1983, real wages stagnated and increased by only 1 percent (Naughton 1986). However, the same period witnessed the installation of
the household responsibility system, rapid increases in peasant income, the emergence of "ten-thousand-yuan households" (wanyuanhu), and the proliferation of prosperous getihu in the cities. In
terms of sectoral income inequality between agriculture and industry, the traditional "urban bias" was substantially reduced during
this period, in which the benefits of the reforms fell mainly in rural
areas (Adelman and Sunding 1987). But urban residents complained
loudly about the deterioration of their income position, and reformers did not hesitate to take advantage of this situation to make a
case for urban reform (Shirk 1988: 360). This constituted one of the
major reasons for the introduction of the industrial reform in 1984.

Instead of tightening wage control to stave off inflation, as in
the Hungarian NEM, Chinese reformers made substantial upward
wage adjustments at the end of 1984, before raising consumer
goods prices early the next year. The idea was to reduce the shock
of the price reform by compensating workers beforehand (Naughton

1986). This policy made political sense when put in the context of the wage stagnation of the previous three years, but the result was huge excess demand for consumer goods and a disastrous inflation that could only be brought down by curbing wage increases. This was repeated in cycles: when the economy expanded, the wage bill rose; the regime's policy then shifted to contraction, and the wage bill was slashed. It was obvious that the regime put great emphasis on the goal of maintaining labor's income position even at the risk of incurring inflation.[31]

The state was ill prepared for this inflationary situation. As the reform transferred more and more income power to the provinces and enterprises, the center commanded fewer and fewer financial resources. Overextended investment, the rapidly expanding wage bill, and huge government subsidies then directly translated into the state budget deficits. Because the central bank, the People's Bank of China (PBC), was directly controlled by the State Council, there could be no independent monetary policy. The Ministry of Finance simply covered its budget deficits through unrestricted overdrafts on its account with the PBC (Y. Li 1989: 657). As a result, the growth rate of the money supply was determined by government spending. As state enterprises spent more, more money was created. Local branches of the PBC were under pressure from provincial leaders to extend easy credit to enterprises within their jurisdictions. Though the PBC was interested in currency stability, its role was limited to implementing policies decided on by the State Council and local governments (Holz 1992: 20–21, 34). Because both central and local governments were unable to decide on a tight monetary policy, for economic and political reasons, inflationary pressure inevitably built up.

Excess demand in both the factor and product markets, an inflationary monetary policy, and structural distortions such as monopolized markets and a two-tier pricing system (see Chap. 2) created a hotbed for inflation. When prices were decontrolled, the inflation rate surged. Then the state suppressed aggregate demand, and the economy slowed. Unable to tolerate the drop in the single most important indicator of the success of the reform, the regime relaxed its contractionary policy and another cycle began, only on a larger scale. In 1984, at the beginning of the marketizing reform, the state pumped 26.2 billion rmb into the economy, more than the total money supply of the past 30 years combined. The state then took contractionary measures in 1985, and industrial production plunged to a record low. The economy was expanded again in 1986, only to be slashed by the "two tight policies" (tightening money and credit) in the autumn of 1987, when inflation was in the offing. As industrial production began to slide in the first quarter of 1988, reformers reversed their policy yet again. In May, a price reform was implemented that resulted in extremely high inflation. The regime was forced to adopt the harshest austerity policy to date, which gradually devolved into a retreat from reform. From 1984 to 1988, the first-wave industrial reform had witnessed three cycles of expansion and contraction (*Jingji Ribao*, Nov. 3, 1989), ending with an inflation rate of 18.5 percent in 1988.

In sharp contrast with Hungary, where the first-wave industrial reform was accompanied by only one unexpected investment boom and where consumer prices remained under tight control, the PRC clearly failed to provide a stable macroeconomic environment for the reform. Each time major reform measures were implemented, they were accompanied by expansionary economic policies. When overheating ensued, the reform was blamed and a conservative trend set in. This synchronization of reform and business cycles could have been avoided (Dittmer and Wu 1993). The Hungarian model deliberately unlinked the two cycles: it pushed for market reform while checking aggregate demand.

The mode in which the PRC's industrial reform shifted to retrenchment (*zhili zhengdun*) was similar to that in Hungary. First, the paramount leader (Kadar or Deng) sided with conservatives at a critical central committee plenum, calling for a halt to reform and directing national attention to neglected issues (increasing manual workers' wages in Hungary and suppressing inflation in the PRC). Demarketizing and deprivatizing measures followed. Institutional changes accompanied these measures (for example, the installation of the State Planning Committee in Hungary and the dismantling of the Research Institute on Reform of China's Economic Structure in the PRC, the former move intended to reconcentrate planning power, the latter to destroy the reformers' most prominent think tank). A political toll was exacted, and reformers were ousted (Rezso Nyers, Jeno Fock, Gyorgy Aczel, Matyas Timar, etc., in Hungary; Zhao Ziyang, Hu Qili, Yan Mingfu, etc., in the PRC, where, it

should be noted, the political upheaval in Tiananmen Square has-
tened their downfall). The country moved into an extended period
of retrenchment (1972–79 in Hungary, 1988–91 in the PRC). As history shows, Hungarian reformers were able to put the country back
on the reform track in 1979. On the Chinese side, there was every
sign that the PRC's second-wave reform was under way in the winter of 1991–92.

Second-Wave Reform

Hungary was forced back to the reform course by its insatiable
demand for investment goods, deteriorating terms of trade in the
1970's (about 20 percent over the decade), global recession and the
lack of competitiveness of its exports, trade imbalances, huge foreign debts, a 10 percent fall in national income over the period, and
finally, the requirements of austerity (Hare 1988; Kovrig 1987; Marshall Goldman 1987). At the end of 1978 and the beginning of 1979,
Hungary's economic policymakers recognized the gravity of their
problems and the dangers inherent in further delay (Bognar 1984:
46). To be sure, there was no necessary linkage between austerity
and reform. In fact, the instincts of the regime were to strengthen
central control over foreign trade, domestic prices, and material allocation in order to redress macro imbalances. It was the failure of
the reconcentrating strategy and the availability of an alternative
platform that changed the course of the country. In this sense, foreign debt and austerity were the catalyst for the second-wave industrial reform in Hungary.

The Hungarian reformers understood that at the root of the
problem was the extension of the soft budget constraint to Hungary's trade with other countries. Because of the virtually absolute security enjoyed by Hungarian enterprises, they had neither the necessity nor incentive to economize on imports or search out profitable export opportunities (Hewett 1980: 484). Investment hunger
ensued. Even though the government was successful in controlling
consumption through wage and price policy, its control over investment was only sporadically effective. As a result, the average annual growth rate of investment increased from 7.0 percent in 1967–
73 to 7.8 percent in 1973–78, when the world economy was in stagnation after the oil crisis (Kornai 1986b: 1721). The ratio of invest-

ment over gross domestic product also continued to grow, uninter-
rupted by the external situation. During the 1970's, Hungary experienced three investment booms, those of 1970–71, 1974–75, and
1977–78. In 1978, when national income utilized grew by 8 percent
while national income grew by 3.9 percent and the dollar trade
deficit rose to over a billion, central planners were forced to
change their strategy. The immediate goal was to reduce the foreign
trade deficit. The long-term objective was to improve the efficiency
of the economy. A whole series of reform policies followed, with
their emphases gradually shifting from austerity to marketization
and ultimately to privatization. These policies were always
prompted and overshadowed by the persistent debt crisis. In 1979,
an austerity program was introduced and investment and consumption were cut. In 1980, a price reform was adopted in which the government linked domestic prices with world market prices through
a complicated mechanism. In 1981, a single Ministry of Industry
was created to replace the branch ministries, in order to reduce bureaucratic interference in enterprises. In 1982, large state enterprises, ministries, and local councils were allowed to found new
small firms in an attempt to deconcentrate the industrial structure.
At the same time, in a major move toward ownership reform, many
private activities in the second economy were legalized. In 1985,
state enterprises underwent a major transformation as councils and
assemblies were created to assume control of the enterprises, a further move toward curtailing bureaucratic intervention and a transitional step toward creating joint-stock companies. A stock market was created, and wholly foreign-owned companies were allowed to participate in it. The dramatic political changes that had
been taking place since 1986 and the tide of democracy sweeping
Eastern Europe in 1989 pushed the reform even further. Most of the
policies of this second-wave reform, especially the early ones, were
aimed at removing the defects of the old NEM, such as lingering bureaucratic control, monopoly markets, and neglect of the second
economy. The reformers were responding to their experience with
the earlier reform and trying to perfect market socialism. But as the
debt crisis persisted and then deepened, the reform platform was
gradually radicalized, hence the increasing emphasis on privatization.

However, there was a basic contradiction between Hungary's

obligation to service its debts and its need to reconstruct its economy. Austerity requires reduced imports and forced exports, which means, among other things, a lack of market competition in import sectors and a soft budget constraint for export sectors.[32] Hungary's heavy debt burden has been both a catalyst of reform and a big obstacle to it. It has forced recalcitrant politicians to take bold steps toward reassigning property rights. At the same time, it has put serious constraints on what they can do to reconstruct the economy without bankrupting it with a liquidity crisis (Young 1989). The country faces a dilemma.

The PRC was also forced back to the reform track when faced with great financial problems. However, the catalyst that touched off the Chinese second-wave reform was not balance-of-payments problems and foreign debt, as in the Hungarian case, but budget deficits. It is true that serious balance-of-payments problems arose as the PRC moved from reform to retrenchment in the fall of 1988, and foreign debt was piling up. The reason for this was quite the same as that underlying the Hungarian case: partial marketizing reform, soft budget constraint, investment hunger, and import cycles. Austerity was also enforced. However, here the two cases diverged. Though retrenchment in the PRC was as ineffective for improving the efficiency of state enterprises as it had been in Hungary, the export drive launched by Chinese reformers in the spring of 1988 persisted during the *zhili zhengdun* period and greatly improved the country's status on the trade front. After 1990, deficits turned into rapidly expanding surpluses. Foreign debt was serviced without a serious drain on the economy. Foreign exchange reserves accumulated. At the end of the retrenchment period, the PRC was worried about protectionist reaction to its export surge, not a lack of competitiveness of its products on the international market. This is in sharp contrast with Hungary's 1973–79 retrenchment, when its dollar deficit steadily grew and the burden of debt servicing became unbearable.

Timing is obviously one reason for the difference between the two cases. The two oil crises hit Hungary hard as its terms of trade deteriorated and demand for its exports slackened because of the global recession. This did not happen in the late 1980's, when mainland China was in retrenchment. However, even if an energy crisis had erupted, the PRC, with its rich oil deposits, would have been in a better position than Hungary was in the 1970's. The other, and more important, cause of the Hungarian-Chinese divergence is the degree of economic development and the size of the labor force in each country. In Hungary, agriculture's share of gross domestic product was 12 percent in 1975, when the country was in the middle of retrenchment (Kovrig 1984: 104). In mainland China, on the other hand, agriculture accounted for 32 percent of gross domestic product in 1989, a year of deep *zhili zhengdun*. At the time the NEM was implemented, Hungary had already achieved full employment. In the Chinese case, agricultural reform released a large pool of rural labor that became a floating population (*mangliu*) that inundated China's large cities on a seasonal basis. In short, the PRC was a huge developing country with abundant labor that was experiencing large-scale urbanization as it shifted from reform to retrenchment. This meant it had great potential for exporting labor-intensive products to the world market. The same advantage did not exist for Hungary in the 1970's, when its degree of economic development and labor shortage precluded an export strategy based on cheap labor.

An export surge and favorable trade balances after 1990 relieved the PRC of the debt crisis that has haunted Hungary since the 1970's. The overall economy of mainland China also regained its high-growth pattern toward the end of the *zhili zhengdun* period. This remarkable performance, however, had more to do with foreign-invested enterprises (*sanzi qiye*), rural industry (*xiangzhen qiye*), private businesses, and the collective sector than it did with the state sector. For all the favorable treatment it received during the retrenchment period, the state sector, especially large and medium-sized enterprises, deteriorated into a miserable situation quite like that of its Hungarian counterpart in the 1970's. In 1989, profits were down 18.8 percent from the previous year; in 1990, they declined another 58 percent. In 1990, around 36 percent of state enterprises were losing money. The interenterprise "triangular debt" rose to 200 billion rmb. The state sector's growth rate was 2.9 percent in 1990, compared with 9.1 percent for collectives, 21.6 percent for private firms, and 56 percent for *sanzi qiye*. Its share in total industrial output dropped from 76 percent in 1980 to an all-time low of 54.5 percent in 1990. Clearly, the PRC had survived the decade-end economic crisis by riding on a dynamic non-state sector, which overcame the drag of inefficient state enterprises. Subsidies to the latter drained the government budget, and the deficit soared to a high of 50.9 billion rmb in 1990, a 37.7 percent increase over 1989. Here the reformers found an urgent need to launch a second-wave reform.

Deng Xiaoping personally launched the campaign in the winter of 1991–92, though party and government leaders had been making sporadic pro-reform statements throughout 1991. The official language was bold: reform was needed in order to take advantage of capitalist practices and recognize exploitation (*People's Daily*, Feb. 23, 1992). However, the policies suggested by the reformers (Zhu Rongji, Gao Shangquan, etc.) were familiar ones. In this new wave of reform, enterprise autonomy would be respected. The scope of mandatory planning would be further reduced. Administrative intervention would be minimized. Prices would be decided by supply and demand on the market. Finally, loss-making enterprises would be closed down in accordance with the Bankruptcy Law. There was talk of smashing "iron rice bowls" (job security), "iron wages," "iron armchairs" (cadre tenure), and eliminating the practice of "eating from the same big pot" (egalitarianism), or the "three *tie* [irons] one *da* [big]." These were reminiscent of the threats of "eliminating unprofitable production" and "regrouping labor" made by Rezso Nyers and Jeno Fock in Hungary in the early 1970's.

Like most of the reform measures in the Hungarian new NEM after the end of the 1970's, the PRC's second-wave reform is characterized by the regime's efforts to remove the perceived defects of the initial reform of 1984–88. The goal is to perfect "socialism with Chinese characteristics," or Chinese market socialism, and not to change the basic ownership structure of the economy. The emphasis is still on marketization, not privatization. It is hoped that this time enterprises will have real power to make production and exchange decisions without interference from cadres or bureaucrats, that the pricing system will genuinely reflect relative scarcities, and that firms will take full responsibility for their performance on the market, including accepting bankruptcies. None of these measures runs against the fundamentals of market socialism, which prescribes full play of market forces while maintaining public ownership. All the factors contributing to the original reform, such as the guiding philosophy of socialist enlightened absolutism, a disil-

lusioned population, pragmatic leadership, the household responsibility system in agriculture, and so forth, plus the elite's unwillingness to privatize the economy for political and ideological reasons, still militate for a deepening of the socialist market reform. In
this sense, the PRC has followed in Hungary's footsteps for yet another stage of development.

Conclusion

The developmental trajectories of Hungary and the PRC are remarkably similar. Although differences can be found in their reform experiences in agriculture, in their attitudes toward marginal
privatization, in the issue that touched off retrenchment in the two
countries, and in the particular catalyst of the second-wave reform,
the overall pattern is the same. In both cases, a pragmatic leadership
was striving to introduce maximum property rights reform without
damaging the state's ultimate claim on the economy, in an effort to
raise the people's living standards and to boost regime legitimacy in
the eyes of a disillusioned population. The basic philosophy of socialist enlightened absolutism, the traumatic imprinting event, the
victimized leadership, the great success in agriculture, and the thor-
oughness of the industrial reform that followed set Hungary and the
PRC apart from other socialist countries. The reform undertaken in
the two countries was aimed at establishing a guided market. The
strategy was to shift from mandatory planning to guidance planning. This is a version of market socialism: socialist ownership
cum indirect bureaucratic control over the market. Both countries
then evaded the thorny issue of job security, but failed to stave off
the dilemma between the competing values of efficiency versus distributional equality in Hungary and efficiency versus price stability
in the PRC. Both were forced into a retrenchment that stabilized
the situation in the short run but was ultimately unable to improve
the efficiency of the economy. Finally, both countries were under
great financial pressure and as a result launched second-wave reforms to relieve pressure on the state treasury.

That said, the PRC may still diverge from the Hungarian pattern. The Hungarian new NEM had three stages: macro stabilization, marketization, and privatization. A steadily deteriorating
economy first compelled the elite to initiate the second-wave re-

form. It then forced the regime through various other reform stages, until full privatization was set as its goal. The Chinese entered the second reform under much less financial stress: budget deficits and domestic debts are less threatening than foreign debts. With balance-of-payments problems under control and inflation down, the PRC did not need to go through a stabilization process, or take on stabilization and structural reforms at the same time (Fischer and Gelb 1991: 92). However, this smoother start may be a mixed blessing. On the one hand, favorable initial conditions reduce the cost of reform (because painful austerity and contractive policies are not necessary) and make it more feasible economically and more acceptable to the general populace. According to reform economists, this means a relaxed environment (*kuansong huanjing*) perfectly suited for launching bold reform projects (Hua, Zhang, and Luo 1988). The third stage of the new reform—privatization—may then be telescoped into the second stage—marketization—and a genuinely mixed economy may emerge from this development. (This is basically an acceleration of the Hungarian reform process.) On the other hand, an easy start also means less urgency to restructure the economy, and a greater likelihood that when faced with strong resistance from the people, as certainly will arise when their "iron rice bowls" and "iron armchairs" are smashed, the regime will back down. Lack of an economic crisis may thus paradoxically dampen the reform drive and make the second-wave reform short-lived. If this happens, the PRC may move into yet another reform cycle, and a decisive breakthrough may have to wait for the next economic crisis.

Fluctuating within market socialism and leaping toward privatization do not exhaust all of the developmental possibilities open to the PRC. Another is reinstituting a command system. The cause of such a development can be found mainly in agriculture. In order to investigate this route of development, we will now turn to a comparison between Chinese economic reform and the Soviet NEP.

Chapter Four

The Soviet Union and the PRC

The major differences between the economies of Hungary (before the second-wave reform) and the PRC (from 1984 to 1991) are their property rights structures in agriculture and, directly related to that, each regime's attitude toward marginal privatization. Hungarian reformers stuck to the principle of market socialism—that is, delegating control power to property users while retaining income power (or ownership)—more closely than did their Chinese counterparts. Hungary's agriculture remained collective after the reform, and its second economy was not officially recognized until the regime was forced to launch the new NEM in the 1980's. The agricultural reform in the PRC, however, privatized property rights to a degree through the household responsibility system, and the regime quickly recognized small private businesses as they emerged. Though marketization remained the dominant reform strategy in both countries, privatization played a much greater role in agriculture and small industry in the PRC than in Hungary. This divergence points to a riskier and more volatile reform route for Chinese Communist leaders, who must weigh the greater gains in efficiency and growth that are possible using the marketization cum privatization strategy against its potentially greater political costs.

Where can we find a Leninist regime in a similar situation, in which agriculture and small industry and trade are private and the state holds the "commanding heights," that is, large industry and other strategic areas of the economy? The New Economic Policy (NEP) period in the Soviet Union from 1921 to 1929 comes immediately to mind. To compare the PRC in the 1980's and the Soviet Union during the NEP is meaningful not only because of the institutional similarities between the two, but more importantly because in spite of these similarities, the two countries diverged into entirely different systems: from 1984 to 1991, the PRC fluctuated within its NEP-like structure, while in 1929 the Soviet Union plunged into state ownership and state control in both agriculture and industry, becoming the world's first command economy.[1] How can we account for this divergence? Why did the PRC opt for the Bukharinite solution, whereas the Soviet Union chose the Stalinist revolution from above? What were the differentiating factors behind this divergence? And what does all of this mean for the prospects of restoring a command economy in the PRC in the 1990's?

This chapter begins with an analysis of the origins of the NEP and post-Mao reforms, followed by a comparison of their political backgrounds and property rights structures. It then examines the structural tensions in the NEP and the pressure that existed at the time to reassign property rights, compared with the situation under Deng's reform between 1984 and 1991. The major factors militating for installation of a command economy in the Soviet Union in the 1920's will be identified to facilitate a more focused comparison with the PRC. As will become clear in the following discussion, the major differentiating factor in the two cases is the elite value system: CCP old guards in the post-Mao era are no longer committed to the revolutionary goals treasured by the Bolsheviks in the 1920's. Because the restructuring of property rights under Deng Xiaoping had greatly improved economic efficiency and created considerable vested interest in economic reform, the elements conducive to the restoration of a command economy were weakened and were unable to roll back the reform between 1984 and 1991. However, the possibility that the PRC will restore the old command system in the 1990's cannot be lightly dismissed, because its current ominous grain crisis is bound to linger, putting pressure on the property rights structure created by the reform.

Because the PRC's property rights structure since the post-Mao economic reform has been characterized by quasi-privatized agriculture and marketized industry, restoration of a command economy, if it happens, will bring about much greater change in rural areas (where the whole economic, political, and social life of the peasantry would have to be reinstitutionalized) than in the cities (where the greatest change would be a tightening of central control over the state and collective industries, together with a squeeze on the marginal private sector). Restoration of a command economy thus would be a transformative phenomenon heavily concentrated in the countryside. The restoration process might begin in agriculture, where the structural tensions of the NEP-like property rights structure are strongest, and then gain momentum and spill over into industry. Hence in this chapter the analytical emphasis will be cast mainly on agriculture.

Origins of the Reform

As in the case of the reforms in Hungary and the PRC, the Soviet NEP was preceded by a traumatic imprinting event: the civil war and War Communism (*voennyi kommunizm*). From the October Revolution in 1917 to March 21, 1921, when the NEP was officially announced, the new Soviet regime tried to impose on Russian society an improvised command economy in the name of War Communism, one geared to the war effort going on at the time.[2] The Land Decree of November 1917 announced the nationalization of privately held land. The peasants were permitted to use such land free of payment, but its transfer (through lease, purchase, sale, or inheritance) was prohibited in order to prevent any concentration of peasant property. The decree resulted in individual peasant households farming socialized land. In the latter half of 1918, as a major measure of War Communism, Lenin tried unsuccessfully to collectivize agriculture through the *kombedy* (committees of the poor) (Jasny 1972). He then resorted to forcible seizures of grain, confiscating virtually all grain stores, even those needed for the peasants' subsistence. In the cities, War Communism began with the socialization of joint-stock companies and banks at the end of 1917. Foreign trade and heavy industry were nationalized in 1918. In 1920, private enterprises with more than five employees ceased to exist (Piettre 1973). Consumer goods were rationed, payments were in kind, and labor was subject to military discipline.[3]

The results of War Communism were predictable. The regime was not in a position to radically reassign property rights in the way that it desired. As a result, industrial output dropped precipitously (by 1920, gross industrial output was down to 31 percent of that in 1913) and was accompanied by a corresponding decline in labor productivity. Agricultural output was less than that needed for peasant consumption alone. Millions died of starvation. There were armed peasant uprisings in the second half of 1920 and in early 1921, usually led by Communists, and demonstrations by urban workers (whose numbers had been halved, from 2.6 million in 1917 to 1.2 million in 1920, because of the food shortages in the cities). These were followed by the Kronstadt sailors' mutiny. The Bolshevik leadership was forced to retreat in the face of the economic debacle and the rising tide of popular unrest. On March 21, 1921, a decree was issued that replaced requisitioning of farm products by an agricultural tax in kind, ushering in the New Economic Policy.

In a sense, the civil war and War Communism, by forcing the Leninist regime to give up its pursuit of revolutionary goals, performed the same function in the Soviet Union as the Cultural Revolution did in the PRC. In both cases there was a disillusioned population and a realistic understanding by the regime that for reasons of sheer political survival it had to come to a truce with that population, an understanding revealed in Lenin's "Either we prove that [we can deliver], or he will send us to the devil" (see Erlich 1967: 8) and in Deng's "socialism cannot endure if it remains poor" (Deng 1984: 197). There was a major difference, however, in the personal experiences of the elite in each country. Bolshevik leaders did not come out of War Communism victimized and traumatized. The power of the party vanguard was blunted after its initial attempt to impose its will on the population (especially on the peasants), but individual leaders did not experience the torture and disillusionment that Deng and his colleagues did during the Cultural Revolution. Even when the Old Bolsheviks fell victim to Stalin's reign of terror in the 1930's, many of them continued to show allegiance to the party and its ideals by cooperating with their interrogators during the show trials. Thus there is every reason to believe that during the 1920's, Bolshevik leaders were fully committed to their revolutionary goals. True, they were puzzled and scared by the stabilization of an international capitalist order in the wake of World War I, and they quarreled among themselves as to the proper strategy with which to pursue their goals under the new circumstances. But their ideals did not fade in the early years of the revolution, and there were no shattering personal experiences to disillusion them. In their eyes, the possibility of a reimposition of revolutionary goals (i.e., socialization of all the means of production) inspired by the value system of the ideology was still very real.[4] In contrast with these Bolshevik leaders, the post-Mao Chinese leadership demonstrates a disillusionment with the utopian goals of the socialist ideology that is clearly connected with the personal trauma they experienced under Mao's rule. Their philosophy is "socialist enlightened absolutism" (see Chap. 3) and their primary concern is regime stability. In short, the Bolshevik regime in the 1920's was still in the revolutionary stage, whereas the post-Mao regime in the PRC has moved into the postrevolutionary stage.[5]

This difference in elite commitments can be looked at in more general terms. There is a unique feature characterizing the process of the pursuit of goals in Communist countries. The very totalitarian nature of the state enables the elite to pursue a positive, substantive goal single-mindedly, in utter disregard of all other possible goals. All the resources of the system are ruthlessly harnessed in the realization of one great ideal. Such a single-minded pursuit can achieve major breakthroughs in a specific field, but always at the price of extreme imbalance and alienation of the population (C. Johnson 1970). Concessions must then be made at this juncture, but as long as the elite value system is intact, and as long as this value system is not adopted by the population, these concessions suggest only a temporary truce, and the elite will eventually make another attempt to impose their ideal.

However, if the damage inflicted by the initial single-minded pursuit is so devastating that it dramatically changes the elite's value commitments, in essence if not in word, then the possibility of transforming society according to an ideological blueprint is exhausted. The disillusioned elite, their mission lost, will instead be preoccupied with day-to-day affairs and the preservation of power. The property rights structure may be redefined to reflect the reordering of elite priorities. However, the implications of this scenario in terms of property rights are more complicated than they may appear at first glance. The property rights structure in a Communist country is determined by a variety of elite considerations, including the value system (or goal culture) of the ideology of the elite. A specific property rights assignment might lose its appeal as the embodiment of a revolutionary ideal but serve certain functions that are in the political interest of the elite (Djilas 1953). One thus has to examine the specific relations between reordered elite priorities and property rights in order to determine whether the old economic system has outlived its usefulness.

Political Background

Although there is a great difference between Soviet and Chinese elites in terms of their commitment to revolutionary ideals, the major political principles in the NEP period in the Soviet Union and in the PRC under Deng are remarkably similar. In both cases, a Leninist party monopolizes political power by excluding opposition, not only in deed but also, explicitly, in principle. At the same time, the party-state acts more like an authoritarian regime than a totalitarian one and contents itself with maintaining political supremacy while allowing the politically nonthreatening sectors of society a great deal of freedom. Within the party, factions are banned but debate is allowed. The costs of losing party political battles are political (ranging from demotions to expulsions), not physical. These features dramatically separate the NEP and post-Mao periods from the heyday of charismatic despotism in both countries, when each regime exercised totalitarian control over society, indulged in a personality cult surrounding the dictator, and punished the losers in intraregime struggles with physical torture and death. The major difference between the Soviet Union in the 1920's and the PRC in the 1980's, however, is that the Bolsheviks were in the process of gradually concentrating political power in fewer hands, in what was an interlude between Lenin's "democratic centralism"[6] and Stalin's personal dictatorship, whereas Deng was trying to disperse power by directing the party away from Mao's dictatorial politics and back to the original political principles of Leninism.[7]

The NEP was described as the first and (before *glasnost* and *demokratizatsia* under Mikhail Gorbachev) most far-reaching liberalization in Soviet political history—a kind of "Moscow Spring" (Cohen 1985: 75). To be sure, even Nikolay Bukharin, the main theorist of the NEP, maintained that the dictatorship of the proletariat entails the existence of a single ruling party and that that party must be united and not permit the existence of "fractions," which will inevitably lead to the development of separate parties (Kolakowski 1981b: 34). Under this premise, "speculators," "counterrevolutionary agitators," and "agents of foreign powers" were treated without mercy. "Revolutionary legality" granted the authorities the power to arrest, imprison, and put to death anyone who presented a danger to the regime. The Cheka (state security service) and concentration camps were set up to safeguard the regime against internal enemies. As for intraparty democracy, in March 1921, Lenin urged the Tenth Congress to pass the Resolution on Party Unity banning factionalism.[8] This action was taken as the party was making a major retreat from War Communism to the NEP and needed to strengthen internal discipline. Bound by this resolution, Stalin's opponents were not able to organize effectively against the general secretary, who gradually tightened his control of the party through the "circular flow of power" (Hough and Fainsod 1979: 46). However, there was no large-scale purge of the elite during the NEP period. The most dramatic penalty Lenin and Stalin imposed on dissenters at that time was expulsion from the party, and even this penalty was rarely imposed on prominent members. Stalin's personality cult did not form until 1929, the year the NEP was abandoned. Ordinary people and party leaders were not asked to demonstrate their ideological fervor in political campaigns. In short, the regime did not go out of its way to expose "potential enemies," and Stalin contented himself with ousting his opponents from strategic positions in the regime.

Outside the political realm, the NEP period was characterized by a generally relaxed atmosphere. Bukharin's idea of "socialist humanism" and free, anarchistic competition in cultural and intellectual life had a deep impact on regime policies. Though writers and artists were required to show loyalty to the regime by not producing anti-Soviet work, they were not required to glorify it. Art and literature were not restricted to specific canons; experimentation was allowed. Writers such as Boris Pasternak, Anna Akhmatova, and Yevgeny Zamyatin, who by no means favored the system, were active (Kolakowski 1981b: 46). In philosophy, Marxism reigned supreme, but there was no official version of it. The natural sciences were not subjected to ideological scrutiny. John Dewey's "progressive" ideas were welcomed. There was an emphasis on the emancipation of women, and the authority of traditional moral values was challenged.

In post-Mao China, the regime gradually shifted from demanding compulsory political participation on the part of the entire population to requiring only its passive obedience. The Four Insistences—on the socialist road, the democratic dictatorship of the people, the leadership of the Communist Party, and Marxism-Leninism and Mao Zedong Thought—proposed by Deng in 1979 set limits on social expression. These are similar to the political assumptions underlying Bolshevik rule in the NEP period. Like the Bolsheviks in the 1920's, all CCP leaders, including Zhao Ziyang, upheld one-party rule, or "the system of multi-party cooperation and political consultation under the leadership of the Communist Party" (*World Journal*, Mar. 18, 1989). The party's rejection of the Western multiparty system intensified as the Soviet Union and Eastern Europe began to experience rapid democratic transformation toward the end of the 1980's. Under the premise of continued one-party rule, any political challenge to the regime was dealt with harshly, beginning with the suppression of the young democrats of the Beijing Spring of 1978–79. The crackdown on the "counterrevolutionary riots" in Beijing and other major cities in 1989 and the subsequent political regimentation vividly demonstrate the regime's unwillingness to tolerate overt challenges to its monopoly of power. "Socialist legality" thus applied only to areas not politically sensitive to the regime.[9] At the same time, intraparty democracy was limited by Deng's rule as the "head of the household" (*dajiazhang*). Though he held fewer and fewer important official positions,[10] Deng was able to rely on his unprecedented personal authority to bypass institutional constraints, draw on whichever group suited his purpose, and retire or purge top party leaders.[11] In doing so, he showed no respect for the rules and procedures of the post-Mao regime that is partly his own creation.

Despite its authoritarian control of society and the lack of procedural democracy within the party, the regime did not indulge in the kind of stormy political campaigns that engulfed the nation under Mao. The "noncampaigns" launched after Deng's political ascendance were qualitatively different from the movements of the pre-reform period (Dittmer 1987: 264). With class struggle removed from the official agenda, people were no longer subject to discrimination and political persecution based on their class origins.[12] Deng's opponents were not subjected to physical torture or even expulsion from the party.[13] As in the Soviet Union during the NEP period, the top leaders used restraint in exercising control over society and the party. Rather than being on the offensive, the regime was simply holding its political ground. This stance, however, did not preclude extreme reactions when the regime was provoked, as witnessed by the bloody suppression of student demonstrators in 1989.

Under Deng Xiaoping, Hu Yaobang, and Hu Qili, the regime adopted a cultural policy that was much more relaxed than that of the pre-reform period. However, the practice of waging battles in the cultural arena and deliberately transferring their implications to the political and economic realms continued. Both conservatives and reformers tried to occupy the cultural front by controlling the major propaganda machines (such as the *People's Daily*), the party and state organs in charge of cultural affairs (such as the Ministry of Culture), the critical front organizations (such as the Chinese Writers Association), and the dominant topics of discussion (such as the epistemological debate on whether practice is the sole criterion of truth, or the question of whether the discussion of socialist alienation is a form of spiritual pollution). Even so, the momentum unleashed under intermittent government relaxation created an atmosphere in which bolder and bolder ideas were presented. The periodical suppressions championed by conservatives usually threatened to undermine economic reform, the paramount goal of the regime, prompting intervention by Deng to restrict the scope and intensity of the "noncampaigns."[14] Each wave of suppression did claim victims, sometimes as a result of Deng's balancing act between liberal reformers and ideological conservatives.[15] But writers and intellectuals critical of the regime usually did not receive punishment greater than expulsion from the party, and as a result of their confrontation with the regime, they gained social prominence and became more outspoken. Like the Soviet regime during the NEP period, the Dengist regime was generally willing to tolerate various forms of art, literature, and intellectual debate as long as they did not explicitly challenge one-party rule. Writers could deal with nonpolitical subjects freely. The omnipotence of Marxism-Leninism was questioned by the regime itself, which admitted that Marx and Lenin "cannot solve all of today's problems" (*People's Daily*, Dec. 8, 1984). The amorphous official ideology, "socialism with Chinese characteristics," also contributed to the latitude allowed for intellectual thinking. Science and technology were well protected from political vicissitudes. Intensive contact with the West, particularly on the part of Chinese students studying abroad, brought a consistent flow of Western ideas to the cities. In rural areas, the relaxation of thought control and economic reform helped revive many traditional values and behavior patterns. Social, cultural, and intellectual pluralism began to gain ground. In short, one finds authoritarian politics and an emergent civil society in China under Deng, as well as in the Soviet Union during the NEP period.

Property Rights Reform

The property rights structures of the two countries reflect the partially relaxed political background prevalent in each at the time. The NEP, introduced by Lenin in March 1921, consisted of a set of concessionary economic policies devised in response to overwhelming pressure from peasants and workers to end the excesses of War Communism. It lasted until 1929, when Stalin announced the start of a full-scale collectivization drive in a *Pravda* article entitled "The Year of the Great Turning Point." During the intervening years, the Soviet Union had a dual economy in which the state controlled the "commanding heights"—large industry, banking, and foreign trade—while interacting via the market with a private sector that included peasant farms, small manufacturing, retail trade, and service enterprises. Here the rule of scale applies. Exactly as in the Chinese reform, the state made concessions where the scale of the economic units was not large enough to constitute an immediate threat to the regime, while maintaining its grip on the commanding (i.e., large) units of economic activity. The smaller the economic unit, the more property rights were transferred from the state to property users.

Another similarity can be found between the NEP and Chinese economic reform in the leading part played by the rural sector in the reformist drive (Chevrier 1988: 10). The major NEP concessions were to the Russian peasants, and the whole NEP period was overshadowed by the precarious relationship between the Soviet regime and the peasantry.[16] The Dengist reform was launched in rural areas, where the regime made greater concessions to the peasants than it ever made in the cities. Unlike the NEP, which was introduced as a package of agricultural and industrial reforms, Chinese industrial reform lagged behind its agricultural precedent by almost six years. Because the rural reform pattern was so successful, it was transplanted (though in a diluted form) to the cities. Thus the agricultural reform in the PRC not only preceded, but also informed and prompted, the industrial reform. In both the Soviet Union and the PRC, the agricultural reform and the private or quasi-private ownership and small-scale production it brought about in rural areas constituted the base for the whole reform edifice. The following is a discussion of the two main features of the NEP, the "commanding heights" principle and agricultural reform.

The "Commanding Heights" Principle

Under the NEP, the Soviet state held fast to the "commanding heights" of the economy, namely large industry, banking, and foreign trade. These were considered vital to the regime's political survival. These areas remained in state hands after agriculture, domestic trade, and small industry were freed from the improvised command economy of War Communism in order to stimulate production. The momentum to decentralize property rights was first unleashed in the March 1921 agricultural reform that ushered in the NEP. The grain requisitioning system was replaced by a tax in kind, and private trade was legalized on local markets. The regime's immediate goal was to encourage the peasants to produce more grain and to allow private tradespeople (so-called Nepmen) to transport it to the cities that were suffering from food shortages. The focus of reform then shifted to industry. In May 1921, the decree to nationalize small industry was revoked, and in July of the same year, Soviet citizens were allowed to set up small-scale industrial enterprises employing no more than twenty workers. In October, a decree was issued ordering that all enterprises that had been confiscated but not actually put under state management be returned to their owners (Jasny 1972: 17). In some cases, enterprises that had been taken over by the state were denationalized and returned to the former proprietors. Because state-owned enterprises proved so inefficient, in July 1921, the state began instead to lease businesses (5,698 in 1923, for example). The leased enterprises, however, employed an average of only sixteen workers. The small private enterprises grew so rapidly that in 1924–25 they contributed 77 percent of the total output for small industry. In contrast, large-scale industry remained almost completely in state hands; in 1924–25, only 1.82 percent of total output was generated by private enterprises. As the number of private enterprises in industry grew, the Nepmen found new sources of products. Ultimately, large state enterprises, small-scale private industry, and peasant households interacted in markets in which the Nepmen, the state, and the cooperative trade network acted as mediators. The Nepmen dominated retail trade, and the state and the cooperatives controlled wholesale trade.[17] A truly mixed economy was brought into being.

Private traders and manufacturers fared well in the initial stage of the NEP, but there was no consistent policy toward them in subsequent years. In 1923–24, with Lenin dying, criticism of the Nepmen mounting (they were prone to conspicuous consumption and public displays of wealth), and the "scissors crisis" evolving (some party members worried about private traders separating the socialist state from the peasantry at a time when peasants were reluctant to produce and market grain for the cities because of unfavorable terms of trade), the triumvirate of Stalin, Grigorii Zinoviev, and Lev Kamenev took measures against private entrepreneurs, imposing heavy taxes, squeezing credit, and limiting deliveries of goods produced by state industry. But in late 1924 and 1925, the whole atmosphere changed as Zinoviev and Kamenev challenged Stalin, who then sided with Bukharin. In 1925, Bukharin was, in effect, directing his famous "enrich yourself" exhortation at the Nepmen as well as the peasantry, because his analysis had concluded that prosperity in the private sector benefited the state (Ball 1985). The April plenum of the Central Committee in 1925, the Fourteenth Party Conference held the same month, and the Fourteenth Party Congress at the end of the year all passed resolutions calling for an end to the kind of restrictive measures taken by the state against peasant households and private enterprises in the cities under War Communism. The initial momentum of the NEP was restored. In this atmosphere, the Nepmen enjoyed lower taxes and an increased supply of goods and credit. The flow of state credit to the private sector was approximately 300 percent greater at the end of 1925 than it had been in October 1924. In 1926, the limit on the amount of property that could be bequeathed to heirs was removed, making it easier for industrial and trade enterprises to remain in business after the deaths of their owners (Ball 1985: 381). From 1926–27 on, however, the economic situation changed and Bukharin's political influence waned. The regime was about to take a dramatic turn in its policy toward the private sector.

At the same time that significant concessions were made to the private sector, the regime retained control of the economic "commanding heights." After the disillusioning War Communism attempt to abolish money, the Bolsheviks recognized the need to restore a money economy and began to set up institutions for that purpose.[18] A People's Commissariat of Finance and a state banking system, composed of the State Bank and several special-purpose banks (for agriculture, industry, electrification, etc.), were created in 1921–22. Under the aegis of these new institutions, financial stabilization was achieved in 1924. The chervonets became the sole currency (the old ruble had suffered a devaluation ratio of 50,000 million to 1 since 1921), and the government achieved its first budget surplus. The financial system created by the Bolsheviks has remained firmly under the control of the regime since its inception.

The state also restored and tightly controlled foreign trade and other economic transactions with foreigners. The country imported grain (to fight the famine of 1921), coal (to rescue state enterprises hit hard by the energy shortage), and investment goods (to help reactivate industrial capacity). A trade agreement with Britain was signed in 1922, and pacts with other countries followed. Lenin spent much time persuading his colleagues to extend concessions to foreign capitalists, on terms much more favorable than those the regime offered Russian capitalists. There were much-celebrated occasions on which Western capitalists visited the Soviet Union and offered ambitious plans, but very little came of them. The 68 foreign concessions which existed in 1928 accounted for only 0.6 percent of total industrial output. This was due in great part to mutual distrust and a lingering hostility that stemmed from past experience (confiscations of foreign property, defaults on past debts, etc.).

Large-scale industry was the single most important "commanding height." The state organ directly in charge of this sector was the Supreme Council of the National Economy (VSNKh, or "Vesenkha") attached to the Council of People's Commissars. After abandoning the philosophy of War Communism, during the NEP years VSNKh leased small-scale enterprises to private individuals and implemented a system of *khozraschot* (cost accounting) in large state enterprises, thereby reintroducing currency as the basis for calculations and payments and tightening budget constraints. Dominated by prominent Menshevik economists, VSNKh embarked on the first administrative decentralization ever attempted in a socialist country by creating "trusts" (in total control of factories under them) that had a high degree of autonomy and financial responsibility. Profit maximization was recognized as the chief goal of the trusts. Transactions among trusts, the state trade network, and the private sector were made on the basis of market principles. However, VSNKh had the authority to control planning and personnel matters within the trusts. Another planning agency, Gosplan (the State Planning Commission, also dominated by Mensheviks), fell under the jurisdiction of the Council of Labor and Defense. Both VSNKh and Gosplan issued plans whose degree of authority varied from one trust to another. Generally speaking, this was not yet a Stalinist command economy, and the plans served more as guidelines or forecasts than as detailed, authoritative orders. Only the key sectors of heavy industry that produced strategic items were subject to detailed supervision and control. Despite its extensive efforts at decentralization, the regime made no attempt to privatize state enterprises in large-scale industry. This area was considered the core of the economy and the base upon which an industrialized socialist power would be built.

The "commanding heights" principle is also obviously at work in post-Mao China. As in the Soviet Union, the reform first gained momentum in agriculture, where the household responsibility system created numerous highly motivated petty producers without causing a concentration of landownership. The small scale of agricultural production made it easier for the regime to grant property rights to peasant households that verged on full privatization (as we will see in the next section, in the NEP case the transfer of rights actually amounted to full privatization). Agricultural markets were revived to provide outlets for peasants' surplus produce, and private trading thrived. Then the reform was introduced into the cities. In 1982, the *getihu* were protected by the new constitution, in part to ensure that they would absorb the surplus labor released from agriculture after the rural reform. Leasing of state enterprises soon became a prominent phenomenon, and was given national attention together with the ownership reform (*suoyouzhi gaige*) of 1986. In each of these cases, the regime was perfectly willing to grant full property rights (both income and control power) to the users of small units of production. But as the production scale increased, the property rights transferred to users diminished (see Table 4).

As in the NEP case, in China the new property rights forms waxed and waned with the political tide. The discussion of political reform by Deng in 1986 gave a boost to *suoyouzhi gaige*, but the student demonstrations in the winter of 1986–87 that brought down Hu Yaobang, and the following Anti–Bourgeois Liberalization Movement, dampened the reform momentum. Zhao Ziyang's success at the Thirteenth Party Congress in 1987 brought about a new surge of reform, which then stalled in September 1988, following disastrous inflation, and was snuffed out after the June Fourth Incident of 1989. Post-Tiananmen China witnessed the suppression of Chinese "Nepmen" by the state, though reform and openness were still emphasized in official statements.

Throughout the reform period, the post-Mao regime held its "commanding heights" as firmly as the NEP regime did. The PRC's banking system, which was under the heavy conservative influence of Chen Yun, remained least affected by the reform of the country's huge economic bureaucracy. The lack of discipline displayed by the People's Bank of China was a result of its subordination to the State Council, which subsidized state enterprises; and the soft credit policy of local branches of the PBC showed their vulnerability to local governments. Both phenomena are indicative of the lack of autonomy of the banking system.[19] Foreign trade and foreign investment were also under state control, though these were areas where the PRC's reform had gone considerably further than its NEP predecessor. However, one wonders how much of this difference was the result of the regimes' different attitudes and how much was related to the much more difficult international situation in which the Bolsheviks found themselves in the 1920's.[20]

As under the NEP, the post-Mao state directly controlled large-scale industry as the single most important "commanding height." In both cases there was a considerable degree of decentralization, with trusts and enterprises granted the power to make important production and exchange decisions. The functions of the various ministries in the Chinese State Council and State Planning Commission (*jiwei*) were very much like those of VSNKh and Gosplan in that they made and enforced plans generally as guides and forecasts, but where the production of items of strategic importance was concerned, they issued detailed orders. In both the Soviet Union and the PRC, the lack of privatization in large industry demonstrated the regime's intention to keep this strategic sector of the economy under its firm control.

Property Rights in Agriculture

The property rights structure in agriculture under the NEP was first established between 1906 and 1911, as a result of the Stolypin reform. This reform, designed by the last competent minister of Tsar Nicholas II, P. A. Stolypin, was an effort to complete the 1861 emancipation of the serfs, which allotted land to the peasants but required them to pay dues for the redemption of the land and transferred property rights not to individual households but to the *mir* (community).[21] Thus the peasants were still not free to leave the land. The Stolypin reform abolished all outstanding dues, allowed peasants to leave the *mir*, gave them full rights to their holdings, and permitted them to buy and sell land. Stolypin's purpose was to encourage the emergence of a class of peasant proprietors who would be prosperous, efficient, and loyal to the tsarist regime. By 1916, two million households (or 24 percent of the households in forty provinces of European Russia affected by the reform) had left their communities and established individual farms (Nove 1982: 22). Agricultural production rose rapidly and rural income increased. But because the large estates allotted to landlords and the church in 1861 were not included in the Stolypin reform, the peasants remained dissatisfied.

Then came World War I and the October Revolution. Large estates were seized and divided up in spontaneous actions taken by the peasants. The average size of landholdings diminished. Many landless peasants became petty proprietors. This redistribution of land added to the momentum unleashed by the Stolypin reform, creating a widespread propertied class in the countryside. The subsequent Land Decree that nationalized all privately held land, the abortive effort by Lenin to collectivize agriculture, the coercive requisitioning that took place under War Communism, and the tax in kind that ushered in the NEP showed the changing attitudes of the new Soviet regime toward Russian peasants, but not any significant changes in property rights structures in agriculture. The NEP simply recognized the fait accompli in the countryside. An agricultural sector dominated by petty proprietors was Stolypin's ideal. It was realized through measures taken by the tsarist regime before the war, spontaneous actions on the part of peasants during the revolution, and the reluctant endorsement of the Bolsheviks.

In the Chinese case, no significant land reform was carried out by the pre-Communist regime (the KMT government) that was comparable to the Stolypin reform.[22] Confiscation of landlord holdings and the redistribution of land were carried out by the Chinese Communists. Even before it took power, the rural-based CCP was already in a much stronger position in the countryside than the Bolsheviks had been. The experiences of the land reform added to the organizational edge that the Chinese party had in rural areas (Bernstein 1967), which explains to a large extent the much smoother process of collectivization in China compared with Soviet efforts (in 1918 and in 1929–30). Agriculture in the PRC was collectivized in the winter of 1955–56, by the formation of agricultural producers' cooperatives. Despite all the convulsive changes wrought during the Great Leap Forward of 1958–59, the basic features of this system of collective ownership and production remained intact for the next two decades. Although 7 percent of the arable land of each collective was reserved for private plots, and rural trade fairs provided outlets for produce grown in spare-time farming, these were merely marginal phenomena. In short, both control and income power were fully socialized, and they were bundled together. Private farming and private income were insignificant and tightly restricted.

Toward the end of the 1970's, the lack of allocative and motivational efficiency in agriculture forced the post-Mao elite to reassign property rights. After 1979, reform measures were taken to transfer both control and income power to the households. The first step was to free up rural markets and significantly activate sideline farming. This was followed by gradual transfers of property rights in the collective sector through various "responsibility systems" (Perkins 1988). The most radical of these, the household responsibility system (dabaogan), gained dominance as a result of urging by reform leaders and overwhelming support by the peasants.[23] The creation of this NEP-like property rights structure in agriculture was based on the understanding of the reforming elite that the old system could not serve the purpose of restoring regime legitimacy by satisfying the material needs of the population. The regime then embarked on decollectivizing agriculture. Because agriculture based on households inevitably reduced the power of rural cadres, who had tightly controlled collectives in the past, political resistance to reform was strong, and it took the replacement of Hua Guofeng, the principal leader of the rural cadre corps, by Zhao Ziyang and Hu Yaobang in 1980 and 1981, to remove the major obstacle to reform (Pye 1981: 23). By June 1982, the household responsibility system had spread to 86.7 percent of all agricultural production teams, and in January 1983, a uniform policy was announced to officially install the new system at the national level (Harding 1987: 103).

Unlike the NEP, the post-Mao agricultural reform was not a reluctant recognition of a system created by the previous regime and forced on the Communist elite by society in an effort to thwart their abortive efforts to collectivize agriculture. In the PRC, each decisive turn in the development of the property rights structure in agriculture was brought about by the Communist state. Although local momentum played an important role in initiating the process, it was the state that seized the trend and actively spread the system nationwide. In the Soviet Union, the state accepted what it felt unable to change, until the Stalinist revolution ended the NEP.

The Stolypin reform and the peasants' spontaneous seizures of large estates during the Russian Revolution created a diffuse landownership and petty production that remained the dominant features of agriculture under the NEP. However, it took the Bolsheviks eight years (1917–25) to remove the legal restrictions imposed on private agriculture. The Land Decree of November 1917 adopted the program of the Socialist Revolutionary Party by following a traditionalist and egalitarian principle in assigning property rights. It stipulated that "private ownership of land shall be abolished forever; land shall not be sold, purchased, leased, mortgaged, or otherwise alienated," and that "all land . . . shall . . . become the property of the whole people, and pass into the use of all those who cultivate it." The same decree also forbade employment of hired labor and demanded the land be "distributed among the toilers in conformity with a labor standard or a consumption standard" (Silverman 1972: 79–80). Lenin frankly admitted that the decree was a reflection of the popular demand at that time and was designed to let the peasants solve their problems in their own way. As a result, a property rights structure was created that reserved ownership for the state, but granted full income power (actual ownership) and control power to the users of the land, the peasant households. No time limit was put on the property rights thus granted. But transfers of land, in whatever form, were forbidden. As a result, all property rights regarding a specific piece of land were bundled together and permanently assigned to the tilling household.

War Communism witnessed serious state encroachments on these newly granted property rights. The *kombedy* (committees of the poor) of 1918 and the *posevkomy* (sowing committees) of 1920 were short-lived and failed to produce lasting results. Other measures in these war years, however, had great impact. The system of requisitioning grain (*prodrazverstka*) amounted to imposing ill-defined household-specific quotas on peasant families that left only enough grain for their subsistence. The policy was one of either outright confiscation (as when peasants received no payment from the government) or virtual confiscation (as when the government's procurement price was very low and money had lost its utility in the war-torn economy) (Nove 1982: 60). In order to ensure the government's supply of grain and prevent peasants from selling their produce through unofficial channels, the regime banned private trade. Deprived of the incentives to produce any surplus (unless for the black market), peasants reduced their sowings and production plummeted. Starvation ensued.

In 1921, the NEP replaced *prodrazverstka* with a tax in kind (*prodnalog*), which set a fixed quota that fell well below the requisitioning level. Peasants now knew in advance how much of their harvest would be requisitioned, and they could freely dispose of the above-quota portion. However, the peasants' control power was still limited by the quota. Because the main purpose of *prodnalog* was to revive agricultural production in order to alleviate food shortages in the cities, it made sense for Lenin to allow private trade between urban and rural areas (Erlich 1967: 6). The state's monopoly on such trade was thus abandoned. Private tradespeople offered alternative channels in which peasants could sell their products, which gave them some freedom in making exchange decisions and bargaining on the terms of trade. After the currency was stabilized in 1924, a money tax replaced *prodnalog*. The control power of households was further expanded, because now they could freely decide what to produce. Finally, the Central Committee plenum held in April 1925, in the heyday of the NEP and of Bukharin's influence, removed the restrictions on hiring labor and leasing land. This official action endorsed practices that had been common among better-off peasants for years (in 1925, 6.1 percent of all peasant households leased land, and 1.9 percent hired labor). After the April plenum, peasants could make their own production and exchange decisions, appropriate profits from the sale of their products, decide how to distribute their income, and transfer the property rights in exchange for profits. They were subject to taxation, which was not heavy throughout the NEP period (Millar and Nove 1976: 61). This property rights structure, together with the leveling effects of the Stolypin reform and the Russian Revolution, produced a private agricultural sector dominated by millions of peasant households that farmed smallholdings and held full property rights that were outside state control.

In the PRC, *dabaogan* was not a historical given, but a policy championed by reformers in the regime. The new system allotted a certain amount of land to an individual household on a long-term basis, with the family to receive all income from the land after meeting certain obligations to the collective and the state. As in the Soviet case, large estates were divided into small plots and distributed among the households according to their size or to the amount of their labor available for field work. A huge number of petty producers was created in this way. The new system changed collective ownership into quasi-private ownership by transferring income power from the collectives to the households for a specific period of time. Individual families now had the full authority to appropriate profits and distribute income among their members. The reduced size of the economic units (from production teams of 30 families to single households), a traditional family structure that facilitated income distribution, and a familial corporatism that motivated its members all contributed to increased efficiency in agriculture. At a time when reformers were trying to decentralize property rights, rural families provided a ready alternative to agricultural collectives.

Dabaogan provided not only sufficient linkage between retained profits and individual reward, it also hardened budget constraint.[24] The state was not likely to bail out households running at a loss, and state relief was likely only if the peasants were threatened by starvation (Perkins 1988: 613). As under the NEP, income power and financial responsibility resided in the peasant households.

There remains a great difference between the Soviet and Chinese cases in the realm of income power. Had the Chinese state transferred income power permanently from collectives to households, we would have been able to call this reassignment of property rights a proper act of privatization, regardless of official claims to the contrary (as in the NEP case). But the new system was based on leases lasting only fifteen years.[25] Whether a peasant should be legally regarded as the owner of a piece of property or as merely having an interest in the land of another was debatable (Simonton 1926: 288). In any case, the limited time frame made peasants reluctant to invest in permanent improvements to their land. It also prompted them to engage in "predatory farming," the practice of exhausting the utility of the land before it was taken back by the state, and to totally disregard conservation of resources (Ch'en Yu-Ch'en 1988). This quasi-privatization, that is, privatization attenuated by a limited time period, thus generated intensive profit-maximizing behavior in the short term at the expense of long-term profit prospects.

Under *dabaogan*, the power to make production and exchange decisions was granted to households in two stages. Between 1983 and 1985, the first stage of reform witnessed a diluted system of compulsory delivery quotas, under which peasants had to first satisfy the requirements of the state by selling a quota at the state-fixed procurement price, but then could sell the rest of what they produced at a premium above-quota price, also set by the state, or on the free market. The existence of the quotas restricted peasants' choices as to what they could produce and with whom they were to make exchanges. But the above-quota area was unrestrained, and there peasants could exercise their control power to maximize profits. This system was very similar to the 1921–24 tax in kind under the NEP, both in terms of the quota restricting the control power of peasant households and in terms of the above-quota discretion (the terms of exchange under *prodnalog* were of course less favorable than under the Chinese system).

The quota restriction was removed, as in the NEP case, at the second stage of reform, which began in 1985. For political reasons, the Chinese regime did not let urban residents pay the full cost of food items. A portion of the prices of agricultural products was absorbed by the state through subsidies. Because the government had substantially raised procurement prices in the early 1980's to encourage production, state subsidies to agriculture rose rapidly.[26] The tremendous burden on the state treasury forced party leaders to consider relinquishing the compulsory quota system. The record grain harvest of 1984 (407 million metric tons) convinced reformers that quotas were unnecessary. It also exacerbated the state's budget problems, since a great deal of surplus grain was sold to the state at the premium above-quota prices. In 1985, a decision was made to abolish the three-decade-old compulsory procurement system (for all but a few products) and to transfer full control power to households: peasants could produce whatever they wanted and sell their products to whomever they considered appropriate. The state still offered contracts to the peasants, but the latter did not have to accept them.[27] This 1985 system was basically the same as the Soviet system after the introduction of the money tax in 1924. The new, expanded control power of the Chinese peasants, however, like their income power, was subject to time limits stipulated in their leases.

Not only were income and control power granted to households, they became transferable. When the household responsibility system was first introduced, the regime adopted a stance that resembled that reflected in the Soviet Land Decree of 1917, asserting that commune members only had the right to cultivate their contracted land, not the right to rent it out, buy or sell it, transfer it, abandon it, or hire other people to cultivate it. As in the Soviet case, Chinese peasants immediately began to do all of these forbidden things. The family farms created by decollectivization were either economically inefficient or simply not viable because of their small size or unfavorable location. The free flow of factors of production—land, labor, and so forth—was necessary for economic growth and efficiency. The profit-maximizing peasants acted in the direction of this economic logic by leasing land and hiring labor, tactics which were then endorsed by the reform leadership. The regime's Central Document No. 1 of 1983 approved private hiring of labor, and in 1984 the regime agreed to the practice of leasing land, though the attenuated nature of the property rights of households required that such transfers be called *zhuanbao* (transfers of contract), that is, transfers of a bundle of time-constrained property rights. Overall, like the Soviet peasants between 1925 and 1929, Chinese peasant households at the second stage of agricultural reform enjoyed the control power to make production and exchange decisions, the income power to appropriate profits and distribute income, and the power to transfer property rights for a profit (though all rights were burdened by a fixed tenure). This basic property rights structure, together with the egalitarian way in which the collective lands were divided up,[28] created a quasi-private agricultural sector characterized by peasant households farming smallholdings and claiming almost complete property rights that were outside state control.

Structural Tensions

The NEP and post-Mao reforms demonstrated an impressive array of similarities. Both were prompted by a crisis situation in which the dictatorial imposition of the ideology of the elite undermined regime legitimacy. Politically, both regimes acted in an authoritarian, rather than a totalitarian, way. In both cases one finds a mixed economy characterized by the "commanding heights" principle and an agricultural sector that played a leading role in property rights reform. The NEP ended in the Stalinist revolution from above, which transformed Russian society to a much greater extent than did the October Revolution. Property rights were radically reassigned, and a command economy replaced the mixed economy of the NEP. Between 1984 and 1991, a similar structure in post-Mao China produced some of the same tensions evident under the NEP, tensions that militated for the restoration of a command economy. However, other factors offset these tensions and prevented a rollback of the reform.

During the 1920's, the debate among Bolshevik leaders on whether to continue the NEP centered on two groups of considerations. The first group had to do with the perceived need for industrialization. Three major factors contributed to this need. One was the international isolation of the Soviet regime and the fear of foreign invasion, hence the need to build up heavy industry and military capacity in order to defend the revolutionary homeland. This consideration was reinforced by the deep-rooted desire of Soviet leaders to catch up and compete with the West. The third factor contributing to the regime's commitment to industrialization was based on the Marxist teleology embraced by the Bolsheviks: social progress is measured by productive forces that in modern times can only be expanded through industrialization. In more practical terms, industry and urban proletariat were considered the pillars of the Soviet regime, the "dictatorship of the proletariat" brought about by a socialist revolution.

The second group of considerations emphasized the need to change rural institutions under the NEP. Here ideology played an even greater role in defining the desires and fears of the elite. Throughout the NEP period and across political factions, there was a consensus among the Bolsheviks regarding the need to check the power of the kulaks, which was considered a direct threat to the regime's survival. In the minds of the Bolsheviks, who used Marxist class analysis to understand their environment, any economic power in private hands translated into political power against the socialist state. Politics was considered a reflection of the underlying economy. The distribution of power in the political realm was directly related to the distribution of power in the economic realm. The threat perceived by the regime was defined through an ideological prism that identified property rights with political power. The rights structure thus gained paramount importance. The regime was also faced with the practical problem of procuring grain under a system of private agriculture and multiple channels of trade in which it could only indirectly control the flow of agricultural produce. Finally, it was only natural for the Bolsheviks to question the efficiency of petty production based on old technology and outdated communal practices.

These two groups of considerations were present from the beginning of the NEP, but discussion of them intensified as the economic situation worsened toward the end of the decade. Opponents of the NEP (the Left) argued that the property rights structure of the day could not achieve the goals of the regime (such as industrialization), but would only weaken its political power and moral commitments. NEP supporters (the Right), however, pointed out that it was a dependable, though perhaps slow, vehicle for the ideals of the elite, and that there was no alternative to it. The champions of these two positions did not always stick to their original stances, as witnessed by Stalin's maneuvering between the Right and the Left.[29] Factional and personal interests were obviously involved, but the changing environment, as perceived by the elite, played a dominant role in bringing about transformation under the First Five-Year Plan.

The two groups of considerations—those surrounding industrialization and those surrounding agricultural reform—began to interact intensively in an anti-NEP direction in 1926–27, when prewar levels of production were reached. The restoration period ended at that time. The high rates of growth experienced up to 1926 were attributed to the utilization of production capacity already in existence but temporarily demobilized by war. Hence the growth pattern of the first half of the NEP did not require much input of fixed capital. But once this easy source of growth had been exhausted, the country could expect only a much lower growth rate if the investment pattern of the past was maintained.[30] Under the pressure of this dismal prediction, the regime began to change its course. The total volume of investments increased by 31.7 percent in 1926–27. At the same time, the procurement price for grain was cut by as much as 20–25 percent. Clearly, agriculture was forced to shoulder the burden of capital accumulation for industry. As the terms of trade for agricultural goods deteriorated, peasants brought less produce to market. In 1928, a grain crisis erupted. Forceful confiscation à la War Communism ensued. The result was a further decline in procurement figures. Finally, Stalin decided to launch an all-out attack on the peasantry by collectivizing agriculture in a frenetic campaign. This attack was synchronized with an urban offensive against the Nepmen, so that when the First Five-Year Plan was completed in 1933, both agriculture and industry had been put under state ownership and state control.

From 1926 to 1929, the perceived need for industrialization— that is, the first group of considerations—prompted the regime to take actions against the peasantry that raised all the fears in the second group of considerations (fears about the power of the kulaks, the inefficiency of petty production, and the state's ability to procure grain) and activated a chain of actions and reactions that ultimately led to Stalin's collectivization cum industrialization drive. This scenario shows how vulnerable an NEP-like economy is to a

Leninist regime under great economic constraints. With a set of similar economic and political institutions, post-Mao China experienced some of the same structural tensions between 1984 and 1991. But in this case, there were mitigating circumstances that acted in the opposite direction. The following discussion focuses on the dichotomy of industrialization considerations versus the considerations of agricultural transformation. As we will see, the pressure for a more centrally directed economy stemmed mainly from agricultural transformation considerations. Industrialization considerations were diluted, redefined, or directly linked with economic reform; hence they contributed to decentralization of property rights.

Industrialization

The fact that the Soviet Union during the NEP period was ruled by a revolutionary elite whereas the PRC in its post-Mao phase was ruled by a postrevolutionary elite makes a great difference in terms of each regime's perception of the threats it faced in the international arena. Marxist-Leninist revolutionary regimes are committed to spreading socialist revolution throughout the world, as in the case of the Bolsheviks in the 1920's, when they had the Third International at their disposal, and the Chinese Communist regime during the 1960's. The goal of exporting revolution to foreign countries inevitably fosters tension between the revolutionary regime and foreign governments (Van Ness 1970). Military confrontation is always a genuine possibility. The regime perceives this threat acutely and directs its attention to its means of defense. However, a postrevolutionary regime is not by definition locked into a zero-sum game with foreign countries with different social institutions. To be sure, traditional strategic interests may dictate the defense posture of the regime and make it play an assertive role in international politics. However, other things being equal, the passing of the revolutionary stage tends to reduce tensions between the regime and the outside world. The perceived threat is diluted and preoccupation with defense is reduced.

The Bolsheviks in the 1920's had fresh memories of the intervention by the West and Japan that took place during the civil war. Stalin's "socialism in one country" represented a realistic recognition of the fact that no immediate socialist revolution could be expected in Western Europe. However, the regime was still fully committed to its revolutionary goals and was aware of the inherent tensions in its relations with the West. The state of isolation in which it found itself and the overwhelming military and technological power of the capitalist countries "encircling" the Soviet Union caused great fear of another foreign invasion. The "plots of Chamberlain and Poincaré," the breaking off of diplomatic relations by Britain in 1927, and the activities of the Japanese in the Far East all added to the threat perceived by the regime. Although some war scares were fabricated by factions in the party, the general belief in the party as a whole was that the regime would face war before very long (Nove 1964: 23).[31] In order to defend the revolution, rapid industrialization was considered a necessity.[32] More than that, the perceived foreign threat determined the direction of industrialization by causing the regime to give top priority to heavy industry, which provided the basis for an arms industry. However, this contradicted the NEP formula, under which the regime was to let the market, which was the major allocating mechanism, dictate the pace and direction of the country's economic development. National resources would then naturally flow to the production of consumer goods, that is, light industry, and defense would not receive the priority considered necessary by the regime. Clearly, the slow-paced, consumption-oriented development of the NEP was incompatible with the defense needs of the regime.

The post-Mao leadership in the PRC had experienced turbulent ideological politics during the Cultural Revolution and had led the country into the postrevolutionary stage (Lowenthal 1983). It was no longer committed to global socialist revolution. This fact meant that tensions based on conflicting ideological values were absent from the regime's relations with foreign countries. The foreign policy of the PRC under reform leaders can be best understood in terms of a balance of power or a strategic triangle (Dittmer 1981, 1992). Revolutionary idealism was gradually replaced by national sovereignty and territorial integrity as the regime's professed core value (Y. S. Wu 1993). In the late 1970's, the PRC elevated its role in the triangle from that of a "wing" courting America's favor to that of a "junior partner" in a united front with the United States against the Soviet Union. It upgraded its status further by improving Sino-

Soviet relations (Griffith 1985) and distancing itself equally from both superpowers in 1982, hence capturing the advantageous "pivot" position. The advantages associated with this position were dramatically demonstrated by the visits of the leaders of both superpowers to Beijing in 1989. In a move that reflected its confidence in its international position and the reduced possibility of foreign invasion, the regime embarked on a unilateral reduction of its armed forces, cutting the size of the People's Liberation Army by one million troops. At the same time that the regime's fear of foreign invasion was reduced, the capabilities of the army were improved through abandonment of Mao's "people's war" philosophy and through collaboration with the West. The fact that the country's military might could be augmented by transforming its military doctrine and receiving foreign technological assistance diminished the need to divert resources to the production of weapons.[33] In fact, the leadership forced many enterprises in the defense industry to shift to the manufacture of consumer goods and many others to put heavy emphasis on arms sales, so that the state could save funds for economic development. Finally, the nuclear capabilities of the People's Liberation Army provided an effective deterrent to foreign invasion, hence further reducing the need to draft industry for defense purposes.

This trend was reversed in the second half of 1989, when the June Fourth Incident increased the threat perceived by the regime as it underwent unprecedented criticism from abroad. The democracy movement that swept Eastern Europe and the Soviet Union in the following months further heightened the regime's sense of being under siege. The failed coup against Mikhail Gorbachev in August 1991 and the demise of the Soviet Union at the end of that year raised the regime's anxiety to a new high. The process of "peaceful evolution" in these socialist countries was attributed to "international reactionary forces" that had "never given up their basic stand of hostility toward the socialist system and their attempts to subvert it" (*People's Daily*, Sept. 30, 1989).[34] However, this perception of renewed threat located the major danger in cultural, economic, and political infiltration by the West, not in direct military confrontation. The army's defense posture was not significantly altered, and there was no discussion of sacrificing the economy to build up military capacity. On the contrary, reformers put even more emphasis on economic development as the best strategy to stave off political turbulence and fight "peaceful evolution" (Ch'en Te-Sheng 1992a: 8). According to Deng Xiaoping, "So long as economic work is done well and we have an adequate material base, all issues will be settled" (*The Economist*, Feb. 1–7, 1992, p. 23). The launching of the second-wave reform at the end of 1991 was thus closely connected with the rapid collapse of the Soviet Union and the reformers' determination to fight the global anti-Communist trend through economic, not military, means.

In addition to a perceived external threat and growing defense needs, two other factors militated for rapid industrialization in the Soviet Union during the NEP period. They were the desire for national development (to catch up and compete with the West) and Marxist teleology (to realize socialism through the growth of industry). The aspiration to development has been shared by all economically backward countries when faced with the overwhelming material power of Western forerunners. For these countries, development means industrialization (Gerschenkron 1962). In the Soviet case, this aspiration did not fully reveal itself during the early years of the revolution, when the cosmopolitan outlook of the regime was still strong, but it gradually gained prominence as Stalin made his political ascent. Industrialization was then directly linked with competing with the West, just as it had been under the tsarist regime (Ulam 1968). Thus, from the tsars to the Bolsheviks, one can find Russian leaders acting as hasty modernizers and industrializers of their country.

Nationalism played a much more prominent role in post-Mao reform than it did under the NEP. For the Chinese Communists, nationalist aspirations were from the very beginning the motivating force behind their movement, and they had worked to their advantage during the civil war (C. Johnson 1962). The early ambition of the CCP to "catch up with and surpass Great Britain and the United States" (*chao ying gan mei*) in industrial production and the post-Mao formula of the Four Modernizations were both indicative of the mentality of the regime. However, there have been great differences in how the regime has defined national development at different times. Following the Soviet pattern, the CCP under Mao chose heavy industrialization as the major vehicle for national development. Investment was biased toward heavy industry vis-à-vis other sectors of the economy, creating a serious imbalance.[35] The death of

Mao gave rise to Hua Guofeng's overambitious Ten-Year Plan, which ran along old Stalinist lines and which finally exhausted the country and forced a change of course. The policy of "readjustment, restructuring, consolidation, and improvement" announced in 1979 marked a turning point in economic thinking in the PRC. From that time on, national development was given an entirely different interpretation. To be sure, the national aspiration for development did not abate. In fact, the realization that the world was experiencing a technological revolution while the PRC was still suffering from its past isolation only heightened the elite's perception of the development gap.[36] A heavier emphasis on nationalism as a source of legitimacy for the regime further highlighted the urgency of catching up with the West. However, national development was no longer defined in terms of rapid heavy industrialization. Economic efficiency now became the major criterion (Brugger 1985: 7). As a result, the input-output ratio replaced direction and pace as the most important aspect of development. The pursuit of efficiency was given such priority that the regime was willing to radically reassign property rights along the lines of marketization and, to a lesser extent, privatization. Iron and steel were no longer the "major link." Every farm and enterprise was pressured to maximize efficiency and turn a profit. The goal of transforming China from an economically backward country with 80 percent of its population engaged in agriculture to a modern industrial nation where nonagricultural workers constituted the majority did not fade, as witnessed by the goal of quadrupling the gross national product in the 1980's (Z. Zhao 1987) and Deng Xiaoping's burning desire to accelerate China's economic growth in the early 1990's (Deng 1992). However, it would now be realized through a new strategy: efficient use of resources and a shift from extensive management to intensive management. Because the requirements of economic efficiency and intensive growth are different from those of rapid heavy industrialization, beginning in 1984, the regime committed itself to reforming the industrial structure. The old command system was considered obsolete for the regime's present task.

The other motivating force for industrialization during the NEP period was Marxist teleology. For Marx, material productive forces were the prime movers of history. The relations of production, class stratification, legal and political superstructure, and social consciousness were all conditioned by these productive forces and were dragged along the predestined stages of human historical development toward socialism by these underlying forces (see Marx in Tucker 1978: 4). Industrialization as an elevation of the productive forces and as a necessary condition for the growth of the proletariat, the chosen class of the revolution, was both inevitable and desirable. The Bolsheviks, by embracing the value and belief systems of Marxism, naturally identified themselves with industry, which was understood to be the only vehicle to socialism. However, because socialist revolution was supposed to take place only in industrialized societies, Marxists were not to be concerned with industrialization. This was the mission assigned to the bourgeoisie, a condition dictated by history, not one created by the Communists. The fact that the Bolsheviks grasped power and created a dictatorship of the proletariat in an economically backward country posed an unprecedented problem. In direct opposition to the Marxist tenets that gave primacy to the productive forces, an "advanced" political superstructure was imposed on a set of "intermediate" relations of production (those of a mixed economy), which in turn was based on "backward" productive forces. The disjunction among the three created tension that had to be relieved.

After realizing that it was impossible to seek help from the proletariat of industrialized countries, the Bolsheviks were forced to set about creating the very conditions for their own political survival.[37] The level of the productive forces was to be brought up to the requirements of the advanced system through industrialization. The Right believed that the productive forces would grow naturally under the relations of production of the NEP, and that massive state intervention was not necessary. The Left, on the other hand, was from the very beginning suspicious of the NEP's ability to unleash the productive forces and recommended strong actions by the state to stimulate industrialization. The final solution, Stalin's ultraleftist policy, was to transform the whole set of relations of production (i.e., the property rights structure) to industrialize the country and bring up the productive forces. The bottom-up approach of orthodox Marxism was rejected. However, the fear that a dictatorship of the proletariat could not coexist with a mixed economy and backward productive forces was based on the belief system of Marxism. Clearly, the Bolsheviks looked to Marxism for a means of safeguarding their regime and realizing socialism, but discarded those tenets that proved useless for their purpose.

For all the reform measures adopted in post-Mao China, Marxist teleology was not abandoned there. Unlike the Bolsheviks, who tried to raise the level of the productive forces to meet the requirements of an advanced system, Chinese reformers proposed to modify the socialist system to make it more "backward," so that it would become commensurate with the underlying forces of production. The purpose was not to retreat, but to allow the development of the productive forces under a set of more appropriate relations of production. This is the strategy of "going backward in order to go forward" (Sullivan 1985). The forces of production became the telos of the reformers.[38] Along this line of thought, Deng proposed "socialism with Chinese characteristics" in 1982. At the Thirteenth Party Congress in 1987, the theory of "the primary stage of socialism" was made an official doctrine. The past policies of the Left were criticized for having put undue emphasis on a single form of ownership and creating an overconcentration of political power. The fundamental task of a socialist society during the primary stage was to expand the productive forces through reform, a process by which the socialist relations of production and the socialist superstructure improve themselves. However, to make institutional concessions to the backward production forces did not mean sliding back to capitalism, for "to believe the Chinese people cannot take the socialist road without going through the stage of fully developed capitalism is to take a mechanistic position on the question of the development of revolution, and that is the major cognitive root of Right mistakes" (Z. Zhao 1987: iii), that is, the mistake of going too far backward in order to go forward. What transpired from this new doctrine was a three-tier structure of society: one-party rule (an improvement on one-man rule) was imposed on a mixed economy in which public ownership remained dominant, which in turn was based on underdeveloped productivity. In other words, an "advanced superstructure" was juxtaposed with a set of "intermediate" relations of production, which was based on "backward" productive forces: a distinctly NEP configuration. In the 1920's, the Bolsheviks debated among themselves as to whether the hybrid system of the NEP could develop the productive forces and lead the country to socialism. The increasingly dismal prospects for this in the latter half of that decade prompted the regime to question the rationale of the NEP. By contrast, from 1984 to 1991, Chinese reformers under Deng were able to link the development of the productive forces with economic reform and the three-tier NEP-like system and rationalized their radical reform policies in terms of Marxism.

The perception of acute international threat, a desire for national development, and Marxist teleology were major factors militating for rapid heavy industrialization that shook the foundation of the Soviet NEP toward the end of the 1920's. In the PRC between 1984 and 1991, one finds instead a diluted perception of external military threat accompanied by growing defense capabilities; national development that was redefined in terms of economic efficiency and intensive growth; and Marxist teleology working to the advantage of economic reform that could presumably expand the productive forces. Under these circumstances, there was no urge for China to plunge into draft heavy industrialization. In fact, during this period the pressure to move in the opposite direction was much stronger.

Agricultural Transformation

The threat perceived by the Soviet regime in the 1920's came not only from international capitalist forces, but also from Russian peasants—the more than 100 million private petty producers in agriculture who constituted 80 percent of the population. All the Bolsheviks, from the Left to the Right, recognized the danger of instituting a dictatorship of the proletariat in an overwhelmingly petty-bourgeois environment. Lenin, the father of the NEP, unequivocally stated that "petty production gives birth to capitalism and the bourgeoisie—continuously, every day, every hour, spontaneously, and on a mass scale" (in Ulam 1974: 294). The Left, including Leon Trotsky, Evgeni Preobrazhensky, Kamenev, and Zinoviev, emphasized the danger of the peasants' undermining Soviet power and working for the restoration of capitalism (Deutscher 1949: 303). Even Bukharin, the staunchest defender of the NEP, agreed that the emergence of a powerful, commercially minded peasantry was a deadly danger to the Soviet regime.[39] This particular perception of a peasant threat sets the Bolshevik regime of the NEP apart from its tsarist predecessor and other non-Marxist states pursuing the strategies of authoritarian modernization. For those regimes, a prosperous class of petty proprietors in the countryside was the staunchest supporter of the state (hence the Stolypin land reform). For the Bolsheviks, the same petty proprietors were their deadly enemies. Here ideology played a critical role in defining the perceptions of the regime.

The Kulak Threat

The perception of a peasant threat was based on three Marxist propositions. First, class is the unit of social action, the carrier of specific interests or historical missions, as well as the basis for a scientific analysis of society. Here class is defined in terms of its relation to the means of production and hence its ability or inability to dispose of wealth. Second, the distribution of political power reflects the distribution of the underlying economic power, which resides in ownership of the means of production. Third, the propertied classes that exploit laborers have a great vested interest in maintaining the class society. On the other hand, hired labor, the exploited stratum, has an opposite interest in a socialist revolution that can overthrow the exploitative social order. The middle stratum, the self-employed, stands between the two but tends toward conservatism because it is possible for its members to accumulate wealth and move upward. By undertaking a class analysis of NEP society (proposition one), the Bolsheviks found that the peasants actually owned land, the most important means of production in a preindustrial country. The regime interpreted this economic power as political capacity (proposition two), a supposition partly based on its experience with the peasants who resisted the Bolsheviks' attempts at collectivization and requisitioning under War Communism and ultimately forced the regime to grant them property rights under the NEP. The attitude of the peasantry toward the Soviet state was considered potentially hostile because the peasants, as small proprietors (the self-employed middle stratum), naturally tended to support the institution of private property and to act against the socialization of the means of production that the regime was committed to (proposition three). Based on this analysis, Russian peasants had both the capacity and intent to threaten the dominance and even survival of the socialist state.

The peasantry was divided into three subclasses. The rich peasants, or kulaks, were those who hired labor. They presumably constituted the greatest danger to the regime (in terms of both capacity and intent), and were thus designated the primary enemy in rural areas. The poor peasants, or *bednyaks*, had smallholdings but were also hired by others as laborers. Between the kulaks and the *bednyaks* were the middle peasants, the *serednyaks*, who neither employed laborers nor were hired by others. Out of a total of 25 million peasant households, 1.5 to 2 million were kulak households, 5 to 8 million were *bednyak* households, and 15 to 18 million were *serednyak* households (Deutscher 1949: 301).[40] The kulaks pressed for the abolition of restrictions on the hiring of labor, long-term leasing of land, and accumulation of private capital from the early days of the NEP. Most of these demands were met at the April plenum in 1925. The Left then accused the state's policy of encouraging accumulation of wealth by small producers through the uninhibited play of capitalism. In their eyes, this policy directly benefited the most productive peasants, the kulaks, by allowing credit, facilities, land, and labor to become concentrated in their hands (Kolakowski 1981b: 30). The stronger the kulaks grew, the easier it would be for them to withhold food from the urban population and to wrest concessions from the state. They would then demand political power, would want to form their own party, or would even rise up in open warfare against Communism. The increasing influence of the kulaks in informal peasant organizations, the land associations based on prerevolutionary communes, particularly aroused the regime's anxiety. Until they were officially abolished by the Fifteenth Party Congress in 1927, these organizations led by well-off peasants were more influential than the village soviets (Lowenthal 1970).

As the grain crisis evolved in 1928, Stalin interpreted it as an attack by the kulaks. In June, he announced a new principle: as socialism continued to advance, class struggle and the resistance of the exploiters would become more and more violent, a doctrine that later served as justification for the physical extermination of the kulak class. Because it was the property rights structure of the NEP in the countryside that gave rise to the kulaks, the threat perceived by the regime could only be diluted by changing that structure. This reasoning led the Bolsheviks directly to collectivization. In short, the political interests of the Bolshevik regime called for preventing the unhampered growth of an individualistic peasant economy beyond a certain point, because such growth inevitably led to the emergence of a class of incipient rural capitalists, a development perceived by the regime as a serious threat to its survival.

In post-Mao China, the reforming elite did not perceive the emancipated peasantry in general, or its upper stratum in particular, as a political threat. When the three Marxist propositions that determined the perceived kulak threat under the NEP are examined in the Chinese context, the reasons for an entirely different reading of the situation by the post-Mao leadership become clear. First, class analysis was not used to determine the composition of the peasantry. In the early 1950's, a full array of class strata had been applied to Chinese peasants, creating categories of poor peasants (*pinnong*), lower-middle peasants (*xiazhongnong*), upper-middle peasants (*shangzhongnong*), and rich peasants (*funong*). Following the NEP formula of "seeking the support of the *bednyaks* (poor peasants), having the *serednyaks* (middle peasants) as allies, and combating the kulaks" (Lewin 1968: 69), the CCP adopted the slogan "Rely on the poor and lower-middle peasants" (Bernstein 1967: 36). The strategy of differentiating categories among the peasantry and forming a united front against the major enemy there played an important role in the collectivization drive in the mid-1950's. But as collectivization eliminated the possibility of hiring rural labor, the basis for stratifying the peasantry disappeared, though the categories were artificially sustained under Mao. The agricultural reform after 1978 provided a material basis for redifferentiating peasants by granting property rights to households and allowing market forces to dispose of labor and land. Although the initial division of collective land was egalitarian in principle, very soon income gaps emerged, land was transferred between households (via *zhuanbao*), and labor was hired (Unger 1986). Free markets for land and labor gradually developed. Rural workers, detached from their land, moved from place to place seeking employment (White 1987a: 421). The equivalents of rich peasants, middle peasants, and poor peasants, as well as a rural proletariat, were created. In this new situation, the traditional categories based on ownership of the means of production and the employment of labor were not applied to the emerging social strata. Other aspects of their economic activities gained dominance in characterizing the peasantry, such as income and type of work. Thus, members of the upper stratum were no longer called "rich peasants" but "ten-thousand-yuan households" (*wanyuanhu*), in reference to their income level, or "specialized households" (*zhuanyehu*), in reference to the type of activity they were engaged in.[41]

The regime was eager to have high-income households demonstrate to other peasants how they got rich and encourage those who lagged behind to follow suit. Class labeling was the last thing the regime wanted to undertake because it was certain it would undermine the agricultural reform upon which the whole reform edifice was built. The growing inequality in the countryside was understood primarily in terms of deteriorating income distribution, not class differentiation and class struggle. In short, class analysis was abandoned by the regime as an approach to understanding rural China.

For the Bolsheviks, class categories provided a basic framework for approaching the Russian peasants. Their perception of a concrete threat was based on a close analysis of the intents and capacity of the peasantry in general and the kulaks in particular. The Bolsheviks assumed that Russian peasants were basically hostile to the regime because its goal of abolishing private property was incompatible with the fundamental interests of the peasants as small proprietors. This assumption was in line with the teachings of Marx and the traditional theory of the international socialist movement.[42] It is true that Lenin was flexible enough to tap the revolutionary energy of the Russian peasants and pragmatic enough to concede to the peasants' demands when he introduced the NEP. But neither he nor any other Bolshevik leader had ever thought of the peasants as natural allies of the proletariat, and all of them were aware of the fragile nature of the temporary alliance (*smychka*) between the regime and the peasantry. This fundamental conflict of interest, however, was based on the assumption that the regime was determined to realize its socialist ideals in the countryside.

In post-Mao China, at the "primary stage of socialism," when expanding the forces of production was considered the paramount goal, this assumption did not hold true. By decollectivizing agriculture in practice, the Chinese reformers pushed their socialist ideals into the future. The disillusioned elite had abandoned the values of Communist ideology, and by doing so eliminated the incompatibility between the goals of the party and the interests of the peasants. It was in this context that Deng spoke of "the misunderstanding, dogmatic interpretation and erroneous application of Lenin's statement that small production engenders capitalism and the bourgeoisie daily, hourly, and on a mass scale" (Deng 1984: 296). This change meant that the calculations of the post-Mao leadership became similar to those of Stolypin or any other authoritarian ruler who depended on land reform to recruit support from the peasants.[43] The regime's trust in the emerging class in the countryside was reflected in its changing alliance policy. There was no longer any mention of relying on the lower strata of the peasantry (the poor and lower-middle peasants), but a lot of emphasis on recruiting the "advanced elements" (*xianjin fenzi*) into the party (Kelliher 1990). These were specialized households, successful farmers, and new entrepreneurs, that is, the beneficiaries of the reform. They had the education, skills, and entrepreneurial spirit to succeed in a market environ- ment, and thus could serve the regime's goal of modernization. They were also considered politically reliable because of their vested interest in economic reform. As the regime's key task changed from making and consolidating a socialist revolution to realizing the Four Modernizations, the intents of the peasantry and its upper stratum were reassessed, and the attitude of the state toward the peasants changed accordingly.

Its abandonment of class analysis and favorable reassessment of the intents of the peasantry did not mean that the post-Mao elite was not conscious of the emergence of an independent economic power in the Chinese countryside. Marxism holds that economic power (defined in terms of ownership of the means of production) translates directly into political power.[44] This explains why, under the NEP, the Bolsheviks were so sensitive to the relative strength of industry versus agriculture and the terms of exchange between the two. For them, state industry was the economic foundation of so- cialism, and agriculture was the base of petty capitalism. If industry could not keep growing, and growing faster than agriculture, the balance of power between the two sectors would turn against the proletariat.[45] For the Chinese reformers, peasants as a class, or rich peasants as a subclass, were not inherently hostile to the regime. However, the rising economic power of the peasants still aroused concern.

At the local level, agricultural reform in the PRC brought about a separation of political and economic authority, which in the Maoist era had been combined in a single line of command (White 1987b). Township and village institutions now performed the functions of communes, production brigades, and production teams in areas such as civil government, public security, judicature, taxation, birth control, and health care. With the introduction of the household responsibility system and the dismantling of agricultural collectives, the peasant household became the dominant unit of production (Croll 1988b: 28). The regime had forecast that contracting of land, diversification of the economy, and development of specialized households would give rise to new forms of cooperatives and economic associations that would provide the services made necessary by increasing specialization. However, the households managed to dominate areas where the cooperatives and associations were supposed to prevail by accumulating producer goods, augmenting labor resources, and developing networks of cooperation based on existing kinship ties (Croll 1988b: 36). The strengthening of these kinship ties combined households into aggregate families and directed their attention beyond the village to small towns and urban centers. The households' control of land and their resources outside the village put them in a strong position vis-à-vis local cadres. A dual power system had come into being, in which political power was based on institutionalized authority while economic power was based on private control over economic resources. Various modes of interaction had developed between these two powers that bore witness to the increasing strength of the private sector.

The increase of household economic power, however, did not translate into a clear political threat to the regime. First, a peasant society composed of numerous petty producers is a fragmented body, not an integrated whole capable of challenging state power (Chevrier 1988: 16). Second, reformers were careful not to relinquish control in strategic areas. The regime's withdrawal from villages was voluntary and selective. In the 1920's, the Bolsheviks suffered from the fact that they came to power through urban insurrections and had not succeeded in penetrating villages and recruiting local political leaders who were both influential among the peasants and loyal to the regime (Skocpol 1979: 222). The rise of the kulaks in local political organizations understandably raised great anxiety among Bolshevik leaders, who simply lacked the organizational means to reach and lead the peasantry. The CCP, on the other hand, was a rural-based party with ample experience in dealing with the peasants. In China, the foundations for political control in the villages were laid during the land reform period and consolidated in the years after. The collectivization of agriculture further tightened these established controls (Bernstein 1967: 27). After the reform, not only were there still political institutions (township governments, village committees, village groups) hierarchically organized to perform administrative functions, but also an array of new policy tools that the regime employed to influence peasant behavior (such as the economic levers—prices, credit, taxes, etc.; the use of ten-thousand-yuan households as models for other peasants to strive for; and the recruitment of new cadres from the advanced elements) (Kelliher 1990).

It is true that rural cadres who had been transferred from the collectives to the new township and village institutions felt demoralized because their power was curtailed, their prestige was undermined, their privileges and connections were reduced, and their values were repudiated. At the same time, the regime's efforts to recruit cadres from among the successful peasants met with difficulties as the cadre's job became more demanding and less rewarding (White 1987a: 423). The indirect control based on economic levers and the use of certain classes as economic role models was not as effective as the administrative command of the old system. However, none of the encroachments on state power had translated into weaknesses that rural political forces took advantage of in order to challenge the political authority of the party. Their major impact was rather on the efficacy of state economic policy.[46] Unlike the Bolsheviks, Chinese reformers did not interpret this reduced efficacy as a political threat. They were sure that the rural transformation of the late 1970's and the 1980's had not created an independent political force rooted in rural capitalism that would endanger the overall political balance of the system (Chevrier 1988). On the contrary, they thought reform had created a rural constituency for them and that the proliferation of interests (the emergence of traders, entrepreneurs, hired laborers, investors, etc.) in the countryside had broken the peasant solidarity of the pre-reform era and further reduced the possibility of a peasant political challenge to the Communist state (Kelliher 1992: 249). Thus the regime was not compelled to roll back reforms for fear of losing political control over the peasants.[47] In September 1991, the Eighth Plenum of the Thirteenth Central Committee was content to pass a decision on agriculture that called for strengthening party organizations in the countryside and teaching peasants through patriotism, collectivism, and socialism while sticking to the household responsibility system (Ch'en Te-Sheng 1992a: 7). This decision shows the regime's concern over the power ratio between the socialist state and rural capitalism. It also suggests that the ruling elite was confident that political control over the peasantry could be achieved within the current property rights structure. This stance was affirmed at the Fourteenth Party Congress in October 1992 and at the First Annual Meeting of the Eighth People's Congress in March 1993, which amended the PRC's constitution to officially install the household responsibility system as a replacement for rural communes and cooperatives.

In sum, the NEP regime perceived the Russian peasants in general, and the kulaks in particular, as a serious political threat because Bolshevik leaders embraced the values and beliefs of Marxism that led them to apply class analysis to the peasantry, recognize the incompatibility between their socialist goals and the material interests of peasants as petty proprietors, and interpret the peasants' economic power as political power. Because the structure of property rights was the root of rural class stratification and the kulak threat to the Soviet regime, the Bolsheviks ultimately transformed the rights structure through collectivization. In post-Mao China, the reform regime no longer applied class analysis to the Chinese peasants. It also abandoned the socialist ideals embodied in collective agriculture, thus removing the conflict between its goals and the interests of the peasants. The regime remained sensitive to the balance of power between the state and rural society (a consideration affected by the belief system of Marxism) and determined to maintain strict political control in the countryside. However, because there had been no concrete political threat from the private economic sector in the countryside, reformers were content to preserve the status quo, at least in the political sense.

The Grain Crisis

The whole NEP period was overshadowed by the Soviet regime's fear that it could not secure enough grain to feed the cities and the army. The Bolsheviks were keenly aware of the fact that the Russian Revolution had been set in motion by food riots in Petrograd and the mutiny of the capital garrison. The grain issue was thus their most urgent concern (Ulam 1974: 298). When crises arose, the regime was forced to respond with all of its capacity and imagination. A decade-long learning process took place in which Bolshevik leaders tried and rejected various formulas.

In the 1920's, the Bolshevik regime employed four different strategies in order to secure grain from the peasants: compulsory procurement, Left price policy (the "scissors"), Right price policy, and collectivization. The War Communism solution—the physical seizure of grain (*prodrazverstka*)—was tried first. Peasants naturally responded by reducing production. In 1921, the regime was forced to introduce the NEP and shifted to a tax in kind (*prodnalog*), which set a grain quota and allowed peasants to dispose of any above-quota portion as they saw fit. In 1924, *prodnalog* was replaced by a money tax.

During the NEP period, taxation was not a major economic lever for the state, and the money tax remained rather low until near the end of the decade, when it was used as a penalty as part of the policy aimed at destroying individual peasant farming. The major policy tool was price, or the terms of trade between agriculture and industry. Generally speaking, state policy favored industry, so that peasants' terms of trade under the NEP never reached more than about three-quarters of the prewar level. However, two price policies were proposed at the time, one by the Left, the other by the Right. Members of the Left, notably Trotsky and Preobrazhensky, pushed for rapid industrialization at the expense of the peasants. They wanted to fix the prices of industrial products at levels much higher than the prices the state paid for farm produce, so as to achieve "primitive socialist accumulation." They had their way in 1922–23, when an immense disparity developed between the prices of industrial and farm goods, a disparity Trotsky called the "scissors" (*nozhnitsy*).[48] By October 1923, the ratio of industrial to agricultural prices was three times as high as it had been before the war.

Peasants dramatically reduced their marketings, and a grain crisis erupted. The state then forcefully eliminated the price imbalance by ordering a reduction of industrial prices.[49] The experience of War Communism and the "scissors crisis" convinced members of the Right, led by Bukharin, that the only way to assure a sufficient supply of grain was to provide peasants with material incentives by offering them favorable terms of trade and abundant producer and consumer goods. Not only would *prodrazverstka* à la War Communism remove the motivation for peasants to produce enough surplus grain for the cities, but even a subtle form of exploitation, like the "scissors," would cause peasants to withhold grain from the market. Bukharin thus proposed his soft, Right price policy to appease the peasants. From 1924 to 1926 (except for a short interruption in late 1924), his policy held sway. Terms of trade improved for the peasants, and the blades of the "scissors" gradually closed.

However, in 1926–27, with the residual capacity of the economy fully mobilized and the need for investment in industry becoming urgent, the regime reverted to the hard, Left price policy. Procurement prices for agricultural produce were cut dramatically, and the shortage of manufactured goods became perennial (this was the so-called goods famine, *tovarny golod*). Peasants responded as they had during the "scissors crisis" of 1922–23, by reducing grain production and marketings (they hoarded the grain in anticipation of higher prices, or fed it to livestock) and by shifting to more production of more profitable items (such as industrial crops and livestock products). As a result, a grain crisis erupted in the spring of 1928.[50] This time the regime was unwilling to tinker with relative prices and immediately resorted to forceful seizures, actually reinstating *prodrazverstka*.

As Bukharin had predicted, neither the Left price policy of the "scissors" nor *prodrazverstka* proved effective with the peasants. Grain production continued to drop in 1928. The regime had now come full circle, from compulsory requisitioning through Left price policy, Right price policy, a second Left price policy, and back to requisitioning. From its point of view, all of the policy alternatives possible within the structure of a private, market-oriented agriculture had been exhausted. A continuation of compulsory procurement would only worsen the situation by further reducing the amount of grain the government could secure from peasants. On the other hand, to go back to Bukharin's soft-line price policy meant either higher food prices for industrial workers, which would certainly result in urban unrest, or pressure on the state treasury to pay unaffordable subsidies, which would dampen the prospects of the industrialization drive launched under the First Five-Year Plan (1928–29 to 1932–33) (Deutscher 1949: 318). The regime lacked the foreign currency needed to import grain, and foreign credit was unavailable because the financial embargo imposed on Russia after the revolution was still in effect. In 1929, under the overwhelming pressure of these events (and here Stalin's personality and the regime's perception of the threat posed by the kulaks also came into play), the regime finally broke the old policy cycle and opted for collectivization, an institutional revolution that transformed the property rights structure in the agricultural sector. Unlike past policies (see the summary below), which had been confined to the existing system, collectivization created new devices for extraction and vested the power to make decisions about production and disposal of agricultural output in the state. For Stalin, this was the most effective way of securing supplies from the peasants. Under collectivization, all land except household garden plots was owned and worked collectively for the overriding purpose of delivering predetermined amounts of specified products to the state (Skocpol 1979: 229). Thus, the grain crisis was solved by radically reassigning property rights in agriculture.

1918–21   War Communism; compulsory procurement (*prodrazverstka*) and failed collectivization (*kombedy*)
1921–22   Start of NEP; tax in kind (*prodnalog*) imposed
1922–23   Left price policy implemented; "scissors crisis" ensues
1924   Money tax replaces *prodnalog*
1925   Heyday of NEP; Right price policy implemented, scissors close
1926–27   State emphasis shifts to industrialization; Left price policy reinstated, peasant prices suppressed, scissor blades reopen
1928   Grain crisis; reinstatement of *prodrazverstka*
1929   Collectivization drive begins

The NEP gave rise to grain crises in two ways. One had to do with the inability of the regime to secure grain from peasants in ways other than by providing manufactured goods at favorable prices. This price policy of the Right proved impossible given the regime's financial constraints, hence the need to restructure the system by reassigning property rights. The second link between the NEP and grain crisis is more technical in nature. The egalitarian redistribution of land during the Russian Revolution produced not only a private agriculture, but one dominated by a huge number of petty producers.[51] After 1917, the estates of nobles and rich peasants, which before 1914 had produced half of the total grain crop and 70 percent of the grain brought to market, were divided into many extremely small holdings (Lewin 1965: 163). A large portion of these small producers now operated near subsistence level. As a result, the average ratio of marketed grain to total production declined. Petty production also made it impossible to implement mechanical methods of farming. This meant a lower production potential. As Marxists, the Bolsheviks believed strongly in the technical superiority of large-scale agriculture, and they considered agricultural production under the NEP extremely inefficient. The NEP also brought back many medieval practices associated with the *mir*, such as the three-field system, separate plots, and periodical redistribution. These antique features worked against efficient use of the land (Millar and Nove 1976: 56). These weaknesses, together with the peasants' lack of the knowledge and skill required to apply modern farming techniques and the regime's inability to provide peasants with technical assistance (e.g., selected seeds, better soil cultivation methods, improved implements, and skills in multiple crop rotation) made agriculture under the NEP inefficient.

It is true that none of these factors was inherently Nepian, that is, one can remove them without changing the basic structure of the NEP. Hence the regime could allow consolidation of smallholdings in order to facilitate large-scale farming. State policies could be implemented to discourage periodical reallotment of strips of land, and the government could grant peasants technical assistance. In fact, except for the latter, this was exactly what the regime did in 1925, when it sanctioned the hiring of labor and leasing of land and prohibited frequent redistribution of land by the communes (Jasny 1972: 19). But then the regime began relying on the NEP to function automatically, expecting growth from the concessions it had made in 1925 and neglecting to make further investments (Lewin 1965: 166). When agriculture failed to perform as hoped, the ultimate rationale of the NEP was undermined. Lenin had introduced the NEP mainly as a concession to peasants, in the hope that they would raise and deliver more produce (particularly grain); the continuously declining production and marketing of grain inevitably doomed the NEP.

Grain production in post-Mao China is an issue as prominent as it was in the Soviet Union during the NEP period. Good grain harvests have always been considered crucial to general rural prosperity and overall political stability. Throughout China's history, rarely was a dynasty overthrown without a preceding grain crisis and rural famine. Mao Zedong emphasized this point by asserting that "agriculture is the foundation of the economy and grain the key link" (yi nong wei ben, ye liang wei gang). Mao's assertion was not missed by his successors. "An economy without a strong agriculture will be fragile, that without a sufficient grain supply will be chaotic" (wu nong bu wen, wu liang ze luan) was a belief shared among the post-Mao elite. However, after six years of rapid growth in agricultural production and rural income following the reform of the late 1970's, in the mid-1980's, the country was plunged into a grain crisis. The 1984 record grain harvest was followed by four consecutive years of failure to meet production targets.[52] The situation improved somewhat in 1989, when the harvest regained the 1984 level. This means grain production basically stagnated over the five years, at a time when the country was experiencing its third baby boom.[53]

The causes for the grain crisis were multiple. However, they were mostly embedded in the new property rights structure that came into being with the reform. Like that of the Soviet Union in the 1920's, Chinese agriculture in the 1980's was characterized by a huge number of private households engaged in petty production. This was the result of an egalitarian land reform, the decollectivization of Chinese agriculture that allotted land to households based on family size or number of the laborers. By the mid-1980's, with the removal of compulsory delivery quotas and the sanctioning of the practices of hiring labor and leasing land, agriculture in the PRC had reached the same degree of liberalization as its Soviet counterpart in 1925 (the only difference lay in the time constraints imposed on the property rights transferred to Chinese peasants). After the major marketization move of 1985, the remaining limits on household farming were not administrative in nature, but were based on the state's monopoly of the input and output markets. The state

provided diesel oil, fertilizer, pesticide, and other scarce capital
goods to peasants and procured the bulk of agricultural products at
prices it set. This meant that manipulation of the terms of trade between industry and agriculture had become a major policy tool, one
used by the state to influence the behavior of peasants—a distinctly
NEP-like situation. As has been shown, the NEP in the Soviet
Union directly contributed to the grain crisis in the 1920's. A similar property rights structure in the PRC also created great tension
between the supply of and demand for grain and resulted in a crisis
situation.

The NEP grain crisis was touched off by the regime's decision in
1926–27 to shift to the hard, Left price policy. This decision was
prompted by the perceived need to increase investment in industry
as the country moved from restoration to reconstruction (i.e., from
utilizing the residual capacity of the previous phase to creating new
capacities for growth). It was also based on the Bolshevik leaders'
optimistic assessment of the capacity of agriculture after important
property rights concessions were made in favor of peasants. In the
PRC, the regime was not under great pressure to achieve rapid industrialization, but was mainly worried about the tremendous burden that agricultural subsidies placed on the state treasury. In 1985,
it tried to relieve this burden by introducing a price reform for agricultural products in urban areas. This action was taken at a time
when industrial reform was being introduced into the cities; workers had been given wage increases in advance to offset the negative
effect the price reform would have on their real income. Naturally
inflation erupted, and the regime was forced to terminate its experiment with price reform.

Because it was politically impossible to let agricultural prices
fluctuate to balance supply and demand, and the state was no longer
willing to shoulder huge subsidies, the only alternative was to
lower the procurement prices for agricultural goods, that is, to tilt
the terms of trade against the peasants. This was done in the context of rising input costs.[54] As in the second phase of the NEP, the
CCP now put great confidence in the incentives provided by the
1985 household responsibility system and expected this "Chinese
NEP" to function more or less automatically, without much state
investment. During the Sixth Five-Year Plan (1981–85), state investment in agricultural capital construction totaled 17.8 billion

yuan, or 5.2 percent of total state investment in capital construction. Under the Seventh Five-Year Plan (1986–90), agriculture received only 14.7 billion yuan, or 3.9 percent of total state investment (Fewsmith 1988: 81). Thus, in both the Soviet Union and the PRC, a financially constrained state (though they were constrained for different reasons) tilted the terms of trade against the peasants at the second stage of its reform, expecting agriculture to generate growth automatically, based on property rights concessions made to peasants. In each case, a grain crisis ensued.

If peasants are faced with deteriorating terms of trade for all of their products, rather than for just one particular product—grain, for example—they may simply work harder without shifting resources away from production of that one crop (Millar and Nove 1976: 52). But both the Bolsheviks under the NEP and post-Mao Chinese reformers lowered the state's procurement prices for grain while those for other agricultural products remained stable. With peasants fully capable of making their own production and exchange decisions and the opportunity cost of grain production increasing, it was inevitable that they would shift to more profitable products. This tendency was stronger in the Chinese case, as a result of the state's policy of encouraging diversification and specialization of commodity production (that is, non-grain production) in order to develop the rural economy. The former slogan of "treating grain as the key link" had been dropped. Specialized commodity production was also deemed a ready solution to the unemployment problem as the reform released surplus labor from traditional grain production (Croll 1988a). As a result, large numbers of households began to turn away from grain growing in favor of raising more lucrative cash crops, specializing in animal husbandry, even engaging in trading and setting up rural industries (township and village enterprises, or *xiangzhen qiye*).[55] This development was fostered by the government's decision to allow the subcontracting of land between peasant households. Those engaged in specialized production thus could contract their land to neighboring households that had surplus labor. It is not surprising that many peasants chose this path when faced with "wrong" price signals from the grain market (which was dominated by the government) and the lack of prestige and status accorded grain growers (a result of low income and the state's emphasis on specialized production). Whereas the ten-thousand-yuan households were hailed as models by local authorities, the poor, uneducated grain-growing peasants were neglected (Kelliher 1990). The rural incentive system was weighted entirely against grain production.

As in the NEP case, factors other than the terms of trade between agriculture and industry contributed to the grain crisis. One of these, the intensive use of land without regard for its conservation (predatory farming), was a direct result of the time constraints imposed on peasants' property rights and was linked to the basic features of the household responsibility system. Other factors included the parcelization of land and subsequent lack of economies of scale (the result of the egalitarian distribution of land at the beginning of the reform), deterioration of the rural infrastructure in the areas of transportation, irrigation, education, social welfare, and so on, and natural calamities.[56] Finally, the rapid growth in grain production in the early 1980's was due mainly to the one-time release of pent-up productive capacity brought about by decollectivization (Perkins 1986: 77). Institutional reforms geared toward motivational efficiency cannot sustain high growth rates if not accompanied by continuous investment. It was thus only natural for the growth rate to drop to a lower level.

The regime was aware of the seriousness of the grain crisis when it first erupted in 1985, as witnessed by Chen Yun's stern warnings at the Conference of Party Delegates of that year (Fewsmith 1988). However, the regime was unable to significantly improve the peasants' terms of trade, either by substantially increasing procurement prices or by lowering input costs. Urban price reform proved too politically destabilizing, while the subsidies necessary to boost grain production were beyond the state's financial capacity.[57] Grain production was still much less profitable than other economic activities such as cash cropping and rural industry. The regime responded to the budding crisis mainly by reimposing limits on the peasants' power to make production and exchange decisions. Grain sales across provincial borders were strictly limited (*Jingji Ribao*, Jan. 6, 1989). The availability of inputs (diesel oil, fertilizer, and pesticide) was made dependent on the delivery of an amount of grain stipulated in contracts between peasants and the state. Harsh administrative measures were taken to enlarge the amount of land devoted to grain production. Voluntary contracts in many cases became mandatory quotas. Peasants were paid for their grain with worth-less IOUs, a move amounting to outright confiscation. The militia was even mobilized to carry out searches for hidden stores of grain.

Together with these administrative measures came discussions about the virtues of cooperatives: their economies of scale, concentration of capital, mechanization of large farms, investment in infrastructure, and so forth. After the agricultural conference of November 1988, great emphasis was put on contracting much larger areas of land to several families or to specialized teams, as opposed to single households, as under the 1983 system (Y. Chen 1989). Peasants were encouraged to rely on collective economic bodies for "socialized services" (*shehuihua fuwu*) in seeding, irrigation, marketing, and so on. The ideal for agriculture was a "two-tiered management system" (*shuangceng jingying tizhi*) combining the "socialized service" and household responsibility systems. The pressure for some form of agricultural recollectivization was mounting.

In short, the regime tightened its grip on peasants in order to extract the surplus it could not otherwise acquire (Friedman 1990: 34). However, it was unwilling to roll back the property rights reform on a large scale. This left importation as the last solution to the grain shortage. The PRC was in a much more favorable position than its Soviet counterpart had been in the 1920's, though it also faced tightened constraints after June 4, 1989. In 1988, the PRC procured 7 million tons of wheat from the United States and another 8 million tons from other countries, making it the third largest grain importer in the world. The practice of importing large amounts of grain no doubt brought about the PRC's balance-of-payments problems. The much-improved trade position of the PRC in 1990–91 made importation more financially feasible. However, the sheer volume of grain that mainland China has to import to cover, say, a 10 percent shortfall in its domestic production is enough to disrupt the world grain market (J. Wong 1992: 41). The transportation of grain to needy areas in times of emergency has also proved a huge problem for the PRC.

In 1989 and 1990, favorable weather, improved terms of trade for agricultural products, rising state investment, and more restricted property rights for peasants resulted in increased grain production (1989 production reached the 1984 level of 407 million tons; 1990 production surpassed it, reaching 446 million tons).[58]

The grain crisis was temporarily relieved. However, in 1991, floods dealt a heavy blow to agriculture, bringing down total grain production by 11 million tons, a drop of 2.47 percent over the previous year. Irrigation and drainage systems that failed during the floods highlighted the lack of investment in this crucial area. The importance of the grain issue was stressed in September, as the Eighth Plenum of the Thirteenth Central Committee proclaimed that agricultural development should be the nation's first priority in the 1990's. The plenum's solution to the grain problem included a little bit of everything: continuing the household responsibility system, gradually strengthening the collective economy, rationalizing price ratios between agricultural and industrial products, expanding market regulation, emphasizing education and technology, improving the irrigation system, and increasing state investment in agriculture (Ch'en Te-Sheng 1992a). All had been done to some extent to bring about the good harvests of 1989 and 1990. But the strategy only raised per capita grain production to 390 kilograms in 1990 and 375 kilograms in 1991, both still below the record 392 kilograms set in 1984. The current target is 400 kilograms, the bare minimum for meeting basic nutritional requirements. However, assuming a population of 1.3 billion by the end of the decade, this suggests a total production level of 520 million tons, or about 100 million tons more than the current production level. The PRC's current strategy of muddling through is obviously not going to satisfy such a need. China's grain shortage could erupt into a crisis at any time.

In sum, both the NEP and post-Mao regimes found themselves facing a grain crisis caused primarily by the reformed property rights structure in the agricultural sector. The fundamental feature of this structure was the ability of private peasant households to freely produce and dispose of their products in pursuit of profit. Under this system, the state could direct rural resources to grain production only by providing economic incentives. At the same time, the state had to keep food prices low in the cities to prevent urban unrest (the primary consideration in the PRC) and to accumulate industrial capital (the primary consideration in the Soviet Union). The difference in food prices was initially covered by state subsidies, but this financial burden became unbearable, forcing the regime to change its policy. In both cases, the terms of trade were changed to the detriment of peasants, and a grain crisis ensued as peasants reduced grain production and marketing and shifted to other economic activities.

In response to this situation, the Bolsheviks swiftly escalated from Left price policy to requisitioning and then to collectivization. From 1984 to 1991, post-Mao reformers resisted the pressure for recollectivization, but they did partially restrict peasants' property rights. They also resorted to grain imports. The peasants' terms of trade improved. State investment in rural infrastructure increased. However, the resultant increase in grain production was only limited, and the means of payment and availability of foreign credit for grain imports remained in short supply. Unlike some of the other concerns of the two regimes, a grain crisis demanded an immediate solution. The effects of such a crisis were felt directly; it was concrete and not a matter subject to different ideological interpretations. Both Stalin and Deng had to deal with it in a practical manner. Because in each case the grain crisis was embedded in the property rights structure created by the reform, both the Bolsheviks and Chinese reformers were forced to take a hard look at property rights to find solutions. Thus, we find that compelling nonideological problems dictated a reconsideration of the basic structure of the economy.

Conclusion

There are striking similarities between the Soviet Union during its NEP period and the PRC in the latter half of the 1980's. Both countries were huge in size and complex in local variations. They were highly autonomous. They were both developing countries in which peasants constituted 80 percent of the total population. In institutional terms, they shared a particular version of a Leninist political system in which authoritarian political control, rather than compulsory participation, was the norm. The economic structure of both countries was characterized by a private agriculture with a huge number of peasant households engaged in petty production, by small-scale private tradespeople and private manufacturers in small industry, and by the fact that the "commanding heights" of the economy—banking, foreign trade, and large-scale industry—remained firmly under state control. The organizing principle of this structure was for the state to assign property rights to private individuals where the economic unit was small and thus politically nonthreatening, and to retain rights where the unit was large and thus inappropriate for private possession. In Marxist terms, the two countries shared a three-tier system: the top tier was a one-party Leninist superstructure, the middle one was a mixed economy with property rights distributed between the public and private sectors according to the "commanding heights" principle, and the bottom tier was the "backward" productive forces expressed in the predominant rural population. Despite all of these similarities, however, the PRC continued to muddle through within its NEP-like structure between 1984 and 1991, essentially taking the Bukharinite line, whereas the Soviet Union took the Stalinist solution and made a grand shift from NEP to command economy. This divergence demands an explanation.

Toward the end of the 1920's, the NEP structure in the Soviet Union was perceived to be less and less conducive to the goals treasured by Bolshevik leaders. Mounting tensions ultimately resulted in Stalin's revolution from above, which destroyed the NEP. In the Chinese case, a similar structure did not give rise to the same degree of tension, mainly because of different commitments on the part of the elite. This difference is based on the fact that Stalin and other Bolshevik leaders were fully committed to the values of Marxism, in spite of the failure of War Communism, while Deng and other rehabilitated cadres in China had had disillusioning personal experiences during the Cultural Revolution that emancipated them from the commitment to socialist ideals. The impact of abandoning the value system of Marxism was tremendous. A whole group of important factors that militated for a transformation of the NEP in the 1920's was absent from the considerations of Chinese reformers. For one thing, the PRC no longer practiced ideological diplomacy and had stopped exporting revolution, which in turn diluted international hostility and its own perception of foreign military threat. For another, China's emerging class of rich peasants was no longer considered an enemy, and its capitalist practices were tolerated and even encouraged by the regime in order to develop a rural commodity economy. The Bolsheviks' fear of foreign invasion gave rise to the need for rapid heavy industrialization, and their perception of a kulak threat led directly to collectivization, both of which were incompatible with the NEP.

There were areas in which Soviet and Chinese leaders shared the same goals but designed different strategies to realize those goals. For example, both regimes aspired to catch up with the West and develop their productive forces. The Bolsheviks placed their hope in rapid heavy industrialization and primitive socialist accumulation, whereas Chinese reformers defined national development in terms of economic efficiency and equated it with productive forces. The Soviets emphasized the pace and direction of development, the Chinese focused on the input-output ratio. The former aimed at extensive growth, the latter opted for intensive growth. The property rights requirements of these two strategies clearly diverged. Hence the same set of goals doomed the NEP in the Soviet Union but provided the rationale for China's NEP-like economic reform.

Finally, there are areas in which the two regimes shared the same concerns and agreed with each other on the defects of a mixed economy. The single most important issue was grain procurement. In both cases, a financially constrained state found it difficult to provide price incentives to private peasant households and at the same time to keep urban food prices low. With foreign credit available only on hard terms and urban interests considered more important than rural interests, the terms of trade for agricultural goods deteriorated and a grain crisis evolved. Clearly, the liberated property rights structure was at the root of the problem because it gave peasants the right not to produce what the state wanted and not to sell their produce to the government. The reformed system also gave rise to a whole host of production problems: the lack of economies of scale, the dispersion of capital, the declining investment in rural infrastructure, and so on. In the Soviet Union, the grain crisis and associated production questions touched off the collectivization drive. In the PRC, there were clear signs of pressure for recollectivization. Between 1984 and 1991, this pressure did not translate into fundamental changes in the agricultural system, although the property rights of individual peasants were often violated. Obviously, the lack of reinforcing factors (such as a desperate desire to rapidly modernize the defense industry, or the emergence of an opposing political force based on rural capitalism) dramatically reduced the weight of arguments in favor of the restoration of collective agriculture.[59] Because economic restructuring had brought about a considerable increase in productivity (Perkins 1986) and created a great deal of vested interest in reform, the grain crisis alone did not generate enough pressure to roll back the liberalizing changes in property rights made between 1984 and 1991.

That said, one should not underestimate the importance of the grain issue or lightly dismiss the possibility of recollectivization if China's grain crisis reaches disastrous proportions in the 1990's.[60] Some discussion of this scenario is in order here. First, if there is a rollback of rural reforms it is highly possible that the marginal private sector in the cities and in rural industry will also be squeezed out of existence. The result will be full restoration of a command economy in both rural and urban areas. In the Soviet case, private industrialists, tradespeople, and artisans were driven out of business in conjunction with the agricultural collectivization drive because Stalin wanted to prevent possible collaboration among the outraged elements of society (Lewin 1965). The same might also happen in the PRC, especially in view of the close link between the marginal private sector and agriculture. When Stalin launched his attack, capitalists engaged in small-scale trade and manufacturing were totally defenseless because their supplies of raw materials, and hence of goods to sell, depended on state industry (Nove 1982). The marginal private sector in the PRC displays the same vulnerability. The ease with which the state can squeeze small private businesses out of existence is demonstrated by the fact that the austerity measures of 1989 alone resulted in the closing down of 3 million township and village enterprises and caused a net flow of rural labor from trade and manufacturing back to agricultural production.[61] Thus, if the PRC does decide to restore a command economy, the regime only need worry about resistance from the peasants.

Second, recollectivization need not be undertaken using Stalin's stormy method. In fact, the PRC's own experience in the 1950's clearly shows that the Chinese Communists were aware of the tremendous human and material costs of Soviet collectivization, and that they were able to tailor their strategies to smooth the process. The features that contributed to China's relative success at collectivizing agriculture—limiting the goal to achieving economic control of agriculture without class struggle, allowing peasants to farm private plots and engage in other peripheral economic activities, compensating former owners for property that had been collectiv-

ized, ensuring that rural cadres were well organized, and so on—
might well reappear in a second attempt. It is true that today many
cadres have transformed themselves into rich peasants, and many
new recruits come from ten-thousand-yuan households. But a
similar development was evident in the 1950's, when many poor-
peasant activists became middle peasants after the land reform, and
important leadership positions gravitated into the hands of these
peasants. The party then launched a rectification movement and
managed to recruit new members from among the still-poor peasants. As has been shown, the ranks of the rural proletariat and poor
peasants swelled after the agricultural reform of the late 1970's and
the 1980's. They are the reserve army of a regime committed to recollectivization.

Third, recollectivization for the PRC would mean restoration,
not installation, of a command economy in agriculture. The cost
difference between the two is huge. The whole infrastructure of collective agriculture is still present (including, for example, the many
cadres who were shifted from the communes to the township
[xiang] governments), as are the management skills.[62] The calcula-
tion that the initial installation cost of agricultural collectivization
in the PRC was much lower than in the Soviet Union and many
Eastern European countries, and that the cost of restoring it would
be lower still, may strengthen the arguments in favor of recollectivization if the grain crisis justifies a reconsideration of the basic agricultural structure.

Fourth, when the reform first started, the centrist position of
moving back to the "golden years" of the 1950's (as embodied by the
Eighth Party Congress of 1956) was quite strong. This position was
against Mao's ultraleftist policies and Deng's radical reform measures. It can be argued that the PRC, with its egalitarian and anti-
materialist legacies, really had not exhausted the full potential of
the centralized economic model (Hare 1988: 57), and that the pattern of extensive growth can be salvaged for China because it is a
developing country with an abundance of labor and at this point
does not really need to shift to intensive growth and corresponding
economic reform, unlike the industrialized socialist countries. The
basic orientation of the commanding state and party bureaucracy,
as well as other losers in the reform game, also favors the solution
of restoring a command economy.[63]

However, the future development of Chinese agriculture does not necessarily have to conform to either the current formula, that is, the 1985 household responsibility system, or recollectivization. Another probable scenario would be for the state, faced with the varied and conflicting constraints of rural interests, budget limits, the high cost of imports, urban interests, and the current property rights structure, to vacillate and adopt no decisive policy, while serious grain production problems persist and political disturbance becomes perennial. This is the Polish scenario. In Poland, after the death of Stalin and the installation of Wladyslaw Gomulka as first secretary of the Polish Communist party in 1956, decollectivization took place. As in post-Mao China, a family-based private agriculture came into being, and unprecedented growth and increases in rural income ensued. Gomulka abolished obligatory delivery quotas for small farms (the whole system of obligatory delivery was abolished under Edward Gierek in the 1970's), raised procurement prices substantially, freed the product and land markets, stressed the profit principle, challenged the superiority of large-scale socialist farming, used various incentives to infuse private farmers with new confidence, and abandoned class struggle, a package of policies almost identical to that observed in the Chinese agricultural reform (Szurek 1987).

But the one-time release of pent-up economic energy brought about by a major institutional reform could not fuel growth in the long term unless accompanied by the necessary inputs. In the 1960's, Polish investment in agriculture dropped, industrial supplies were inadequate, procurement prices were relatively low, private land was parcelized and undermechanized, the rural labor force was moving into the cities, and the specter of future collectivization constantly haunted peasants. As in the PRC, all of these factors prevented the newly privatized and marketized agriculture from providing enough grain products and other major food items, and yet, again as in the PRC, the market was not allowed to send the right demand signals to peasant producers because of the state's commitment to urban price stability. In addition, the state was under great fiscal pressure as agricultural subsidies competed with investment in industry for a share of the national budget. The Polish regime then restricted wheat imports in 1967, in an attempt to achieve self-sufficiency in grain production. Thus, all of the possible solutions to the food shortage were blocked by the Gomulka government itself. Finally, when the regime decided to implement an urban price reform in December 1970 in order to bring food prices in line with production costs and relieve the state of heavy agricultural subsidies, inflation was touched off and workers revolted in Gdansk, Szczecin, and other industrial cities. As a result, Gomulka was replaced by Gierek.

Gierek blocked the food price increases, as he had promised workers he would do, and raised the procurement prices paid to farmers. He then resorted to foreign loans to bridge the gap. He also launched a very ambitious plan to increase Poland's industrial productivity by importing Western technology and to create a competitive export sector to pay for imports and loans. But as this strategy became more and more expensive, the regime began to cut imports and launched an unpublicized collectivization drive. From 1970 to 1978, state agriculture's share of arable land rose from 24.9 to 31.6 percent, while that of the private sector shrank from 75.1 to 68.4 percent. But foreign borrowing and partial recollectivization failed to save the regime from the perennial agricultural crisis. In June 1976, the government raised the retail price levels for food, but the ensuing demonstrations and strikes were strong enough to force it to withdraw the increases. On July 1, 1980, a new price reform was introduced, only to cause a repeat of the 1970 scenario of worker unrest and strikes, and the predictable collapse of the Gierek regime.

The difference between the Polish scenario (perennial crisis) and the Soviet scenario (collectivization) was the inability of the Polish United Workers' Party (PUWP) to radically reassign property rights when faced with a grain crisis.[64] With this alternative removed, the Polish regime could only depend on imports to relieve the tension inherent in its NEP-like structure. But the viability of this solution hinges on a competitive export sector, which Poland failed to build. The position of the CCP in the countryside is much stronger than that of the PUWP, and the possibility of recollectivization or considerable expansion of the collective sector in Chinese agriculture cannot be excluded. However, because this solution inevitably incurs great costs, it will not be adopted before the regime has exhausted all alternatives. Another way out of the agricultural crisis is to resort to imports and acquire the means to pay for them. Here the PRC has some advantages over the Soviet Union and Poland. This observation leads us to the model of export-led growth and the capitalist developmental states in East Asia, especially the Republic of China, right across the Taiwan Strait.

--•--•-•-•-•-•-•-•-•-•-•-•-•-•--•

Chapter Five

The ROC and the PRC

In Chapters 3 and 4, we compared the PRC and Hungary and the PRC and the Soviet Union. In this chapter we will discuss a third alternative for the PRC: state capitalism, as exemplified by the Republic of China in Taiwan in the 1950's and 1960's. Our main purpose in exploring the Taiwan case is to examine the reasons behind the ROC's shift from an NEP-like system to one characterized by private ownership in both agriculture and industry and state control of the market. We will examine these factors in the context of the PRC's industrial reform between 1984 and 1991.[1]

We will start with a comparison of the political background for economic reform in the two cases and then move to a comparison of property rights reform, beginning with agriculture (land reform in Taiwan and decollectivization in mainland China). Our focus will then shift to industrial reform. The factors that contributed to Taiwan's adoption of state capitalism in its First Four-Year Plan and its grand shift to export-led growth will be identified and discussed in the context of the mainland's post-Mao reform. Finally, we will evaluate the prospects for the PRC of adopting state capitalism in the 1990's.

Political Background

Taiwan in the 1950's was characterized by a stability unknown in the preceding decade. In the 1940's, the Kuomintang (KMT) was first engulfed in the protracted Sino-Japanese War, and then, immediately after the Japanese surrender in 1945, became embroiled in the civil war against the CCP. In 1949, the Nationalist government lost the mainland to the Communists and fled to Taiwan. During the same period, Taiwan itself was depleted by Japanese exploitation during World War II, thoroughly bombarded by the United States toward the end of that war, deprived of its administrative, professional, technical, and bourgeois strata as the Japanese were deported after the war, economically devastated by the burden of supporting the KMT against the Communists in the civil war, and finally, forced to absorb more than two million political refugees (1.5 million civilians and more than half a million military personnel) from the mainland. However, none of these misfortunes was as traumatizing as the sub-ethnic conflict between mainlanders and native Taiwanese that culminated in the Erh Erh Pa (February 28th) Incident of 1947. The Taiwanese uprisings of that time were ruthlessly put down, leaving bitter feelings between the two groups that have plagued the society ever since.[2] Adding to these political difficulties was the military threat from the Communists, who launched an attack on the Nationalist stronghold on the island of Quemoy in 1949. In the same year, U.S. aid was cut off, and in 1950, the U.S. Department of State issued a white paper holding the Nationalist government fully responsible for the loss of mainland China to the Communists. Thus at the beginning of the 1950's, an exhausted KMT state was surrounded by an alienated population, overwhelmed by an external security threat, and abandoned by its most important ally.

All this began to change with the outbreak of the Korean War in June 1950. Two days after North Korea's Kim Il Sung launched an all-out offensive against South Korea, U.S. President Harry Truman ordered the Seventh Fleet to cruise the Taiwan Strait in order to prevent a Communist attack on the island. U.S. aid to Taiwan resumed in 1951. With the external threat alleviated and its confidence restored, the KMT state began to rebuild itself. While on the mainland, the KMT had suffered from internal strife, incompetent administration, and entanglements with local elites; the rebuilt party-state in Taiwan achieved unprecedented organizational cohesiveness, enhanced state capacity, and secure state autonomy.

Prior to 1949, the KMT was actually a coalition of factions headed by former warlords. The Northern Expedition that formally unified China in 1928 was followed by continuous infighting among factional leaders that often erupted into full-scale warfare. Though Chiang Kai-shek managed to assert his position as national leader in this process, he had to deal with disobedient and powerful generals (such as Li Tsung-jen of Kwangsi and Yen Hsi-shan of Shansi) who dominated their provincial bases, which were by and large outside the central government's control. The fiasco of the civil war and the retreat to Taiwan purged the party-state of any elements not loyal to Chiang, because none of them was willing to follow him to the island (Gold 1986b: 58–59). The generalissimo-turned-president thus became the paramount leader of the Republic of China in Taiwan when he resumed office in 1950. Chiang then set about reconstructing (*kai-tsao*) the KMT in a two-year program (1950–52) that eliminated any remaining factional influence and installed a hierarchy with Chiang acting as the supreme *tsungtsai*.[3] Chiang was also commander in chief of the armed forces; he thus combined command of the Nationalist Party, the government, the military, and the security apparatus in his own hands. The internal coherence of the party-state was achieved through Chiang's personal dictatorship.

Chiang brought to Taiwan a large group of experienced administrators and professionals who filled the vacancies left by the Japanese. The rebuilt state and party apparatus penetrated deep into Taiwanese society. Here the organizational edge of the KMT's Leninist structure (specialized organs targeting different population groups, regional branches, party cells in schools, enterprises, residential communities, front organizations, etc.) fully revealed itself.[4] Finally, the autonomy of the KMT party-state was secured in the unique historical context of the late 1940's: the KMT, as an alien regime from the mainland, had no connections with local elites in Taiwan. The Erh Erh Pa Incident eliminated the intelligentsia on the island and rendered the society leaderless and intimidated. There was no domestic bourgeoisie to speak of, because the Japanese had not allowed them to emerge during the colonial period, and the landlord class had been gradually removed in the land reform that started in 1949. As a result, no social forces were capable of challenging the KMT or penetrating its establishment. In sum, with an internally coherent organization, enhanced administrative capacity, and secured autonomy, the KMT occupied a position comparable to that of a Leninist party. Without the retreat to Taiwan, this would have been impossible.

With the modern organizational weapons of a Leninist-type party in his hands, Chiang nevertheless ruled Taiwan in a very traditional manner. On the one hand, the KMT monopolized political power at the national level, suppressed dissent, controlled the mass media, and preempted social organizations that might constitute bases for opposition. On the other hand, the party-state paid utmost attention to improving the material well-being of the population and considered economic performance the ultimate source of legitimacy for the regime. The underlying philosophy of this approach is paternalistic authoritarianism, a traditional feature shared by other East Asian countries (Pye 1988a). Within this tradition, an ideal ruler is concerned with the livelihood of the people and exchanges material benefits for obedience and reverence from his subjects. This relationship between ruler and ruled is an extension of familial behavior patterns into the political realm. Chiang was conservative in his education and convictions and believed in the virtues of traditional Chinese political philosophy, that is, paternalistic authoritarianism. In part because of the circumstances in which he found himself, Chiang concentrated his attention on military affairs and until 1949 did not put enough emphasis on economic construction. The mainland fiasco taught him a lesson. After painstaking reflection on the KMT's failure there, Chiang came to the conclusion that the loss of the mainland was due to the Nationalist government's inability to bring economic benefits to the population; or, in his words, "the neglect of the principle of people's livelihood (min-sheng chu-i)" (Kindermann 1987: 384). Though still committed to retaking the mainland by military means, Chiang realized that the survival of the KMT state in Taiwan depended on its economic performance, particularly in view of the aftermath of the Erh Erh Pa Incident. Its experience on the mainland and the political imperatives of surviving in Taiwan thus reinforced the paternalistic tradition of the KMT.

A 1950 communique on party reform stressed the resolve of the KMT leadership to make a fresh start from Taiwan, and Chiang declared that "what we should be concerned with is not that we are unable to take the mainland back but that we are incapable of developing Taiwan" (Di 1988: 24; Pang 1988: 58). The U.S. used all of its influence to push the KMT toward economic development in Taiwan and to suppress its lingering desire to retake the mainland. The Seventh Fleet was sent to the Taiwan Strait at the same time that the U.S. asked the ROC government to cease air and sea operations against the mainland (*Republic of China* 1986: 382). The US$2.5 billion in military aid from the U.S. was used to strengthen Taiwan's defenses, not to prepare a military campaign against the mainland. The U.S. Military Assistance Advisory Group (MAAG) understandably exercised great influence on the island. The 1954 Mutual Defense Treaty between the U.S. and the ROC ensured the security of Taiwan while effectively prevented Chiang from using the island as a military base from which to launch a major offensive against the mainland (Crozier 1976: 365). Taiwan was thus safe but circumscribed. Although skirmishes between the mainland and Taiwan continued throughout the 1950's and Quemoy was heavily bombarded by the PRC in 1958, the separation of the two Chinas became an established fact, and the KMT's prospects for retaking the mainland became dimmer with the passage of time. Chiang was then forced to turn more attention to the economic development of Taiwan.

The *kai-tsao* (reconstruction) period (1950–1952) was a turning point for the ROC. The KMT established the Central Reform Committee in July 1950 as an ad hoc organization to substitute for the Central Executive Committee during the *kai-tsao* campaign. In October 1952, the Seventh National Congress of the KMT marked the conclusion of the reconstruction period. *Kai-tsao* tightened the KMT's political control, stifled factions within the party, and shifted national attention to Taiwan's economic development. The configuration of Chiang's paternalistic authoritarianism emerged clearly from this transformation. From then until the late 1970's, when the process of democratization accelerated, economic concerns prevailed in Taiwan, and politics was demobilized. The two realms were purposely separated, and different principles were applied to each. The government pursued economic growth and equitable distribution as its major legitimating devices, while a "frozen democracy" (in which democratically elected national representatives from the mainland were granted life tenure) limited political participation to the provincial and local levels. Martial law was imposed in 1949. No opposition party was allowed to form, and until

1988, no new journals, magazines or newspapers were permitted to enter the market.[5]

In a sense, what emerged from the *kai-tsao* period in the ROC is similar to post–Third Plenum developments in the PRC after 1978. In both cases, a Leninist-type party was in full control of the country. An indisputable leader (Chiang in Taiwan and Deng on the mainland) ruled supreme. A traumatizing event had alienated the population, and the leader was keenly aware of the crisis of legitimacy the regime faced (the legitimacy of the KMT as a national liberator was undermined by the Erh Erh Pa Incident, and the utility of Marxist-Leninist-Maoist ideology was exhausted by the Cultural Revolution). Both regimes concentrated their efforts on consumption-oriented economic development ("uphold the *min-sheng* [people's livelihood] principle" in the ROC, "resolve the principal contradiction between the growing material needs of the people and the backwardness of social production" in the PRC) because improving people's livelihood was considered their most important legitimating device. Any competing goals (in the ROC, retaking the mainland; in the PRC, class struggle) were relegated to a secondary position.[6] However, while listening to their economic advisors and making the necessary structural changes in the economy, Chiang and Deng held fast the political commanding heights in their countries and harshly suppressed dissent. The party-state monopolized political power because presumably it knew what was best for the country and needed concentrated authority in order to overcome obstacles when implementing its policies. Economic reform thus advanced much faster than political reform. People were asked to accept the enlightened rule of the technocrats, backed by the supreme leader, because by so doing they could expect economic prosperity in return.

Despite their overall similarities, there remain differences between the two cases. For one thing, opposition to the party-state's policies was stronger in the PRC, where it led to open protests in 1986–87 and 1989. There were no such protests in the ROC in the 1950's and 1960's.[7] One important reason for this difference is the history of student activism on the mainland, dating back to the May Fourth Movement of 1919, and the experience at organization and struggle that students gained during the Cultural Revolution. In the 1960's, Mao broke the rules of the power game in mainland China by inviting outside forces (particularly young students) to join the factional struggles in the party in order to change the balance of power in the establishment. Even after the Cultural Revolution, Deng continued to maneuver young democracy activists, using them in the Beijing Spring of 1978–79 to defeat his archenemy, the then CCP chairman Hua Guofeng, after which he slapped the democrats with the Four Insistences. The idealism and energy of young students were repeatedly tapped and then suppressed when their utility was exhausted, a process that finally gave rise to spontaneous student demonstrations in the late 1980's. In sharp contrast to the activated society on the mainland, Taiwan had never experienced comparable political mobilization before the 1950's. The Erh Erh Pa Incident further silenced the local population and forced them to accept the new rulers. On the other hand, the provincial and local elections dating from the early 1950's provided opportunities for political participation in which independents freely competed and won major positions (the first popularly elected mayor of Taipei, Wu San-lien, was an independent).

Another major reason for the relatively greater political activism on the mainland was the fundamental conflict between economic reform and the principles of the socialist ethic, which included stable prices for consumer goods, a relatively flat income distribution, and guaranteed full employment (Kornai 1986a). Though the KMT was hypersensitive to inflation and, to a lesser extent, income dispersion, and was willing to sacrifice growth for stability, the people of Taiwan were generally more tolerant of price fluctuations, disparities in income, and, especially, lack of job security than were their compatriots on the mainland. This was only natural, since Taiwan had never experienced socialism. As a result, Taiwan's economic reformers in the 1950's were less constrained than their counterparts on the mainland in the 1980's, where the combined effect of a politically activated society and a population unwilling to bear the cost of economic reform meant that the formula of economic liberation cum political authoritarianism met with greater difficulty, especially once the PRC's market socialist reform failed to keep people's living standards rising at a consistently high rate and the side effects of reform set in.

It was against this background that the theory of "new authoritarianism" (*xinquanweizhuyi*) emerged. In late 1988 and early

1989, when the mainland economic reform was frustrated and the country moved into a period of retrenchment, Zhao Ziyang's supporters summarized the successful experiences of Taiwan and other East Asian NICs in combining economic freedom and authoritarian political control.[8] They believed the PRC could succeed only by following in the footsteps of these new authoritarian countries. An absolutist leader (presumably Zhao), surrounded by a group of reforming technocrats (presumably Zhao's advisors), would create a power core responsible for implementing decisive policies to transform the PRC's economic system and ensure accumulation of capital and efficient allocation of resources. Democracy would have to wait until economic development reached a certain level and society can afford it. Although "new authoritarianism" was heavily criticized by the official newspapers, this had more to do with the origins of the theory than with its perceived validity. The theory's very existence was indicative of the strong sense of frustration prevalent among PRC reformers, who were constrained by an articulate society that did not want to accept the formulas dictated by the reforming elite of the CCP. What they aspired to was a political environment as manageable as that in Taiwan in the 1950's.

Another major difference between the political backgrounds of the two cases was the presence of a strong American influence on Taiwan. The Korean War shifted U.S. policy toward the ROC, making Taiwan an important strategic asset in America's global containment of communism. At the time, U.S. military and economic aid was vital for the ROC's survival, and American advisors wielded a strong influence over KMT policies. In the 1980's, no foreign country exercised comparable influence over the PRC, which skillfully played the enviable "pivot" role in the game of international strategy. However, this difference should not be exaggerated; American influence was limited, even in the ROC's early years in Taiwan, when it was extremely vulnerable. Because the U.S. considered strengthening the KMT state to be in its strategic interests, and Chiang did not allow any alternative political forces to emerge in or outside the party, the U.S. had to cooperate with him.[9] It is true that the KMT's mainland adventures were discouraged and checked by the U.S., but Chiang was allowed a much freer hand in dealing with domestic issues. Thus, for example, all U.S. aid was funneled through the central government and became a powerful instrument in the KMT's implementation of its policies. Generally speaking, during the 1950's and 1960's, the strategic interests of the U.S. coincided with the KMT's goals of consolidating political control and developing Taiwan's economy.[10] In these respects, the U.S. presence acted as a reinforcing, rather than a constraining, factor.

Property Rights Reform in Agriculture

The KMT and the CCP began their respective economic reforms against a common political background. First, both party-states had full control of society and were in a position to radically reassign property rights. Second, traumatic imprinting events—for the KMT, the loss of mainland China and the Erh Erh Pa Incident; for the CCP, the Cultural Revolution—changed the priorities of elites and prompted them to make economic reforms in order to restore their legitimacy among an alienated population. Thus both the capacity and motive for a restructuring of the economy were present.

Reform began in agriculture, though different approaches were used in the two cases. In Taiwan, a land reform eliminated the traditional landlord class and redistributed land to the tillers. On the mainland, the state decollectivized agriculture and allotted land among peasant households. The results were similar. Both reforms created a large number of peasant proprietors farming smallholdings. The production motive was maximized as income power was transferred to individual producers. As it turned out, the land reform laid the foundation for Taiwan's rapid economic development over the following four decades, and the restoration of family farming initiated the whole reform process on the mainland in the 1980's.

The land reform in Taiwan was a politically motivated economic transformation dictated by the KMT state. Its purpose was very clear: to equalize property rights in rural areas, where the majority of the population lived, and to create a contented, propertied class that would be supportive of the government and immune from Communist influence (Di 1988). The reasoning behind the reform was in line with the rationale of the Stolypin reform in imperial Russia and was exactly what had prompted the U.S. to undertake similar land reforms in Japan and South Korea.[11] There were facilitating factors: the Sino-American Joint Commission on Rural Reconstruction (JCRR) provided planning, organizational and technical advice, and partial funding (US$1.4 million); the landowning class did not have connections with the KMT state and was terrified by the Erh Erh Pa Incident; the inflow of political refugees from the mainland demanded a rapid increase in agricultural production unavailable under the old system; and the min-sheng chu-i of KMT ideology stressed land ownership by the tiller, a tenet that had been neglected by the KMT on the mainland.[12]

In 1949, General Ch'en Ch'eng was appointed governor of Taiwan. Immediately after taking office, Ch'en proclaimed that "the people's livelihood is the first priority of the government [min-sheng chih-shang]" and launched a three-stage land reform. Between 1945 and 1949, the number of tenant farmers in Taiwan grew to about 70 percent of the rural population (39 percent were landless tenant farmers and 31 percent were part owners), and rents were as high as 50 to 70 percent of the anticipated harvest (Pang 1988: 91; Di 1988: 28). As the first step of the reform, Ch'en decreed that farm rents could be fixed at no more than 37.5 percent of the anticipated annual yield of the main crops.[13] Then, in 1951, the government began to sell public land formerly owned by the Japanese to its cultivators and other landless tenants at a price of 2.5 times the value of the annual main crop yield, with repayments in kind set to coincide with the harvest season over a ten-year period. In accordance with this policy, 174,600 hectares of public land (21 percent of the arable land on the island) were sold to peasants. Finally, the most radical land-to-the-tiller program was implemented in 1953, when landlords were compelled to sell to the state any land they held in excess of a specified amount.[14] The government then resold the land to the tenants at the same prices and under the same repayment conditions as had been set for the sale of public land. One significant feature of this program was that landlords were compensated for 70 percent of the purchase price with land bonds in kind, and for the remaining 30 percent with shares of stock in four government enterprises selected for privatization—Taiwan Cement, Taiwan Pulp and Paper, Taiwan Agriculture and Forestry, and Taiwan Industry and Mining. The land reform thus converged with the policies of state capitalism.

The immediate result of the land reform was the creation of a huge number of small peasant proprietors who became the dominant force in Taiwan's countryside.[15] The old landlord class disappeared.[16] With the dispersion of ownership rights, income differentiation on the island was significantly reduced. It was estimated that the 1953 Land to the Tiller Act alone had a net wealth redistribution effect—measured in 1952 prices—of NT$2.2 billion, or roughly 13 percent of Taiwan's gross domestic product in 1952 (a fact contributing greatly to a decrease in the Gini coefficient from 0.558 in 1953 to 0.440 in 1959, or, measured in terms of the ratio of the income share of the top 20 percent households to the bottom 20 percent, a drop from 20.47 to 8.95 during the same period of time) (Thorbecke 1979: 176). Another major positive impact was increased motivational efficiency. Landownership provided a strong motive for peasant proprietors to apply family labor more intensively per unit of land, to invest more in accretionary activities that improved the quality of the land (such as leveling the land, digging small irrigation canals, and employing better crop rotation methods), and to adopt a more appropriate agricultural technology. This favorable situation, together with great improvements in the physical and organizational environments of agricultural production, increased its annual growth rate to 5.6 percent between 1953 and 1958.

The property rights granted to owner-cultivators were not complete, however, especially in the area of rice production. The government established various mechanisms for extracting surplus rice from the peasants. Land repayments and the land tax in kind forced peasants to give up a portion of their produce to the state, thus encroaching on their income power. Compulsory sales of rice to the state and a rice-fertilizer barter system (*fei-liao huan-ku*) were also implemented. The former required peasants to sell to the state a certain amount of rice at prices considerably lower than market prices. The latter was based on the government's monopoly on chemical fertilizer and amounted to another compulsory purchase at fixed barter ratios unfavorable to rice growers. These collection methods constrained the control power of rice farmers, who could not make production and exchange decisions freely. The rice-fertilizer barter program was the most important of the state's devices, accounting for between 60 and 70 percent of total government rice collection in the 1950's and 1960's. In 1954, the state garnered 73 percent of all rice marketed, a figure which was gradually reduced to about 50 percent by the late 1960's (Thorbecke 1979: 180). Agricultural surplus was thus extracted to feed the urban population (especially the *chun-kung-chiao jen-yuan*—members of the armed forces, their dependents, government employees, and teachers), to stabilize prices, to earn foreign exchange, and to fund industrialization.

The various collection mechanisms employed by the state clearly created unfavorable terms of trade for rice farmers. In addition, the government guaranteed the prices for sugarcane, corn, mushrooms, asparagus, fruit, pork, and other agricultural products, thus widening the profit differential between rice growing and the production of other commodities. Because owner-cultivators were no longer obliged to produce rice with which to make rental payments, as under the old tenant system, many of them shifted to non-rice production. The result was rapid product diversification. The share of rice in total agricultural production fell from 50.2 percent in 1952 to 36.8 in 1965 (Kuo, Ranis, and Fei 1981: 57). Not only was there a shift from rice to other agricultural products, but also a trend toward off-farm activities. As the number of part-time farmers increased rapidly, so did the proportion of nonfarm receipts in total farm household receipts (Thorbecke 1979: 178). However, most of the household members engaged in off-farm activities were part-time or seasonal workers who maintained their residence on the farm. This phenomenon corresponded with the regional and rural decentralization of industrial development that took place on the island after the mid-1950's. Rural industry absorbed the labor released from agriculture in a highly productive way. It also reduced rural-to-urban migration and contributed to further income equalization (because poorer and smaller households earned a larger proportion of their income from off-farm activities).

Up to this point, one can find a great number of similarities between Taiwan's land reform and agricultural decollectivization on the mainland. Both employed a radical reassignment of property rights to change the incentive scheme of the old system and maximize motivational efficiency. As a result, in both cases agriculture became dominated by a large number of peasant proprietors farming smallholdings. Both reforms followed the principle of an egalitarian distribution of land among peasant households, in Taiwan through compulsory redistribution of excess landlord property and on the mainland via the allotment of plots according to household size or number of laborers available for field work. Agricultural growth was evident following the reforms. From 1953 to 1958, Taiwan's agriculture grew at an annual rate of 5.6 percent. On the mainland, the annual agricultural growth rate between 1979 and 1984 was an amazing 8.6 percent, compared to an average of 2.9 percent over the previous two decades.[17]

With the dispersion of ownership, property users gained a much larger share of the income generated by their efforts, though the transfer of income power was not complete in either case (it was limited by land repayments and the land tax in kind in Taiwan and by time constraints on the mainland). Control power was partially in the hands of the state, as evidenced by compulsory state procurement in both countries (these were abolished in principle on the mainland in 1985) and the government policy of linking the provision of agricultural inputs to the delivery of grain (e.g., through the rice/fertilizer barter system in Taiwan and the practice of tying the sale of diesel oil, fertilizer, and pesticide to the delivery of grain on the mainland). Finally, the transferability of property rights was not completely unfettered. In Taiwan, only tillers could purchase farmland, and on the mainland, the sale of land had to take the form of *zhuanbao* (transfers of contract).

There were both developmental and extractive aspects in the two reforms. The change in the incentive scheme offered the greatest momentum for growth, and the various extractive mechanisms transferred surpluses to the state. The latter was considered necessary because it was politically imperative to secure a basic food supply for the urban population (especially state employees) and to maintain price stability.[18] Both the KMT and the CCP considered the hyperinflation of the late 1940's a major factor in the defeat of the Nationalist government on the mainland (Pang 1988: 103; Huang 1990: 33).[19] This historical lesson provided a strong incentive for each of the two parties to pursue stability as its chief policy priority. It was against this background that property rights in agriculture were both dispersed and constrained. Generally speaking, the income position of peasant proprietors improved greatly, whereas their control power was limited, especially with regard to the extractive price policy the state adopted for the most important staple crop.[20] Because in both cases the terms of trade worsened for grain but not other commodities, and rural industry, trade, and high-profit services were open to peasants, it was inevitable that rural labor would shift from grain production to cash crops, animal husbandry, and non-agricultural activities. On the mainland, grain production plummeted, and a crisis emerged in 1985. However, the same did not happen in Taiwan. Here the two cases diverged.

The restructuring of property rights is by nature an institutional reform that, if successfully planned and implemented, can release pent-up economic energy and bring about a spurt of growth. However, unless accompanied by sufficient inputs, this one-shot growth may quickly peak and plummet. Agricultural reform in the PRC (decollectivization) was initially very successful, to such an extent that the CCP leadership cut both the absolute and relative amounts of investment in agriculture, expecting it to grow more or less automatically (see Chap. 4). At the same time, the terms of trade for grain declined, and further property rights reforms provided peasants with an easy exit from grain production. The subsequent precipitous drop in grain production was hardly surprising. Taiwan's similar agricultural reform shared this price policy that discriminated against its major crop, together with an easy exit to production of other goods and services. However, favorable colonial legacies and consistent efforts by the KMT state to improve the physical and organizational environment of Taiwan's agriculture made a great difference in the outcome of the reform in that country.

Agriculture in Taiwan was blessed with a set of positive features from the colonial period. These included an appropriate labor-intensive technology that relied on modern inputs (particularly the new Ponlai rice variety and chemical fertilizers), a greatly improved infrastructure for irrigation, drainage, and transportation, and a group of rural institutions that conducted agricultural research, disseminated knowledge, provided extension and credit services, and marketed inputs and outputs (Thorbecke 1979; Myers and Saburo 1984). After 1949, the KMT fostered further development in these areas. The most important role was played by the JCRR, a de facto superministry of agriculture jointly created by the ROC and U.S. governments. Well funded by the U.S., semi-independent from the government, and staffed by both Chinese and American experts, the JCRR planned and carried out the transformation of Taiwan's agriculture in the 1950's. It formulated agricultural development plans and implemented a large number of projects using U.S. funds. Between 1951 and 1965, US$213 million, or 22.5 percent of total U.S. aid to Taiwan, was allotted to agriculture. This represented 59 percent of net domestic capital formation in that sector. The JCRR controlled the bulk of the local currency counterpart funds that were generated through aid-financed imports, undertaking nearly 6,000 projects. These encompassed crop and livestock improvement, water resource development, soil conservation, rural health improvement, and agricultural research. The JCRR also played a decisive role in land reform and the reorganization of farmers' associations, which then acted as local branches of the central agricultural agency.[21]

The activities of the JCRR and the farmers' associations in particular, and the KMT's strategy in general, demonstrated how "Taiwan's agricultural sector received gross resources from nonagriculture in a variety of ways that by increasing its productivity allowed it to provide a net transfer to the rest of the economy" (Thorbecke 1979: 203). In Taiwan, the continuous provision of sufficient inputs into agriculture, together with the institutional restructuring that took place during the land reform, more than offset the negative impact of a discriminating and extractive price policy, and prevented the emergence of a grain crisis such as occurred in mainland China.[22]

The KMT's development cum extraction policy worked well in the countryside for nearly two decades. Then, despite farmers' incentive to produce and the technology and infrastructure that supported it, toward the end of the 1960's Taiwan's agriculture began to stagnate, reflecting the growth limits of intensive small-scale farming. In the early 1970's, the government shifted its agricultural policy from extraction to protection, a decision prompted by a 1973 rice shortage and a high rate of inflation caused by the first oil crisis. The rice/fertilizer barter system was abolished in 1973, followed by guaranteed rice prices beginning in 1984 (Li Kwoh-Ting 1988: 117). The government now maintained farm incomes and subsidized food prices to satisfy both rural and urban interests, an approach typical of a developed country (Gray 1988: 193). This grand shift was made at a time when the country's per capita gross national product (GNP) had reached roughly US$2,800 (in 1989 prices) and the government budget had registered a continuous surplus since

1964—that is, when the state was no longer financially constrained and the economy could afford a supportive policy toward agriculture.

Mainland China was also compelled to shift to a price policy favorable to peasants as a grain crisis emerged and the agricultural growth rate dropped in the late 1980's (from an average of 9.9 percent for 1981–84 to 3.6 percent for 1985–88). Clearly the growth spurt brought about by decollectivization could not be sustained without sufficient inputs in technology and infrastructure in the context of small-scale farming. However, this early decline in the growth rate caught the PRC in a situation that was much more difficult than that of the ROC in the early 1970's: per capita GNP on the mainland was only US$303 in 1989, and the government was heavily in debt (the budget deficit for 1989 was 9.54 billion rmb). Subsidizing agriculture on a long-term basis was unfeasible in view of the financial constraints on the state and the degree of development of the economy. Hence the regime, in its policy statements, assigned top priority to agriculture (People's Daily, June 26, 1990) and emphasized the development of an infrastructure and technology (keji xingnong), although the government's commitments were still questionable.

The change in Taiwan's agricultural policy in the early 1970's brought about a surge in rice production on the island, but the overall growth rate remained low (an average of 2.9 percent in the 1970's, compared to 4.6 percent in the 1960's). The major constraining element was the small-scale farming brought about by the egalitarian land reform. It lacked economies of scale and made it very difficult to implement mechanized farming. The 1973 Statute for Agricultural Development and the "second land reform" in 1981 thus called for joint management of individual farms, contract farming, and enlargement of the average farm size. The government's goal was to encourage the separation of ownership and management so that farmlands could be consolidated and made amenable to mechanized farming (Li Kwoh-Ting 1988: 116). However, these measures were not successful in bringing about any significant changes, because small-scale farming as an institution proved very difficult to remove.

Mainland China went through a similar egalitarian land redistribution, so small-scale farming was also a constraining factor in its agriculture. The lingering Marxist view that praised large-scale production particularly sensitized CCP leaders to this issue. The problem in the PRC was also one of encouraging the consolidation of land without damaging peasants' motive to produce. In Taiwan, this was not a serious problem because the growth momentum of private small-scale farming was not exhausted until fifteen years after the reform. On the mainland, where agricultural growth peaked much sooner after decollectivization, the issue of small- versus large-scale farming became more prominent and constituted a powerful argument for recollectivization (*Central Daily News*, Jan. 23, 1990).

In sum, the agricultural reforms in Taiwan and mainland China were similar in their political backgrounds (both were crisis induced), the property rights structures that they brought about (a large number of peasant proprietors farming smallholdings), their initial results (high growth and product diversification), and some of their constraining elements (extractive price policy and small-scale farming). Each of the two countries initiated a reform process that spread to the whole economy (import substitution and export expansion under state capitalism in Taiwan and industrial reform based on market socialism on the mainland). The major difference was the PRC's relative lack of investment in agriculture, which caused an earlier exhaustion of the reform's growth momentum in that country.

Pre-Reform Industry

In addition to their similar political backgrounds and agricultural property rights reforms, we can detect structural similarities in pre-reform industry in the ROC in the 1950's and the PRC in the 1980's. Both industries were characterized by the dominance of state enterprises and strict government controls. It is true that in the PRC, miscellaneous reform measures were introduced between 1979 and 1984 to improve industrial efficiency. However, these measures did not alter the fundamental command structure of mainland industry. Similarly, prior to the First Four-Year Plan (1953–56), which emphasized privatization, most industry in Taiwan was owned and controlled by the government (although a small traditional private sector did exist). In short, industry on both sides prior to the major reform—1984 in the PRC, 1953 in the ROC—was firmly in state hands.

This situation requires more explanation in the case of Taiwan than in that of mainland China, which has had a state socialist economy since the 1950's. The prominent role of the KMT state in Taiwan's industry was brought about by its takeover of the Japanese corporations set up during the colonial period. Due to the policy of "agricultural Taiwan, industrial Japan," there was little industry on the island under Japanese rule. Japan wanted to develop Taiwan into a major source of food and focused its attention on developing the island's agriculture. This policy produced an agricultural surplus (mainly of sugar and rice), which, following a typical colonial pattern, was then exported to Japan in exchange for industrial products (Ho 1975: 421).[23] However, toward the end of the colonial period, Tokyo modified its policy and began to increase the island's industrial capacity in order to process raw materials extracted from Southeast Asia and to increase Taiwan's self-sufficiency with regard to consumer goods. Taiwan was to become Japan's bridgehead to the newly conquered territories to the south. Industrial chemicals, ceramics, aluminum, machine tools, and textiles were introduced to the island (Pang 1988: 26). This preliminary industrialization was concentrated in the colonizers' hands, partly because of initially restrictive regulations regarding capital ownership and partly because very few Taiwanese had accumulated enough wealth to participate (Fei, Ranis, and Kuo 1979: 25).[24] Industrial production was consolidated in a few very large, modern companies owned by the Japanese. These companies controlled approximately 90 percent of the corporate capital in mining and manufacturing (Ho 1975: 422).[25] Transportation and communication were also dominated by government monopolies and government enterprises.

This Japanese-dominated industry was strictly controlled during World War II. In 1945, it was turned over to the Chinese government, hence the dominant role of the KMT state in Taiwan's industry. It had been the policy of the colonial government to staff Taiwan's industrial establishments with Japanese rather than to train Taiwanese as administrators, technicians, and skilled industrial workers; the mainlanders who came to the island with the KMT state readily filled these positions. Moreover, some mainland state enterprises were relocated to Taiwan before 1949, adding to the weight of the state sector. Juxtaposed with this large and modern state industry dominated by mainlanders was a small traditional sector, also a part of the colonial legacy, that was made up of handicraft shops and small manufacturing establishments run by Taiwanese.[26] They were undercapitalized and applied traditional production techniques. A few mainland capitalists came to Taiwan with the Nationalist government (the bulk of the bourgeois class moved to Hong Kong or the U.S.), but they were deterred from investing there because of rampant inflation and political uncertainty.

Thus, before industrial reform began in 1953, the Taiwanese government not only owned the bulk of industry, it directly managed it. Under conditions of extreme scarcity of all goods and state control of foreign aid, materials and products were allocated mainly by the government, not by the market. Prices were strictly controlled by the Resources Bureau created in 1952. Interest rates were determined by the government through the public banking system. Imports and exports were heavily regulated and largely managed by government agencies (Ho 1978: 128). Foreign exchange controls were imposed in 1949 (Shen 1972: 97). With inflation running as high as 1,145 percent in 1948, the government assigned top priority to economic stability, a move that reinforced the tendency to concentrate economic control in state hands.

Between 1949 and 1953, that is, between the relocation of the central government to Taipei and the beginning of the First Four-Year Plan, state industry in Taiwan was under the control of the Taiwan Production Board (TPB). The board was chaired by the provincial governor (Ch'en Ch'eng in 1949, Wu Kuo-chen from 1950 to 1953), but the real power was held by vice chairman K. Y. Yin, arguably the single most influential economic policymaker in Taiwan during the 1950's and early 1960's. The TPB not only monitored all state enterprises, it took charge of planning production and supply, financing projects, and determining export arrangements (Pang 1988: 35). It directed resources to the production of defense-related products and necessities (Shen 1972: 96). It placed top priority on restoring infrastructure damaged by Allied bombing and on developing the production of electrical power, chemical fertilizers, and textiles. The TPB acted as Taiwan's first economic general staff, the pilot agency that directed the country's economic activities.[27] The plans of the TPB were supported by the Council for United States Aid (CUSA), which was in charge of selecting aid-financed imports, allocating the sales proceeds of such imports (the aid-generated counterpart fund in local currency), and supervising aid projects. After trade with Japan resumed in 1950, Yin was appointed director of the Central Trust Board, the largest trading agency, hence combining his power in industry and trade and making the allocation of materials more effective. During this period of time, the TPB under Yin directed state enterprises, controlled foreign trade, and applied various administrative levers (such as rationing) to manage the economy.

Though not yet a command economy, Taiwan at the beginning of the 1950's was characterized by dominant public ownership and administrative allocation. This brought about a whole range of problems associated with state enterprises: inefficiency, overstaffing, rigid pay structures, and bureaucratic interference (Kuo, Ranis, and Fei 1981: 61). Still, there was strong pressure to maintain or even strengthen state dominance of industry. Conservative forces in the party and the government favored the public sector as a very effective state instrument for managing the economy and achieving important goals like economic stability. Their memories of wartime economic mobilization and the economic bureaucracy originally established in mainland China also predisposed them toward direct administrative control of the economy.[28] Furthermore, Sun Yat-sen's *min-sheng chu-i* (principle of the people's livelihood) contained elements that favored state capital in strategic sectors of the economy—for example, where natural monopolies occurred and in areas requiring more capital than private entrepreneurs could provide (though he also mentioned that entrepreneurs should be given a free hand in all other areas of the economy). This ideological tenet was easily co-opted by those in favor of establishing a command economy. Finally, the mainlander-Taiwanese cleavage that reinforced the public-private division in the economy acted against the expansion of the private sector. As a result, public enterprises were glorified and the intrusion of private enterprises was resisted.

Pre-1984 industry in mainland China was also characterized by public ownership and state control, though the industrial reform measures introduced after 1978 had brought about marginal privatization and limited marketization. In the 1950's, instead of confiscating former colonizers' assets, as was done in Taiwan, the Chinese Communists socialized the industrial means of production owned by the Chinese bourgeoisie and began building a command economy through Soviet-style five-year plans. Unlike in Taiwan, the traditional small-scale handicraft sector on the mainland was also socialized, together with retailers in the cities, under the three socialist transformations of the 1950's. In the 1960's and 1970's, there were repeated campaigns against private business and individualism, competition, personal ambition, and inequality. Large-scale state enterprises were considered the ideal form of ownership and received top priority from state planners.

The urban private sector began to reemerge in the late 1970's as a result of economic reform. The party tolerated private business mainly because it could absorb surplus labor (youths awaiting job assignments, Red Guards from the countryside, etc.). However, only very small establishments were tolerated in this "individual economy" (*geti jingji*). The 1982 Constitution extended protection to those engaged in the individual economy (the *getihu*) and recognized the right of PRC citizens to inherit private property. As a result of this policy shift, individual industry began to develop rapidly. In 1984, individual industrial output reached 1,480 million rmb, a 97.3 percent increase over the 1983 level (from 1981–84, the average growth rate for the individual economy was 108.8 percent) (Sah 1986: 21). However, its share in the country's total industrial output was still a negligible 0.2 percent in 1984, much smaller than that of Taiwan's private industry in the early 1950's.[29]

From 1979 to 1984, industrial reform in mainland China mainly took the form of piecemeal and uncoordinated measures that were experimented with at certain trial points (Solinger 1985: 88). Most of these reform measures aimed at marketization, that is, loosening state control over enterprises by gradually shifting from mandatory planning (using administrative levers) to guidance planning (using economic levers) without changing the socialist ownership structure. Under this scheme, the success indicator for enterprises became profitability, bonuses were reinstated, "profit contracts" were introduced, taxes were substituted for profit (*li gai shui*), capital allocation via the state budget was gradually replaced by credits extended by financial institutions, limited decision-making power in production, exchange, and pricing was delegated to managers, the number of commands issued to enterprises was reduced, and the scope of central planning and material allocation was reduced (C. Wong 1985). However, the new incentive schemes (e.g., egalitarian distribution of bonuses) remained ineffective, the problems associated with the soft budget constraint (such as investment hunger) were exacerbated, and the diffusion of decision-making power without an accompanying price reform and a competitive market failed to match production with demand. There was no gain in industrial productivity (C. Wong 1985), in sharp contrast to the growth pattern in agriculture. More importantly, the central ministries, and increasingly the local governments, continued to interfere with enterprise decisions. Thus, the state remained the dominant allocator.

In contrast to Taiwan in the early 1950's, there was no economic pilot agency on the mainland that was capable of integrating the various functions involved in managing the economy. The State Planning Commission, the State Economic Commission, the Ministry of Foreign Economic Relations and Trade, the various production ministries, the provinces, and the "key cities" all shared considerable power in the country's economic decision making. Neither was there a figure comparable to K. Y. Yin, to whom Taiwan's leaders had delegated full power for guiding the economy. Political intervention by party cadres was much more widespread on the mainland, following the time-honored tradition of a "director responsibility system under the leadership of the party secretary" (Sah 1990: 296). This fragmented institutional and power structure made decisive economic policy making extremely difficult (Lieberthal and Oksenberg 1988).

The shortcomings of the old command system were well-known and recognized by the CCP leadership in the early 1980's. However, prior to the 1984 industrial reform, guidance planning was still subordinate to mandatory planning, not to mention ownership reform. As in Taiwan, there was strong resistance to economic liberalization, which was reinforced by a deep-rooted fear of its socio-political-ideological implications, hence the party purge and the Anti–Spiritual Pollution Campaign in 1983. Official ideology was also used by conservatives to attack the reform. Marxism–Leninism–Mao Zedong Thought proved to be a much stronger ideological barrier to economic liberalization than Sun's *min-sheng chu-i*, though there were no sub-ethnic conflicts complicating economic restructuring in mainland China as there were in Taiwan.

Industrial Reform:
State Capitalism Versus Market Socialism

The ROC in the early 1950's and the PRC in the early 1980's shared similar political backgrounds (authoritarian rule cum crisis-induced developmental policy aimed at improving the people's living standard), agricultural reforms (egalitarian land redistribution), and state-dominated industries (in terms of both ownership and control). In 1953, the ROC launched its First Four-Year Plan, which emphasized privatization of industry and the creation of a bourgeois class. In 1984, the PRC adopted the Decision on Reform of the Economic Structure that focused on marketization and the shift from mandatory planning to guidance planning. With the continuous growth of its private sector, Taiwan gradually developed into an economy characterized by dominant private ownership and state guidance of the market, or state capitalism. On the other hand, with only marginal privatization and more power delegated to state enterprises, the PRC followed the Hungarian example and moved closer to the model of market socialism. How can we account for this divergence?

As in the case of pre-reform industry, the strategy taken by the ROC requires more explanation than that taken by the PRC, which basically adopted the reform package established by Hungary in its New Economic Mechanism. In the 1980's, the reforming elites in the PRC were what Janos Kornai called "naive reformers," who wanted to introduce market into the rigid command structure while retaining the state's capacity to direct the economy.[30] Naive reformers chose to transfer control power to property users in order to enliven the economy (*gaohuo jingji*), while maintaining public ownership as a guarantee of state dominance. The resultant hybrid of market socialism was presumed to combine the efficiency of the market and the security of socialism. Income power (ownership) was not chosen for transfer because it was considered vital to the definition of socialism (the elimination of exploitation) and the rule of the party (as *the* owner and employer in the national economy).

In the PRC, privatization in small-scale establishments and capitalist enclaves was a prominent phenomenon, but the post-1984 industrial structure in general demonstrated the defining feature of market socialism: marketization without privatization. As in Hungary, this scheme was considered sufficient to stimulate the economy without undermining the fundamental interests of the party.[31] It was a great advance from the old command system and compared favorably with the more limited administrative reforms made by other socialist countries. The Chinese market reform would have been impossible without the disastrous Cultural Revolution and its reordering of elite priorities. However, market socialism still aimed at minimizing the cost of systemic changes in property rights and resistance from conservative forces (Kornai 1986b). It did not touch on the fundamental issue of ownership reform because such a strategy was considered too costly.

Taiwan's state capitalism was created in two stages: primary import substitution in the 1950's and export expansion in the 1960's. Going a route opposite to that taken by the mainland, Taiwan began with ownership reform (privatization) while maintaining tight state control of the market. The shift from primary import substitution to export expansion in the late 1950's and early 1960's created a booming export sector based on private enterprises producing labor-intensive products, tilting the balance further against the state sector. Taiwan thus gradually grew into a private economy, with the means of production mostly in private hands and profits mostly appropriated by private entrepreneurs (White and Wade 1988: 6). At the same time, the state continued to manipulate both administrative and economic levers to guide private enterprises toward goals set by the technocrats. Income power was in private hands but the state exercised great control power, though in a fashion that was increasingly indirect and market conforming. In the following discussion, we will concentrate on those critical decisions that transformed Taiwan's economy in the 1950's and 1960's and make a comparison with mainland China.[32]

The ROC: Initiating State Capitalism

State capitalism was given a big push by the ROC government in the early 1950's, mainly through various policies that expanded the share of the private sector in industry. Both structural and auxiliary elements can be found behind the critical decisions made at that time. By structural elements I mean the economic constraints imposed on Taiwan's economy: import dependency, balance-of-payments problems, and a hard budget constraint were the critical triad. Auxiliary elements included U.S. aid, Chinese technocrat-privatizers, and the KMT's ideological pragmatism. It was through the combined effect of these structural and auxiliary elements that resistance to privatization was overcome and an indigenous bourgeoisie was created.

During the colonial period, Taiwan was a primary exporter of agricultural products (mainly rice and sugar). At the same time, it was almost completely dependent on imports for manufactured consumer goods. Its economy was highly trade dependent and relied on Japan as its single export market.[33] That market, however, was cut off by the U.S. military government that occupied Japan in 1945. Taiwan's trade then shifted to mainland China in 1946–48, but that market closed in 1949 as a result of the Communist victory there. The loss of the Japanese and mainland markets dealt a fatal blow to Taiwan's war-devastated economy, which was already having great difficulty absorbing 2.1 million political refugees from the mainland (a number that represented more than 30 percent of the island's original population). In the early 1950's, Taiwan's economic survival depended on U.S. aid–financed imports, which were required in order to meet the basic needs of the population.[34] Its large balance-of-payments deficit almost exhausted the government's gold and foreign exchange reserves.[35] Its trade deficit was as high as 6 to 10 percent of the GNP. This extreme dependency on imports and the balance-of-payments crisis forced the government to develop domestic industries that could produce substitutes for imports. Because the items imported in the largest quantities were chemical fertilizers and textiles, these two industries, together with electrical power, were targeted as priority industries by the TPB. Fertilizers were critical to the government's barter program with the peasants, while electrical power plants were clearly above the capacity of the private sector to develop, so both were kept in state hands. However, the TPB made a critical decision to nurture private entrepreneurs in the textile industry. This was the starting point of the privatization drive that ultimately changed the ownership structure of Taiwan's economy.

Import dependency and balance-of-payments problems made primary import substitution (the replacement of nondurable consumer goods imports with domestic production) a necessity. However, they did not predetermine the ownership structure of the import-substituting industries. The decision to promote private enterprises in the textile sector cannot be understood without taking a look at the last structural factor: the hard budget constraint facing Taiwan's government in the early 1950's. It was because of this constraint that policymakers were forced to restrict state investment in textiles and resort to the private enterprises. Like many other developing countries at the time, Taiwan suffered from large budget deficits. They were covered only by the sale of U.S. aid–financed imports (Di 1988: 26). However, Taiwan was different from most less-developed countries in the early 1950's in that its government was fully committed to maintaining economic stability and a balanced budget while implementing import substitution.[36] This policy was the direct result of the KMT's loss of the mainland, which was attributed primarily to the rampant inflation caused by unchecked government spending and uncontrolled increases in the money supply. The hyperinflation in Taiwan in 1946–49 also reinforced the government's anti-inflationary stance (Lundberg 1979: 269). As a result, the government began to exercise rigid budget control (Li Kwoh-Ting 1988: 120). Under a hard budget constraint, deficit financing of other than absolutely necessary state enterprises was out of the question. It was only natural, then, for policymakers to resort to the encouragement of private enterprises in designated industries.[37] Private enterprises in the textile sector were given much more favorable consideration under these circumstances.

Auxiliary political factors also contributed to Taiwan's policy shift vis-à-vis private industry. Among them, U.S. aid was arguably the most important. From 1951 to 1965, over US$4 billion was made available to the ROC government in the form of grants, loans, and military equipment. The nonmilitary share alone, US$1.42 billion, was equivalent to over 6 percent of Taiwan's GNP and financed about 40 percent of the country's investment and imports during that period of time. Expressed on an annual per capita basis, U.S. aid represented US$8 per capita per year for fourteen consecutive years (Thorbecke 1979: 205). During the critical 1951–53 period, aid-financed imports of US$150 million in basic foodstuffs and consumer goods helped bring down the inflation rate and probably ensured the very survival of the ROC.

U.S. aid was jointly administered by AID and CUSA. This financial assistance was the most powerful leverage that Americans held in influencing ROC policies (Gold 1986b: 73), though the strategic need for the U.S. to stabilize the economy of the island and strengthen its defense posture against the mainland limited its use as a policy tool. This meant that a large part of U.S. aid had to go to subsidizing budget and trade deficits, stabilizing prices, and financing investments in infrastructure. However, AID did have full discretionary power in allocating resources to different enterprises, and it had a strong preference for the private sector (Di 1988: 26). Thus, its program imported the raw cotton needed for development of the infant private textile industry. It also established the Small Industry Loan Fund and Model Factory Program and offered preferential interest rates to private enterprises. A total of US$20 million and NT$283 million from the sale of aid imports was channeled to Taiwan's private sector. In 1952–58, U.S. aid constituted 24 percent of total private investment on the island. All major private firms benefited from the aid programs (Li Kwoh-Ting 1988: 58). More significant than direct allocation of aid funds and materials was the American advisors' influence on Chinese officials and their support of the privatization drive, in which they used U.S. aid as a powerful means of persuasion. It was on this level of developmental strategy that the U.S. had the greatest impact.

Another important political factor contributing to the emergence of Taiwan's first entrepreneurs was the role played by technocrat-privatizers. K. Y. Yin was the leading figure in this group of government officials. Trained as an electrical engineer and recruited into the state economic bureaucracy early in his career, Yin established the pattern of having engineers from state enterprises, rather than professional economists, run key economic planning agencies (Gold 1986b: 68). He did not follow any established economic theories but guided Taiwan's economic transformation in a learning-by-doing approach (Pang 1988: 63). Yin was deeply impressed by the rapid industrialization of Japan. The lesson he drew from both the Meiji restoration and the rapid recovery of Japan under American occupation was that the state must combine private ownership and government guidance for economic development. Taking advantage of individual profit motives, the state should mobilize resources that can only be activated by private ownership, but it should control the business environment in order to direct the behavior of private enterprises toward state goals. Private ownership would fuel the economy, and state control would guide its growth.

Thus for Yin, property rights were considered dividable and private ownership much more valuable than a self-regulating market. Based on this understanding, Yin vigorously pushed his plan to create private entrepreneurs by manipulating various administrative and economic levers, that is, by controlling the market.

The last important political factor that favored the emergence of a private sector in Taiwan was the KMT's ideological pragmatism. This does not mean that there was a lack of elite commitment to Sun Yat-sen's *san-min chu-i* (the Three Principles of the People: nationalism, democracy, and the people's livelihood). Rather, the ideology itself was pragmatic and was compatible with a wide range of economic policies that technocrats could choose from.[38] Sun divided the state and private sectors, reserving some industries for the former and leaving all residual areas open to the private sector. However, he also stated the need to restrict private capital and to develop state capital. Sun's teachings led to a mixed economy in which both the state and the private sector played an important role. Sun's general principles were subject to different interpretations that could be mobilized to support opposing policies. What mattered most was that economic technocrats could legitimate their policies of state capitalism in terms of *san-min chu-i*, and their opponents could not monopolize the official ideology. In this sense, *san-min chu-i* was flexible and thus conducive to economic development.[39]

Primary import substitution first took the form of the "entrustment scheme" designed by K. Y. Yin in 1951. The state provided raw cotton to textile "entrepreneurs," paid wages to their workers, and purchased their yarn. The same arrangement applied to fabric, which was then sold by the Central Trust Board at controlled prices (Tung 1988: 73). The government made all production and exchange decisions and the entrepreneurs appropriated the profits. Property rights were divided into two parts: the state held the control power and private enterprises held the income power. This is a perfect example of state capitalism: private ownership cum state control. With profits guaranteed by the state, private enterprises boomed and production accelerated. In 1953, the entrustment program was replaced by price controls. Entrepreneurs continued to benefit from the suspension of textile imports (which dated from 1951), and enjoyed special foreign exchange quotas and preferential rates for imports of raw cotton and machinery. With no foreign competition and with domestic supply exceeded by demand, private textile firms made huge profits and expanded their production. Many of Taiwan's major textile conglomerates emerged during this period, including Taiyuen-Yulong, Tainan, Far East, Hsin-Kuang, and others (Tung 1988: 75; Di 1988: 36; Wen 1984: 15).

In 1953, the TPB was succeeded by the Economic Stabilization Board (ESB), and Yin became the convener of the all-powerful Industrial Development Commission under the ESB. The principles of state capitalism that had been applied to the textile industry were incorporated into the ESB's First Four-Year Plan and were extended to other import-substituting industries. Typically, the government did all the preparation work and then provided planning, capital, equipment, and a market to the private entrepreneurs, making sure that they would benefit from participation in these projects. A good example was Formosa Plastics, a private enterprise established by W. C. Wang and T. C. Chao that later developed into Taiwan's leading industrial conglomerate (Wen 1984: 16). In 1954, the government began to transfer shares of stock in several public enterprises (Taiwan Cement, Taiwan Pulp and Paper, Taiwan Agriculture and Forestry, and Taiwan Industry and Mining) to landlords whose assets had been compulsorily purchased under the land-to-the-tiller program. Large landowning families in particular benefited from this policy, which allowed a few of them to turn themselves into successful industrialists. As a result of the two approaches to privatization (creation of new private enterprises and direct privatization of public corporations), Taiwan's private sector accounted for an increasingly larger share of total industrial production: 27.5 percent in 1949, 44.1 percent in 1953, and 50.0 percent in 1958 (Pang 1988: 109; Kuo, Ranis, and Fei 1981: 60). The goal of replacing nondurable consumer goods imports with domestic production was also achieved. Between 1952 and 1957, the share of consumer goods in total imports fell from 19.8 percent to 6.6 percent (Ranis 1979: 207).

The ROC: Deepening State Capitalism

Taiwan experienced a great change in economic strategy in the late 1950's and early 1960's, when it shifted from primary import substitution to export expansion. This move was hailed as a decisive step toward liberalizing the economy by opening it up to the world market. Much of the country's later success in economic development (rapid industrialization with improved income distribution) was attributed to this policy shift (Kuo, Ranis, and Fei 1981: 7). From the standpoint of property rights, however, the differences between the two strategies were not that dramatic. The fundamental principle of state capitalism, that is, the government guiding private enterprises toward developmental goals, was unchanged. Under changed economic circumstances, the state simply applied a different set of incentives and disincentives in order to turn private enterprises in a new direction (the nature of this new direction did, however, reduce the state's control power).

In the 1960's, the private sector continued to produce an increasingly larger share of total industrial output, thanks primarily to the emergence of a large number of small and medium-sized private enterprises in the export sector. At the same time, shifting the direction of industrial growth from primary import substitution to export expansion did marketize the economy in the sense that the government was no longer able to control the market for Taiwan's producers. That market was now located in foreign countries, where Taiwan's private enterprises faced stiff competition without government protection. However, the competitiveness of Taiwan's exports was to a large extent determined by its production costs, which could be reduced by the state's export-promotion measures. In fact, the technocrats designed industrial policies that targeted strategic industries, provided financial support through credit allocation and various tax policies, fixed exchange rates so that they favored exports, offered market information, and at times exercised administrative guidance.[40] Generally speaking, under export expansion output was liberalized because the state lacked control over foreign markets; however, input was still tightly controlled by the state through an array of administrative and economic levers (though the latter became more important as time passed). Throughout the 1960's, continued privatization was accompanied by limited marketization, so that at the end of the decade, when secondary import substitution began, Taiwan's industry was characterized by a dominant private sector and state control through indirect and market-conforming means.

Structural elements played a decisive role in this policy shift, much as they did in initiating state capitalism under primary import substitution. Balance-of-payments problems and the termination of U.S. aid, a limited domestic market and declining growth rate, and the lack of an alternative strategy predisposed the government to export expansion. Under the existing structure of a strong private presence in labor-intensive industries and a continuous hard budget constraint for the state, this shift in Taiwan's industrialization strategy naturally brought about further privatization, while its outward orientation mitigated state control of the market, though only to a limited degree. Auxiliary factors facilitated the transition process, among them U.S. policy, the influence of Chinese technocrat-privatizers, and the KMT's ideological pragmatism. As in the previous stage, it was through the interaction of structural and auxiliary elements that the critical decision to deepen state socialism was finally made.

Balance-of-payments problems continued to haunt ROC policymakers toward the end of the 1950's. Imports still exceeded exports by a large margin, and trade deficits continued to be alleviated primarily by U.S. aid (Scott 1979: 312). Despite the rapid growth of import-substitution industries and the severe restrictions imposed on consumer goods imports, Taiwan's trade deficit remained at around 5 percent of GDP from 1951 to 1958, and showed no sign of coming down. The inability of Taiwan's import substitution strategy to reduce its trade deficit was due to increased imports of capital and intermediate goods, which were necessary to the growth of the import-substituting industries.[41] This problem was exacerbated by the fact that U.S. aid was coming to an end. Imports had already been restricted, so one obvious alternative solution to the balance-of-payments problems was to increase exports. However, there was little room to expand Taiwan's primary exports, sugar and rice (which constituted 69 percent of total exports in 1958): the International Sugar Agreement imposed a quota on Taiwan's sugar exports, and rice exports were limited by the availability of land and the increasing demands of Taiwan's fast-growing population. Because a significant increase in these traditional exports was impossible, the only alternative was to build a strong export sector in manufactured goods.

The second structural element militating for export expansion was the relatively limited size of Taiwan's domestic market. With a small population (10 million in 1958) and a low per capita income (per capita GNP in 1958 was US$583 at 1985 prices), the domestic market for primary import-substituting industries was quickly saturated. By 1954, Taiwan had pretty much exhausted its import-substitution opportunities in the obvious areas such as textiles.[42] The growth of manufacturing (particularly of textiles and wood and rubber products) slowed significantly as "easy" import substitution came to an end. Surplus production capacity, often higher than 50 percent, was prevalent among manufacturers. Overcompetition on the domestic market drove prices down and forced many private businesses into bankruptcy. At the end of 1957, local businesspeople proposed setting up cartels to restrict sales competition and price cutting (Pang 1988: 113). Clearly, foreign markets were needed for Taiwan's manufactures if the economy was to retain a healthy growth rate.

In many less-developed countries, the conclusion of the primary phase of import substitution is followed not by export expansion, but by secondary import substitution, that is, increased domestic production of previously imported capital goods and durable consumer goods and domestic processing of intermediate goods (Ranis 1979: 218). Following this strategy, Taiwan could have built import-substituting industries in chemicals, urea fertilizer, prevulcanized plastics, and compact cars. This option was put to a lively debate in the late 1950's before being rejected in favor of the export expansion strategy. The major obstacles to the deepening of import substitution were Taiwan's lack of expandable primary exports and its small domestic market. For many less-developed countries that followed the deepening strategy (e.g., the large Latin American countries), primary exports acted to finance the shift from primary to secondary import substitution, while large domestic markets absorbed the capital goods and consumer durables produced by the new import-substituting industries. Neither of these conditions applied to Taiwan in the late 1950's.[43]

An additional reason for choosing export expansion based on the manufacture of labor-intensive products, instead of capital-intensive import substitution, was the labor surplus produced by a high population growth rate and successful land reform. From 1953 to 1958, Taiwan's population grew at an average annual rate of 35.8 per 1,000. A large proportion of this population increase took place in rural areas. At the same time, the land reform released surplus rural labor from farming. These laborers then sought employment in industry. In the 1950's, the economy failed to absorb all the new-comers, and the number of unemployed increased rapidly (Kuo, Ranis, and Fei 1981: 13). In order to solve the unemployment problem, it was imperative for Taiwan to develop labor-intensive industries. The production of capital-intensive products was thus not suitable at this juncture.[44] Furthermore, because a large number of private enterprises had been brought up under the "entrustment scheme" and other measures of state capitalism in the 1950's, and these enterprises were located in precisely the most promising labor-intensive industries targeted for export expansion, it was only natural for the government to encourage them to shift from the domestic to the international market, rather than creating state enterprises to lead the export drive. Also, the government's hard budget constraint and fiscal and monetary conservatism were entrenched elements of the system and deterred any attempt at widening the public sector for export expansion. Thus the choice to go international based on what had already been established in labor-intensive industries predetermined the further growth of private enterprises and the shrinking of the relative size of the public sector.

Among the elements contributing to Taiwan's economic development, K. Y. Yin's role deserves special attention. It is interesting to note that the concentration of economic decision-making power in Yin's hands coincided with the two most important turning points in Taiwan's economic development: the introduction of primary import substitution in the early 1950's and the shift to export-led industrialization in the late 1950's and early 1960's. In 1955, after successfully initiating the process of creating a domestic bourgeoisie, Yin was implicated in a Yangtze case for his approval of a dubious government loan to a private enterprise. He was impeached by the Control Yuan and indicted by the court (Chou 1982: 14). Clearly, the close relationship between bureaucrats and businessmen that was characteristic of state capitalism caused trouble for Yin.[45]

Between 1955 and 1957, Yin lost all of his positions in the government, partly because then prime minister O. K. Yui was unhappy with Yin's aggressiveness in pursuing goals at the expense of Yui's power and so did not come to Yin's rescue when he was under attack in the Yangtze case (Pang 1988: 115). Before Yin's (temporary) fall, he pointed out the defects and limits of the system he had brought into being and suggested export expansion as a solution.[46] However, no reform was implemented while he was out of office, even though the symptoms of an exhausted import-substitution strategy were becoming more and more evident. It was not until Yin resumed important positions within the government (as secretary-general of the ESB in 1957, chairman of the Foreign Exchange and Trade Commission and vice chairman of CUSA in 1958, and chairman of the board of the Bank of Taiwan in 1960) that economic reform regained momentum. In 1958, the ESB was dissolved and merged into a stronger CUSA, which combined the planning function and the power to utilize U.S. aid in one all-powerful agency. As vice chairman of the reorganized CUSA, Yin was actually in full charge of it. From 1958 to 1963, he enjoyed the full support of Chiang Kai-shek and Ch'en Ch'eng, who replaced O. K. Yui as prime minister in 1958. Completing the team that brought Taiwan toward export-led industrialization were C. K. Yen, finance minister from 1958 to 1963, who supported tax exemptions and reductions for export and investment based on a supply-side argument (i.e., the growth brought about by the reform would more than compensate for the loss in tax revenues), and Yang Chi-tseng, minister of economic affairs from 1958 to 1965.

The role of U.S. policy was also quite important. AID was clearly interested in encouraging an export expansion led by the private sector (Ho 1978: 119). It actively participated in drawing up reform measures and made great efforts to convince Chinese officials of the urgency of the reform.[47] At one point, AID threatened to reduce U.S. aid should the ROC government not adopt the policy package aimed at export expansion and offered US$20–30 million for its prompt implementation. It also established an Office of Private Development to promote private enterprises (Gold 1986b: 76–77). In the early 1960's, the U.S. opened its market to Taiwan's labor-intensive products and shifted its support from direct aid to market access. These moves greatly fostered Taiwan's critical policy shift in the late 1950's and early 1960's. As for KMT ideology, Sun Yat-sen was silent on the issue of import substitution versus export expansion. Here the technocrats had a free hand in formulating economic policies without fear of meeting ideological opposition. Bureaucrats interested in maintaining the status quo (such as those on the Foreign Exchange and Trade Control Commission and in the Finance Ministry, both headed by Hsu Peh-yuan) were unable to mobilize official ideology to oppose the reform.

Three important reform measures were introduced between 1958 and 1961. They were a reform of foreign exchange and trade, a nineteen-point program of economic and financial reform, and a Statute for Encouragement of Investment. Through these measures, the overall incentive structure was shifted from one favoring production for the domestic market to one encouraging export. A favorable investment environment was created for private enterprises through various tax exemptions and deductions. The multiple exchange rate system was abolished and the New Taiwan dollar was devalued (from NT$25 to NT$40 for US$1). The allocation of foreign exchange for permissible imports was simplified, and some goods on the controlled and suspended lists were moved to the permissible category. The government thus reduced its protection of Taiwanese producers of a large number of consumer durables. Preferential rates for loans were provided to exporters. A system of tax rebates effectively reimbursed exporters not only for customs duties, but also for the commodity tax, defense surtax, harbor dues, salt tax, and slaughter tax (Ho 1978: 196). Export cartels were allowed to form, exporters were permitted to hold their foreign exchange earnings, and subsidies were provided for exports. As a result, the value of Taiwanese exports (in U.S. dollars) expanded at an average annual rate of 24.5 percent throughout the 1960's, and export's share of GNP rose from 8.9 percent in 1958 to 18.7 percent in 1968. By the end of the 1960's, the growth of Taiwan's manufacturing sector was fueled by export expansion (Ho 1978: 201). The industrialization pattern had shifted decisively from import substitution to export-led growth.

The private sector expanded rapidly. The speedy growth of Taiwan's industry in the 1960's was mainly caused by the expansion of three manufacturing industries: food processing, textiles, and electronics. All three used labor intensively and benefited from Taiwan's comparatively low labor costs. Private firms dominated these industries, and their export-led growth greatly increased private industry's share of industrial production, hence furthering privatization. Of the three, food processing expanded first. Its major product

shifted from sugar in the 1950's to canned mushrooms and asparagus (both introduced by the JCRR) in the 1960's.[48] The status of largest exporter shifted correspondingly, from the government's Taiwan
Sugar Corporation to the private firms in the food processing industry. Later, textiles took the place of food processing in the manufacturing expansion. Here the private entrepreneurs nurtured by K. Y.
Yin in the 1950's took advantage of the government's export-promotion policies and expanded into the export sector.

Finally, in the late 1960's, electronics expanded rapidly.[49] This
was the first industry in postwar Taiwan that was directly linked
with foreign investment that began in the 1960's. Many American
giants, such as Ford, TRW, RCA, and Admiral, set up subsidiaries in
Taiwan to produce goods for the U.S. market. The Export Processing
Zones established by the government clearly facilitated the inflow
of foreign capital at this critical juncture. In 1970, 49 percent of all
the electronics firms registered in Taiwan were foreign-owned.
That foreign ownership accounted for 80 percent of all investment
funds in the electronics industry. Local firms began to catch up only
in the 1970's, increasing their investment share to 60 percent in
1978 (Tung 1988: 86). What mattered here in terms of the property
rights structure was that enterprises in electronics were owned either by foreigners or by domestic entrepreneurs. Rapid growth of
the electronics industry represented a further expansion of the private sector.

Progress toward marketization was much slower than privatization. The economic regime that emerged from the post-1958 reform was far from liberal. It is true that administrative allocation of
materials and products characteristic of the entrustment scheme
was gone, and economic levers replaced administrative levers as the
main instrument of the state. However, many measures designed to
promote export were in direct conflict with free market principles.
Thus, for example, the exchange rate of NT$40 for US$1 was maintained throughout the 1960's, 1970's, and most of the 1980's, regardless of the fact that Taiwan's trade relations with the U.S. changed
dramatically during that time. What appeared to be a "realistic"
exchange rate turned out to be a critical export promotion device.

On the other hand, the reform measures themselves failed to
significantly change the old protectionist system. Thus the number

of controlled and prohibited imports as a percentage of the number of total imports remained high throughout the 1960's: it was 44.0 percent in 1960, 45.7 percent in 1966, and 42.9 percent in 1970 (Pang 1988: 157). The protection of infant industries clearly did not end after the shift to an export-oriented strategy (Haggard 1986: 351). The tax rebate and other government policies were aimed at changing the profit parameters and guiding private enterprises toward strategic industries and production for export, not at establishing a self-regulating market. What happened in the transition of the late 1950's and early 1960's was a shift of government goals and a modification of state tools necessitated by economic imperatives. This shift did not alter the basic structure of state capitalism, but actually deepened it by promoting further privatization while retaining the levers of state control. However, the very nature of export expansion subjected Taiwan's private enterprises to international competition and market discipline, hence contributing to the principle of marketization. It also forced the government to concentrate on those industries that could be competitive on the international market. The principle of comparative advantage thus received greater attention than it had under the strategy of import substitution. This observation is modified, however, by the fact that the state took various measures to promote exports and reduce the shock of foreign competition by regulating the domestic market so that it favored exporters (for example, by using high tariffs to protect private enterprises that subsidized exports through domestic sales). Also, the state interpreted comparative advantage in a dynamic sense, that is, it actively created a comparative advantage through dirigist industrial policies.

In short, the export-led growth strategy made competition on the international market the ultimate test for Taiwan's private enterprises and oriented the state's industrial policies toward that test. The strategy set a broad goal but did not specify the means for achieving it. It was up to the technocrats to design and use the appropriate instruments for doing so. As it turned out, these technocrats had few qualms about applying administrative and economic levers to promote export and growth. For them, the market was simply a tool, like tariffs and quotas. They exercised great influence on the production and exchange decisions of private enterprises, in many cases curtailing the control power of those enterprises. They did, however, promote and respect private ownership, a fact that set them apart from planners in mainland China.

The PRC: Absence of State Capitalism

The structural and auxiliary factors that militated for state capitalism in Taiwan 30 years earlier were by and large absent in mainland China in the early 1980's, which explains to a large extent the PRC's 1984 decision to make marketization, instead of privatization, the major goal of its economic reform. As far as structural aspects of the economy were concerned, the PRC's lower dependency on imports and its capacity for expanding exports meant fewer balance-of-payments problems and less international pressure. The existence of a full array of inefficient light and heavy industries suggests that the most urgent need for the mainland was to import Western technology and to improve the efficiency of the industrial enterprises already in operation, not to create new ones. Finally, the hard budget constraint was less a feature of the economic system in the PRC than it had been in the ROC. This meant that if there was a need to establish new enterprises, the PRC was not under great pressure to resort to private entrepreneurs: it could simply increase state investment.

As far as auxiliary aspects were concerned, in the PRC there was no functional equivalent of U.S. aid pushing for privatization. Nor was there a group of technocrat-privatizers who received full support from top political leaders. Finally, Chinese Communist ideology, even in its current form of "socialism with Chinese characteristics" or "the primary stage of socialism," proved a recalcitrant obstacle to large-scale privatization of industry.

Import Dependency

During the 1950's, the PRC was highly dependent on the importation of Soviet and Eastern European capital and technology. Between 1953 and 1957, the PRC conducted more than 70 percent of its trade with other socialist countries. The abrupt withdrawal of the Soviet advisors in 1960 put an end to this dependency on the Soviet bloc countries. Though with great difficulty, the PRC managed to pay off its debts to the Soviets in 1965. Overall, the 1960's and the bulk of the 1970's were characterized by a policy of self-reliance. Thus, for example, the total value of foreign trade was held to between US$4.3 billion and US$4.6 billion in 1965–1970, which meant that it had a decreasing share in the GNP. In real terms, foreign trade in 1969 was lower than in 1958 (Reynolds 1987: 483). The rapprochement between the U.S. and the PRC, and that between Japan and the PRC in the early 1970's, laid the foundation for expanded trade with the West. Trade then jumped from US$6.3 billion in 1972 to US$11 billion in 1973, in part reflecting a huge increase of defense-related imports from Japan. But a plateau was quickly reached in the middle of the 1970's, so that between 1974 and 1977, foreign trade grew by only 1.5 percent, though it remained heavily oriented toward the West.

A significant change occurred in the late 1970's. In 1978, Hua Guofeng launched his ambitious Ten-Year Plan, the major goal of which was to rapidly increase steel production. To this end, large-scale projects were launched in electricity, transportation, and coal production (Ying 1982). Though the plan had unmistakably Stalinist priorities, the capital and technology for implementing it were to come from the West. This "great leap Westward" increased imports by 44 percent in 1978 and deepened the PRC's dependency on the West. However, the unprecedented investment rate and trade deficit brought about by the Ten-Year Plan forced the CCP leadership to reconsider its feasibility, and in 1979 the plan was replaced by the eight-character guideline of "readjustment, restructuring, consolidation, and improvement."[50] Over the next few years, Deng Xiaoping changed the priority of domestic production, launched a structural economic reform, and slowed the pace of imports. He nevertheless put great emphasis on attracting Western capital and technology. It was under Deng that the PRC established diplomatic relations with the U.S., which boosted trade between the two countries. The granting of most-favored-nation status to the PRC in 1980 and the relaxation of export certification by the U.S. in 1983 further accelerated bilateral trade. The U.S. thus joined Hong Kong and Japan to become one of the PRC's major trading partners in the 1980's.

At the turn of the decade, Hua and Deng redefined the meaning of imports for mainland China. Whereas their purpose had previously been to compensate for the production shortages in China's centrally planned economy, they now provided foreign capital and technology for China's Four Modernizations (Wu Yuan-li 1987: 70).

This new role elevated imports to a more important position and created more room for their expansion. However, because of its extremely low starting point, rapidly expanding trade was not yet a significant portion of gross national product. Import dependency, as measured by imports' share of GNP, was 6.9 percent in 1983 (*International Financial Statistics* 1990: 168). Until 1984, the PRC's total import dependency was lower than it had been during the First Five-Year period (1953–57).

This was a far cry from the import dependency that Taiwan experienced when it initiated state capitalism in the early 1950's. In 1952, imports accounted for 14.8 percent of Taiwan's GNP. Because Taiwan had hardly any industry to speak of, its imports included not only the capital goods needed for economic development, but nondurable consumer goods (such as textiles) to meet the basic needs of the population. The greatest difference between mainland China in the early 1980's and Taiwan in the early 1950's is that the mainland needed imports to improve the efficiency of its industrial enterprises, whereas Taiwan depended on imports for its physical subsistence. Mainland China could produce both consumer and producer goods, though in poor quality and with low efficiency. Taiwan had little light industry and practically no heavy industry, and it therefore relied on imports to satisfy all its needs for manufactured products.

In the early 1950's, Taiwan suffered from both a high degree of import dependency and constraints on its primary exports, rice and sugar. Market disturbances (for example, the loss of the mainland market), rising domestic demand (due to the influx of political refugees and a high population growth rate), and quotas imposed by international trade organizations (such as the restrictions in the International Sugar Agreement) made export expansion along traditional lines impossible, hence the need to develop light industries to lead the export drive. In the early 1980's, mainland China was in a more favorable position. Unlike Taiwan, it exported a variety of agricultural products, textile goods, and petroleum (both crude and refined). Trade in the first two categories followed a historical pattern established before 1949, whereas petroleum and petroleum products were newer additions to China's trade, dating from the 1960's. It is true that both agricultural products and petroleum were subject to fluctuations in production and increasing domestic demand,[51] and textile exports faced rising protectionism in industrialized countries and restrictions imposed by international organizations.[52] However, the very fact that the mainland possessed multiple export possibilities, each subject to different restrictions, meant that its export sector had a much greater capacity for expansion than Taiwan's had had 30 years earlier.[53]

As a result of its lower import dependency and more expandable exports, the PRC in the early 1980's accumulated less of a trade deficit than did the ROC in the early 1950's. From 1978 to 1981, due to the sharp rise in the PRC's imports of Western capital goods, a trade deficit emerged and rose rapidly. Though Hua's Ten-Year Plan was suspended in 1979, the surge in imported investment goods continued in 1980. This prompted central planners to take drastic measures to curb imports and promote exports, which brought about trade surpluses in 1982 and 1983.[54] In 1984, with the urban industrial reform gaining momentum, imports again surpassed exports. However, the trade deficit in that year was only 0.5 percent of GNP, compared with an average of 5 percent in Taiwan during the 1950's.[55] Freedom from desperate balance-of-payments problems made international economic pressure much less acute for the mainland than for Taiwan, which in turn meant much less incentive for Communist elites to transform the economic structure in order to relieve such pressure.

Established Industries

In the early 1950's, Taiwan's mounting balance-of-payments problems forced the government to cut imports. In order to satisfy the domestic need for nondurable consumer goods previously covered by imports, the ROC's economic planners resorted to primary import substitution, replacing imports with domestic production. However, there was no industrial base to begin with, so new enterprises had to be created from scratch. Here one finds the origins of Taiwan's privatization and state capitalism. When the grand shift to export expansion was made around 1958, the government looked for available capacity in the targeted industries and found it in the private enterprises that had been nurtured over the past decade. Economic planners thus shifted the incentive structure from its emphasis on saving foreign exchange to earning it, and they guided private enterprises toward the international market, hence deepening Taiwan's privatization and state capitalism. At both turning points, the absence of state enterprises in targeted areas proved a critical factor shaping Taiwan's economic development. However, the situation in mainland China 30 years later was quite different.

China began to establish its primary import-substituting industries during World War I. In the 1930's and 1940's, light industries (especially the textile industry) had developed in Shanghai and Tianjin, while heavy industry was concentrated in Manchuria. Generally, labor-intensive light industry was much more developed than capital-intensive heavy industry, a reflection of China's factor endowments.[56] After 1949, the new Communist regime dramatically changed China's industrial structure by plunging the economy into a hasty secondary import substitution that, through a series of five-year plans, put a major emphasis on heavy industrialization.[57] The withdrawal of the Soviet advisors in 1960 did not change this basic development pattern. Under Mao's self-reliance policy, import substitution took the extreme form of disengaging the mainland's economy from the outside world. Domestic demand for both producer and consumer goods was met by domestic production. By the 1970's, industry in mainland China already accounted for 50 percent of its GNP (Perkins 1986: 32). Thus, when the open-door policy was adopted toward the end of that decade, the PRC was equipped with a full array of both light and heavy industries, the result of its primary and secondary import substitution. This overall strategy of economic self-reliance meant that the mainland's industrial enterprises lacked efficiency and modern technology and management.[58] However, a huge industrial sector had been established, and it was firmly in state hands.

The PRC entered the international market after the completion of both primary and secondary import substitution. The ROC developed its dependency on international trade before it entered the stage of primary import substitution. The implications of this difference have been made clear. Mainland China needed only to import capital goods to improve the efficiency of existing industrial enterprises, whereas Taiwan depended on imports for all of its manufactured goods.[59] The mainland could export a variety of both primary and manufactured goods, whereas Taiwan had to rely on exports of rice and sugar. As a result, the mainland was less vulnerable to low price and income elasticities of demand for primary products than was Taiwan. The existence of a broad industrial base in the hands of the Beijing regime meant something more, namely that the PRC's balance-of-payments problems would not translate into a need to create new enterprises or to depend on private entrepreneurs. Beijing's central planners could concentrate on upgrading and expanding the industrial capacity already in state hands. The government's inability to put loss-making enterprises out of business further reinforced this strategy.

The Soft Budget Constraint

The last link in the causal chain leading to privatization and state capitalism in Taiwan was the hard budget constraint that the ROC government faced. Because ROC economic planners exercised great discipline in controlling government investment, the need to expand production capacity in order to achieve import substitution and export expansion could only be satisfied by promotion of the private sector.

The situation in mainland China in the early 1980's was quite different. State enterprises there had been facing a soft budget constraint. The piecemeal industrial reform undertaken since the late 1970's had created a system under which enterprises retained a growing share of their profits, so that investment funding came mainly from their own funds or from the banking system and not from government grants (Perkins 1988: 617).[60] However, this delegation of financial power was not matched by increasing enterprise responsibility. The result was overextended investment and massive government bailouts of loss-making enterprises (there had never been a case of bankruptcy in the PRC, and the deliberation of a bankruptcy law was not yet on the government's agenda). The other major expenditure associated with economic reform in the early 1980's was the government's payments for grain procurement. Subsidies to inefficient state enterprises and expenditures for grain procurement coincided with the delegation of more and more income power to the provinces and enterprises, which caused budget deficits for the state. In a situation not unlike that prior to 1949, these deficits were covered by the central bank. Though quite conscious of the danger that might result from its lack of fiscal and financial discipline, the Communist state did not assign top priority to hardening its budget constraint, as the Nationalists did in Taiwan. When pressured to develop industries in order to cut imports or increase exports, mainland China's central planners were not as

adamant as their Taiwanese counterparts in putting a lid on government investment in state enterprises. This being the case, there was
no need for them to promote private enterprise. The soft budget
constraint of the Communist state thus removed the need to encourage private industry even in the face of great international economic pressure.

A good example of this is the development of the mainland's
consumer durables industry. The open-door policy brought a sharp
increase in the number of visitors from Hong Kong and Macao after
the late 1970's.[61] This significantly whipped up the mainland population's desire for the modern consumer products, especially consumer durables, enjoyed by overseas Chinese.[62] In order to boost the
morale of the Chinese people, PRC reformers loosened the import
controls on consumer goods. However, they also decided to replace
imports with domestic production as early as 1979. Import dependency thus brought about the need for import substitution. Because
an elaborate industrial base had been established in state hands, and
the state faced only a soft budget constraint, import substitution
did not lead to the encouragement of private enterprise, but to direct state investment. Between 1979 and 1983, the government invested 10.3 billion rmb to expand the country's capacity to produce
consumer goods such as sewing machines and television sets. This
trend continued into the latter part of the 1980's, so that in 1988 the
PRC was among the world's largest producers of television sets,
washing machines, and refrigerators (C. Y. Cheng 1990: 22).

Lack of International Pressure

Mainland China in the early 1980's was not influenced by the
kind of auxiliary political factors that were instrumental in bringing privatization and state capitalism to Taiwan in the 1950's and
1960's. In the case of Taiwan, U.S. AID played a critical role in allocating aid funds to facilitate the growth of the private sector, drawing up plans to liberalize the island's economy, and influencing
ROC political leaders to take radical economic reform measures.
Because U.S. aid in particular and American support in general were
critical to the survival of the ROC in its early years in Taiwan, the
U.S. preference for a private economy carried great weight in the decision-making process of the KMT state.[63] U.S. aid was important
not only because of its size (it made up 6 percent of Taiwan's GNP
in 1951–65) and function (financing trade deficits, providing invest-

ment funds, stabilizing prices, and offering technical assistance), but also because it was Taiwan's only source of international capital at the time. Private foreign capital and loans from other foreign governments and international financial institutions did not begin to materialize until well into the 1960's, after U.S. aid had been terminated.[64] This meant that Taiwan did not have alternative sources of foreign financial support and had to depend on the U.S. completely when undertaking its economic reform. Small wonder that the U.S. exercised great influence on the direction of economic restructuring in the ROC in the 1950's and early 1960's.

The situation in the PRC was different. In the 1950's, mainland China was heavily dependent on the Soviet Union for financial and technical assistance and institutional emulation. In fact, the centrally planned economy imposed in mainland China at that time was much closer to its Soviet prototype than the state capitalist system in Taiwan was to the capitalist model that the U.S. exemplified. In this sense, the PRC's dependency on the socialist hegemon brought about a greater degree of institutional conformity than the ROC's dependency on the capitalist hegemon. However, the mainland's socialist dependency, together with the political influence of the Soviet Union, came to an abrupt end in 1960. Since then, the PRC has taken a highly independent position in its foreign policy, starting with the "dual adversary" position it adopted vis-à-vis both superpowers in the 1960's.

It is true that the direction of the PRC's foreign trade and its sources of financial and technological support shifted decisively to the West in the late 1960's and 1970's, and it entered a quasi antihegemonic alliance with the U.S. against their common enemy, the Soviet Union, in the late 1970's. However, this shift in mainland China's foreign policy did not signal a new political dependency on the West. In the early 1980's, with relations between Beijing and Moscow improved, the PRC elevated its role in the strategic triangle from that of junior partner to pivot. This move was motivated by Beijing's deepening economic dependency on the West and a growing fear that it might be betrayed by the senior partner. It was also motivated by the realization that there were limits to the Beijing-Washington collaboration: the "Taiwan issue," rising American protectionism, the remaining controls on U.S. technology transfers, and the incompatibility between the value systems of a reforming socialist country and the world's capitalist hegemon.

Thus when Leonid Brezhnev launched his peace initiative in May 1982, Beijing responded swiftly. In September, the CCP's Twelfth Party Congress emphasized the "self-reliance and independence" of the PRC's foreign policy, and declared that mainland China "never attaches itself to any big power or group of powers, and never yields to pressure from any big power," thus signaling the end of its united front with the U.S. in the language of assertive nationalism (Whiting 1983). This was the basic foreign policy stance adopted by the PRC at the time that major industrial reform was to be launched. Clearly there is no parallel between the PRC's autonomy from the superpowers in the early 1980's and the ROC's dependency on the U.S. in the early 1950's. No great political influence from either superpower directed the PRC's economic reform, unlike the way in which the U.S. actively pushed for privatization in Taiwan.

One can nevertheless ask whether there was a functional equivalent to direct foreign aid that might have influenced economic reform in the PRC. This question is particularly relevant to the 1980's, when the debt crisis in the developing world granted a prominent position to international financial institutions and made them capable of influencing, and sometimes dictating, structural reforms in debt-ridden countries. Only these institutions had the resources and operational scale needed for dealing with a crisis of such proportions, and private lenders followed their lead by committing money to countries that adopted their programs. The situation in Eastern Europe, especially in Poland and Hungary, clearly suggests that centrally planned economies were not immune to debt crisis and the influence of international financial institutions. Because rich capitalist countries controlled such institutions as the International Monetary Fund (IMF) and the World Bank, and privatization dominated the domestic politics and foreign policy postures of several key capitalist countries (particularly the U.S. during the Reagan administration), one wonders how much and what kind of influence international financial institutions exercised over the PRC when the country was making critical economic reforms.

The PRC was very conscious of its economic vulnerability toward and dependency on the West, and guarded carefully against the danger of accumulating heavy foreign debt. However, with its increasing integration into the international economic system, borrowing from international financial institutions became almost inevitable. The PRC needed funds to cover its current account deficits and to finance its development projects, areas covered by the IMF and the World Bank respectively. Beijing assumed the China seats in both institutions in 1980 by dislodging Taipei. Between 1980 and 1984, the PRC's cumulative loans with the International Bank for Reconstruction and Development (IBRD) and the International Development Association (IDA) totaled US$1,913 million. These loans were primarily for projects in energy development, agricultural research, and educational modernization. As for its dealings with the IMF, in November 1980, the PRC purchased SDR 218.1 million from its reserve tranche. In March 1981, another purchase was made on the PRC's first credit tranche, for SDR 450 million under conditionality. The PRC also drew SDR 309 million from the IMF's Trust Fund. However, in 1984, the PRC made a repurchase of SDR 450 million for its credit tranche. The purpose of these purchases was to cover the country's deficits. The PRC borrowing from both the World Bank and the IMF in 1980–84 totaled 1.2 percent of its 1984 GNP, considerably less than the ROC's dependency on U.S. aid in the early 1950's (over 6 percent of GNP).

Furthermore, the ability of any capitalist country to use international financial institutions and their lending capacities to influence the PRC was limited by the distribution of the voting power in these institutions. As the most influential member of both the IMF and the World Bank, the U.S. had 19.3 percent of the voting power in the IMF after its Eighth General Review in 1983. In 1984, the U.S. held 19.2 percent of all votes in the IBRD and 20.01 percent of the voting power in the IDA (Gold 1986a). These figures were lower than in the past, suggesting that the power of the U.S. to control those institutions was declining. The countries holding secondary positions, such as Japan, did not have an explicit political preference for privatization.[65] Even though the Reagan administration strongly emphasized the role of the International Finance Corporation—a member of the World Bank group that lends money to the private sector of less-developed countries—and championed privatization as a global cause, this did not translate into concrete actions by the international financial institutions in which the PRC took part to influence economic reform there toward privatization. Because the PRC was doing what the IMF and World Bank explicitly urged their members to do, such as exercising fiscal discipline to redress deficits, increasing exports to earn foreign exchange, and devaluating an artificially high currency, the international financial institutions actively helped the PRC with its market socialist reform.[66] In fact, because borrowed funds were funneled mainly through Beijing, these institutions helped increase the financial leverage of the central government over the provinces and enterprises.

Lack of Technocrat-Privatizers

In the 1950's and 1960's, privatization and state capitalism in Taiwan were supported by a paramount political leader (Chiang Kai-shek), a chief economic policymaker (Ch'en Ch'eng), and a group of technocrat-privatizers. In the 1980's, the PRC likewise had a paramount political leader—Deng Xiaoping—who was committed to economic reform. In the early 1980's, Hu Yaobang and Zhao Ziyang still received full support from Deng, and Zhao, as the prime minister in charge of the reform, was in a position roughly comparable to that of Taiwan's Ch'en Ch'eng.[67] However, in the PRC there was a conspicuous lack of technocrat-privatizers to actively advocate, prepare, and implement privatization programs.

Taiwan's leading technocrat-privatizers in the 1950's and 1960's, such as K. Y. Yin, K. T. Li, C. K. Yen, and Yang Chi-tseng, all received a Western education, had a science or engineering background, started working with the government on the mainland, experienced the difficulties of wartime economic development and postwar reconstruction, and emerged as strong supporters of economic nationalism. Their basic economic concepts came from the West, particularly from the United States. However, for them a more pertinent reference case was Japan, both in terms of its prewar economic development and its postwar recovery. The KMT's mainland experience taught the future technocrats a tough lesson, tilting their priorities toward economic stability and fiscal and monetary conservatism. As it turned out, their exposure to the West predisposed them to a private economy, while their economic nationalism and personal experience convinced them that the state should guide national economic development. The amalgam of these two tendencies was state capitalism, or private ownership cum state control. Although the degree and mechanisms of state control might vary across industries and over time, the fundamental philosophy of the state leading private enterprises toward national goals was firmly established in the minds of these technocrat-privatizers.

The mainland's economic reformers came from an entirely different background. Their basic economic concepts came from the Soviet Union. For them, the most pertinent reference cases for economic reform were in Eastern Europe, that is, the plan-perfecting and socialist market variants of a centrally planned economy. Their experience with the Maoist version of Chinese Marxism constituted a powerful deterrent to extreme distributional egalitarianism and moral incentive. In the late 1970's, early economic reformers in the PRC (such as Xue Muqiao and Sun Yefang) grouped around Chen Yun, whose moderate reform philosophy (that of the "bird cage economy") was similar to that in the Soviet Union and Eastern Europe in the late 1950's and early 1960's. Then came a younger generation of economic reformers, most of whom received their university and graduate education after 1949 and worked in the various research institutes of the Chinese Academy of Social Sciences (e.g., Liu Guoguang and Zhao Renwei), the Ministry of Finance (e.g., Xu Yi), the State Planning Commission (e.g., Fang Weizhong and Liu Suinian), the Economic-Technical Research Center under the State Council, and other government and party agencies.[68] In the early 1980's, it was this group of middle-aged economic reformers who provided political leaders with policy suggestions. Basically, they did not surpass the conceptual framework of limited market socialism, which Yugoslavia and Hungary had achieved in the late 1960's.

It was only after Zhao Ziyang replaced Chen Yun as the PRC's economic tsar in 1983 that a group of young and radical economic reformers began to exercise their influence. Most of these third-generation reformers were recruited into the Research Institute on Reform of China's Economic Structure (Tigaisuo) and the Research Institute on Rural Development (Fazhansuo), the two most important think tanks of economic reform, while Zhao Ziyang was fully in control of the State Council.[69] These young reformers pushed for more radical measures to restructure the economy and reassign property rights. Most of the reform policies in the mid-1980's were designed by them and supported by Zhao. However, in 1984, their influence was still limited, and the general direction of the reform was still well within the framework of the indirect bureaucratic control version of market socialism (Kornai 1986b: 1701). This was the case because all of the PRC reformers, from Xue Muqiao to Zhao's "graduate students," had to start from an established Soviet-style command economy, look for reform precedents from Eastern

Europe, and make policy suggestions based on mainland China's
30-year experience with socialism. These conditions limited their
perspective and predisposed them to the easier, previously tested
strategy of socialist marketization, rather than to privatization.
They were also hampered by the fact that their presence was concentrated within research institutes, rather than in the economic
bureaucracy (as was the case of Taiwan's reformers), thus their proposals, though backed by political leaders, faced much greater difficulty during the implementation process. This fact further restricted the PRC's policies of limited market socialism.

Ideological Constraints

Both the KMT and the CCP have an official ideology that in-
forms, directs, and constrains their respective economic policies.
However, Sun Yat-sen's *san-min chu-i* (Three Principles of the People) does not see eye to eye with Marxism–Leninism–Mao Zedong
Thought on the appropriate property rights structure of the economy. *San-min chu-i* was originally contained in a series of lectures
Sun delivered in 1924. They were geared to a general audience and
couched in language that appealed to common sense, and they contained no rigorous reasoning or grand philosophical themes. Sun
tried to identify China's problems, provide concrete solutions, and
urge his compatriots to take action. As a result, *san-min chu-i* (as
well as Sun's other teachings, such as the *Fundamentals of National Reconstruction*) was more like a package of practical policies
designed to meet China's current needs than a rigorous political
doctrine. The fact that it later became the KMT's official ideology
did not change its basic characteristics.

In *min-sheng chu-i*, the part of *san-min chu-i* that contains
Sun's thoughts on China's economic development, important roles
are assigned to both the state and the private sector. The division
between the two hinges on several considerations: the nature of the
goods in question, the capacity of private entrepreneurs, and the
structure of the market. The state is to provide public goods, participate in production that is beyond the capacity of private entrepreneurs, and act as a direct producer in industries that are natural
monopolies. These are flexible positions compatible with a wide
range of economic policies from which the technocrats could
choose. Because they were relatively free from ideological constraints, the technocrats then concentrated on solving impending

economic problems in a spirit of "healthy pragmatism" (Li Kwoh-Ting 1988: 143; Fei 1988: 46).

This was not the case in mainland China. From Marx to Lenin to Mao Zedong, the original ideology was "enriched" by an increasing number of theoretical modifications. Marx and Engels laid the foundation of the ideology by providing it with a philosophical base, a historical-class perspective, and a critique of capitalism. Lenin added to that an organizational code, an alliance strategy, and an updated international version of the original doctrine. Mao made his contribution by devising policies that made socialist revolution possible in a backward peasant society, and by asserting the permanency of class struggle and the need for continued revolution. Despite this theoretical proliferation, however, the fundamental value judgment of the ideology has remained intact: it denounces private property and demands its abolition. The core principle was based on the desire to eradicate exploitation, which invariably arises from private employment. As long as an employer makes profits, laborers are exploited, because their labor constitutes the sole source of value, which should be fully appropriated by themselves. This basic belief was upheld by Marx, Lenin, and Mao, and it constituted the strongest ideological obstacle to privatization of the PRC's industrial sector.

That said, there remains a theoretical difference between exploitation and private property: exploitation is based on private employment of labor, which private ownership of the means of production does not necessarily entail, at least when the private enterprise in question is small. Obviously, self-employment and the hiring of family members do not constitute exploitation according to the original doctrines of Marxism. In the early 1980's, Chinese reformers made use of this theoretical nuance in order to allow the emergence of getihu (private enterprises with fewer than eight employees) at a time when the problem of urban unemployment was becoming increasingly serious and demanded an immediate solution. Clearly, the size stipulated for the getihu was arbitrary, since small-scale employment does not guarantee the absence of exploitation. However, it did have the blessing of Marx, who first came up with that figure, and it thus carried ideological significance by suggesting that private ownership does not equal exploitation when it is small, and as such is permissible. In this case, ideology did put a lid on the scale of privatization (*siying qiye*, or larger private businesses, did not come into being until much later).[70]

Conclusion

The ROC in the early 1950's and the PRC in the early 1980's shared many similarities. Both political systems were characterized by the rule of an authoritarian regime dominated by a Leninist-type party. After a traumatizing event (the Erh Erh Pa Incident in Taiwan and the Cultural Revolution in mainland China), both regimes were committed to economic reform in an effort to restore their political legitimacy. Agricultural reform was their common starting point. The land reform in Taiwan and decollectivization on the mainland created a large number of peasant proprietors farming smallholdings. In both cases, the production incentive was maximized as income power was transferred to individual producers. Industrial reform was the second step. There the pre-reform structures were similar, both of them characterized by the dominance of state enterprises and strict government control. In short, Taiwan in the early 1950's and mainland China in the early 1980's shared similarities in their political institutions, motives for economic reform, agricultural restructuring, and pre-reform industrial systems. However, these commonalities did not result in similar industrial reforms.

In the early 1950's, the entrustment scheme and the First Four-Year Plan initiated Taiwan's privatization drive and its state capitalist development. The shift from import substitution to export expansion in the late 1950's further enlarged the private sector and deepened state capitalism, while the move toward marketization was limited. The structural elements that accounted for these two turning points were international economic pressure in the form of serious balance-of-payments problems, the lack of industrial capacity needed for import substitution and export expansion, and the hard budget constraint that the state faced. The auxiliary factors were the U.S. role in pushing for privatization, the efforts of a group of technocrat-privatizers led by K. Y. Yin, and the KMT's ideological pragmatism.

By contrast, in 1984, the CCP decided to reform mainland China's industrial structure in the direction of limited market social-

ism, that is, retaining socialist ownership while replacing administrative levers with economic levers. Despite the previous similarities with Taiwan, there was no privatization drive in the PRC's
industrial reform; both the structural and auxiliary factors for privatization were lacking. On the structural side, the PRC's lower import dependency and more expandable exports meant fewer balance-of-payments problems and less international economic pressure. The existence of an established industrial base meant that any
need for import substitution and export expansion could be met by
expanding the industrial capacity of state enterprises. The government's soft budget constraint allowed it to increase state investment in the public sector, rather than resort to encouraging private
enterprises. On the auxiliary side, the PRC was not politically dependent on the U.S., and the international financial institutions it
dealt with did not push for privatization in the PRC in the way the
U.S. had in Taiwan. The economic reformers in the PRC were not
privatizers but market socialists. Finally, Marxism–Leninism–
Mao Zedong Thought forbade exploitation, which was defined
in terms of private employment, so the only type of private enterprise allowed was the small-scale *getihu*. As a result, at the turning
point of their development, Taiwan and mainland China diverged.
Still, one wonders if there is any possibility for the two to converge
in the future.

Because of their different structural and auxiliary factors, the
ROC and the PRC opted for different property rights modes: state
capitalism in Taiwan and market socialism on the mainland. However, this does not mean that they had nothing in common in their
subsequent development. In fact, if we take openness to the international market as our primary concern, post-1953 Taiwan and
post-1984 mainland China did demonstrate considerable similarity.
This situation prompted some scholars to speculate about the possibility of the PRC developing into a huge newly industrialized
country (Perkins 1986). With regard to property rights, however,
this observation needs to be qualified. Sheer openness does not necessarily mean restructuring property rights in a fundamental way.
For example, a socialist country's dependency on foreign trade can
be very high, with state production enterprises and state trading
companies monopolizing all trade activity in accordance with plan
directives. This was in fact the case in the PRC during the 1950's,

when all of its trade with the Soviet bloc was managed by the socialist state. State-planned and state-conducted trade or other external economic activity, even when transacted with private foreign partners, does not suggest great changes in industrial property rights in a socialist country. Thus Hua Guofeng's Ten-Year Plan involved giant projects with private Western companies, but on the Chinese side, these projects were to be implemented without any change in the relation between state and enterprises. What concerns us here is not the extent of openness per se as measured by a country's trade dependency ratio or other such indicators, but the property rights structures of the enterprises involved in external economic activity, that is, the impact of openness on domestic industrial property rights.

Investment has a greater impact on industrial property rights than does foreign trade. In the late 1970's, the PRC adopted an open-door policy in order to introduce Western technology into its outmoded industry and expedite industrial modernization (C. Y. Cheng 1990: 18). However, imports of machinery and equipment had to be paid for with foreign currency, which mainland China lacked. This was the case because the PRC's exports, though expandable, could not rise as rapidly as its import needs, and the government was cautious about borrowing from foreign sources. The only alternative under these circumstances was direct foreign investment (DFI). Thus, with Deng Xiaoping's political ascendancy, the PRC began to take measures to attract foreign investment to mainland China. However, unlike trade or foreign loans, DFI had a direct impact on the property rights structure of mainland industry. Because the PRC was primarily interested in attracting Western capital (including investment by Japan, Hong Kong, Macao, and, ultimately, Taiwan), it invited private foreign companies to invest in a socialist economy. This meant that capitalist institutions and practices that could not be governed by the rules of market socialism would enter mainland China. Furthermore, because Beijing was eager to upgrade its industrial capacity, it could not restrict the scale of enterprises that were founded with the help of foreign investment. In fact, from the PRC's point of view, the larger and more capital- and technology-intensive these enterprises were, the better.

The inevitable conflicts between the mainland's socialist structure and capitalist DFI were initially contained in the four carefully circumscribed Special Economic Zones (SEZs)—Shenzhen, Zhuhai,

Shantou (in Guandong), and Xiamen (in Fujian)—established in 1980. These SEZs immediately remind even a casual observer of the Export Processing Zones (EPZs) established in Taiwan in the late 1960's and early 1970's (Fitting 1982).[71] To be sure, the initial purposes of setting up the Special Economic Zones on the mainland and the Export Processing Zones in Taiwan were not identical: the PRC was primarily interested in bringing in foreign investment that would introduce advanced technology to its industry, while the ROC treated its zones mainly as manufacturing bases for labor-intensive exports and tried to attract foreign companies with ready market outlets. The SEZs were embedded in the PRC's overall strategy of industrial modernization, and the EPZs were an integral part of the ROC's drive toward export expansion.[72] Despite this difference, the SEZs and EPZs demonstrated many similarities in their institutions, partly because they all shared the goal of attracting foreign investment, and partly because the SEZ designers clearly had in mind the successful pattern established by Taiwan's EPZs more than ten years earlier, a pattern that by 1978 had been followed by 22 countries, including South Korea and the Philippines. Among these similarities were tax holidays, duty exemptions on imports, loosened foreign exchange controls, permission to expatriate profits, ready availability of industrial land, government provision of infrastructural facilities (transportation, warehousing, public utilities, port facilities, etc.), and simplified administrative procedures. The special concessions granted to foreign investors in the zones aroused similar criticisms in the two cases. Both the SEZs and the EPZs were attacked as a throwback to the treaty ports and extraterritoriality enjoyed by foreigners in old China. They were also associated with the exploitation of cheap Chinese labor for the benefit of foreigners, a charge that obviously carried more weight in mainland China, where the official ideology was based on the need to abolish exploitation (C. Y. Cheng 1990: 19; Li Kwoh-Ting 1988: 95).

The similarities between mainland and Taiwanese practices increased when the SEZ experience was expanded to include larger and larger areas of the mainland, and when the initial emphasis on technology transfers was gradually replaced by the goal of promoting labor-intensive exports (i.e., the same goal as stood behind Taiwan's EPZs). Following the four original SEZs, fourteen coastal cities were opened to direct foreign investment in 1984. In 1985, the three coastal areas were added to the list. These were followed by

Liaodong and Jiaodong peninsulas, Hainan province as the fifth SEZ, and finally the whole eastern coast of China in 1988. At that time, Zhao Ziyang's grand strategy of international circulation explicitly recognized that the mainland's open-door policy should be reoriented toward export expansion in labor-intensive industries. The mechanisms designed to maximize technology transfers in the old SEZ package, such as the insistence on joint ventures, domestic supply of materials and parts, and introduction of the latest production technology, were dropped. This new open-door policy thus brought mainland practices much closer to the export-expanding measures of Taiwan's EPZs. Here one finds the possibility of a convergence of the two cases.

The original idea to create the EPZs in Taiwan stemmed from the technocrats' desire to create a free trade zone to compete with Hong Kong. However, what they ultimately brought about was a typical example of Taiwan's state capitalism. In the EPZs, the state manipulated all of its economic levers (lower tax rates, duty-free imports, etc.) to assure private enterprises (both foreign and Chinese) that they would reap huge profits by investing in the zones and in the "right" industries, but then no local sales of their products were allowed. High walls, watchtowers, and police patrols were used to ensure that no zonal products were smuggled out to the domestic market.[73] The state set profit parameters and directed private enterprises toward targeted industries and markets. This was clearly not laissez-faire, but state capitalism. The EPZs were not the technocrats' concession to the principle of free trade, but an integral part of Taiwan's mercantilism. This means that when the PRC emulated Taiwan's practices of the 1960's and 1970's, it made a shift not toward laissez-faire capitalism à la Hong Kong, but toward state capitalism. This point becomes obvious when we look at the economic concessions made by Beijing to foreign investors and the numerous controls that PRC bureaucracies continued to exercise at the same time. In short, income power was granted to foreign investors because this was the only way to attract them, while a great portion of control power remained in state hands. Under this scheme, the foreign investors' after-tax profits could be expatriated, but the investment plans, the materials and parts supply, the availability of credits, the wage level, the personnel policy, and other important production and exchange decisions were subject to bureaucratic review, with or without a contractual base (Yeh 1989).

DFI in Taiwan directly and indirectly contributed to the growth of the private sector. This was especially evident in the 1960's in the electronics industry, the fastest growing industry on the island at that time. The EPZs and other concessionary policies lured many giant U.S. investors to Taiwan. Their investment mostly took the form of fully owned subsidiaries (Tung 1988: 84). These firms contributed greatly to Taiwan's electronics export boom and employed a large number of young female workers just released from rural areas. Gradually, parts, components, and related industries prospered, and domestic electronics firms assumed the leading role in the industry in the 1970's. In this way, direct foreign investment in electronics, by its presence and its linkage effect, accelerated the trend toward privatization. On the other hand, though there is some evidence of a similar development on the mainland in the 1980's, privatization based on DFI remains constrained by two factors. The first is the CCP's conservative attitude toward sole foreign ownership, which was only partially relaxed toward the end of the 1980's. Various forms of direct foreign investment have been developed and expanded on the mainland since the late 1970's. Prominent among them are joint ventures, contractual joint ventures, coproduction, sole foreign ownerships, compensation trade, processing and assembling, and international leasing (Yeh 1989). Joint ventures with a 51 percent Chinese share have been the regime's favorite property rights form for DFI, though the more flexible coproduction is much preferred by foreign investors. However, sole foreign ownerships represent only a small fraction of DFI in the PRC.[74] This means that foreign investors have to find Chinese partners, usually in the state or collective enterprises. The resultant joint ventures and operations are not really private (Prybyla 1984). Thus, a rapid increase in DFI does not mean a corresponding increase in the number of private enterprises in mainland China.

The second obstacle is the limited spillover effect of DFI in expanding the private economy. Unlike in Taiwan, where foreign firms found local supporting enterprises that were in private hands, on the mainland foreign investors must do business with the established state and collective enterprises, the only exceptions being the *siying qiye* in the cities and the private portion of township and village enterprises (*xiangzhen qiye*) in rural areas. Though an increasing number of these private enterprises do become subcontractors for firms supported by foreign capital, the small size of the pri-

vate industrial sector puts a limit on the interaction between DFI
and grass-roots private enterprises. That said, the most promising
mechanism for developing the mainland's private economy is still
direct foreign investment and the various property rights forms it
entails. *Getihu, siying qiye,* and *xiangzhen qiye* are either small by
nature or are carefully restricted by the state. But the same state has
a vested interest in bringing in large-scale foreign investment, and
with it, inevitably, some private property rights forms, to modernize the PRC's industry and expand its exports. Here privatization
has a better chance to take root and then link up with the private
enterprises emerging from the bottom of the economy. However,
even if this trend is successful in expanding the private economy in
the coastal areas of mainland China, what will eventually emerge is
a regional capitalism under state guidance, that is, a capitalism that
is limited in terms of both geographical space and the transfer of
property rights.

It is obvious that the success of even this limited version of state
capitalism hinges on continuation of the open-door policy and increases in direct foreign investment. Because openness is a policy
strongly endorsed by Deng Xiaoping and supported by both liberals
and conservatives (such as Wang Zhen), and it has created tremendous vested interests for the PRC's political leaders and bureaucrats
(as well as their children), it is extremely unlikely that the PRC will
move back to self-reliance and autarky in the 1990's. This is particularly so because mounting balance-of-payments problems in the
late 1980's and the regime's strategic shift to export expansion
based on labor-intensive products in 1987–88 deepened mainland
China's dependency on the world market. Direct foreign investment can be expected to increase further, subject not to restrictions
imposed by Beijing, but only to the reluctance of foreign investors
who may consider the investment environment in mainland China
less attractive, especially in view of what happened in Tiananmen
Square in 1989, than opportunities in other parts of the world (such
as Eastern Europe).

However, there has been a surge of investment in the PRC by
Taiwanese businessmen (*taishang*). By 1989, *taishang* had already
committed the largest amount of DFI in Fujian province in general
and in Xiamen in particular. Their investment was the major reason
that Xiamen surpassed Shenzhen as the leading SEZ that year, for

the first time since the SEZs had been created.[75] The Tiananmen Incident did not dampen this momentum. Thus, in the first half of 1989, *taishang* invested US$100 million in Xiamen. The second half of the year registered a surge of DFI from Taiwan to US$360 million. By the end of 1989, total Taiwanese investment on the mainland had reached US$1 billion and involved 1,000 projects. This represented 10.1 percent of the number and 6.5 percent of the value of all foreign investments in the PRC. By the end of 1990, Taiwan's accumulated investment had reached US$3 billion. By the end of 1993, it had hit the US$10 billion mark. Taiwan thus became the second most important foreign investor in mainland China, outpaced only by Hong Kong. Faced with rising labor and land costs and surging global protectionism, Taiwan's enterprises in traditional labor-intensive industries will almost surely continue shifting their production bases to mainland China, and Beijing has every reason to welcome them, particularly because they are situated squarely in the industries designated for export production, and they come with ready market outlets.[76] This means that Taiwan will become a major factor in expanding the private sector on the mainland in the 1990's. However, it is unlikely that Taiwan (together with Hong Kong) will be able to produce anything more than a regional, state-guided capitalism in the southeastern part of mainland China.

Chapter Six

Conclusion

At the beginning of this book, we asked what causes an authoritarian regime that fully controls a society to restructure its economy, and what the relationship is between the causes and the type of economic restructuring undertaken. Taking the post-Mao reform in the PRC as our major case for investigation, we have used a comparative approach to analyze that reform. A property rights typology based on the dividable nature of the rights and control power/income power (ownership) dichotomy facilitates the comparison of three historical cases with the post-Mao reform. The conceptual framework chosen here is capable of grasping the main features of the economic structures in question, namely Hungary's market socialism after 1968, the Soviet Union's command economy after the Stalinist revolution from above, Taiwan's state capitalism since the 1950's, and the Chinese mainland's predominantly market socialism after 1984. The two-by-two typology is useful here because it corresponds to the practices of the states in question, particularly the deliberate attempt of state socialism to marketize but not privatize property rights. This reinforces the notion that property rights pertaining to the means of production can be divided and distributed among different rights holders, that the coalescent concept of property rights is valid only in certain historical times, and that an authoritarian state with great capacity and maximum autonomy vis-à-vis society can divide property rights and distribute them in various ways to achieve the goals of the ruling elite.

The four cases demonstrate great similarities in their authoritarian politics, traumatic imprinting events, liberal agricultural reforms, and state-dominated industry (see summary in Table 6). Their divergence into different property rights modes thus poses an interesting question that can only be explained by locating the differentiating factors among the cases, which include the impact of agricultural reform (a positive or negative demonstration effect), ideological constraints, security threat/war preparation, and international economic pressure. We will examine these one by one. Finally, we will discuss the prospects for the PRC's economic reform in the 1990's in view of the four factors that in the past have proved so important in determining the state's course in restructuring the economy.

Explanations for Divergence

The strong authoritarian state, traumatic imprinting events, liberal agricultural reform, and state-dominated industry shared by all four cases did not lead to a single developmental pattern. Hungary launched the NEM reform in 1968 and adopted market socialism. The Soviet Union plunged into Stalin's revolution from above and installed a command economy. The ROC in Taiwan started a privatization drive in 1953 and developed its state capitalism. From 1984 to 1991, the PRC fluctuated within a predominantly socialist market system. After looking carefully at the four cases, we find that there are four important factors influencing elite decisions at certain strategic points. They are the demonstration effect of the agricultural reform, ideological constraints, external security threats, and international economic pressure. Depending on the results of a country's agricultural reform, its demonstration effect can be positive, that is, it leads to dispersion of industrial property rights, or negative, that is, it leads to a reconcentration of industrial property rights. A country's ideological constraints primarily affect the way it views ownership rights. External security threats affect the degree of marketization. Finally, international economic pressure has a concentrating effect in the short run but a liberalizing effect in the long run, especially when such pressure reaches crisis proportions and world capitalist forces are brought in to salvage the economy.

TABLE 6

Background Similarities Among the Four Case Studies

Country	Authoritarian politics	Traumatic event	Economy in command	Agricultural reform	Pre-reform industry
PRC	"Emancipating the mind" and "seeking truth from facts" cum Four Insistences	Cultural Revolution (1966–76)	Third Plenum of the CCP's Eleventh Central Committee (1978)	Marketization and quasi privatization	Dominance of large and medium state enterprises; market insignificant
Hungary	Alliance policy cum proletarian dictatorship	Anti-Communist revolution (1956)	Eighth Party Congress of the HSWP (1962)	Marketization without privatization	Dominance of highly concentrated state enterprises; market insignificant
Soviet Union	Socialist humanism cum democratic centralism and revolutionary legality	Civil war and War Communism (1917–21)	Tenth Party Congress of the CPSU (1921)	Marketization and privatization	Large industry firmly in state hands; small private sector; market not main allocator
ROC	Local self-government cum revolutionary democracy and martial law	Erh Erh Pa Incident and loss of mainland (1947–49)	Establishment of Central Reform Committee (1950)	Dispersion of private ownership rights with limited marketization	Dominance of public corporations; small private sector; market not main allocator

These factors explain to a great extent the decisions made by elites in the four cases examined here (see Table 7). They also shed light on possible future scenarios in the PRC.

The Impact of Agricultural Reform

In all four cases, agricultural reform had a strong demonstration effect on the restructuring of industrial property rights. In Hungary and Taiwan, successful agricultural reform led to similar industrial reform, whereas in the Soviet Union the failure of the NEP agricultural reform resulted in a grain crisis, which then led the regime to force industry into a commandist structure. Mainland China at first followed the Hungary/Taiwan pattern, extending to industry the general type of reform used in agriculture. Then, because of the ensuing grain crisis, the pressure for agricultural recollectivization increased, and the NEP precedent became more relevant to the Chinese. In Hungary, the marketizing reform in the countryside between 1965 and 1968 strengthened reformers' confidence and paved the way for the introduction of the NEM on January 1, 1968. The NEM followed the same principle of marketization without privatization, or market socialism. The dispersion of property rights in agriculture led to a similar dispersion of property rights in industry. Similarly, the land reform implemented in the ROC demonstrated the benefits of state capitalism to the KMT elite. Privatization with limited marketization meant maximum motivational efficiency as well as state control of rice production and marketing. The privatization drive in industry launched under the First Four-Year Plan (1953–56) followed this developmental strategy, so that while income power was dispersed among the new entrepreneurs, a large portion of control power remained in state hands. Because the agricultural reforms in both Hungary and Taiwan were accompanied by sufficient inputs (technology, infrastructure, etc.), a high growth pattern was sustained for an extended period of time, and its impact on industrial reform was a positive one.

In the Soviet case, one finds the opposite scenario. One of the major reasons Stalin abandoned Bukharin's "enrich yourself" formula in the Russian countryside was the failure of the agricultural sector under the NEP to deliver enough grain to feed the urban population. Privatization and marketization after 1921 had created a highly dispersed property rights structure in rural Russia, which

TABLE 7
Explanations for Divergence Among the Four Case Studies

Country	Impact of agricultural reform	Ideological constraints	Security threat/war preparation	International pressure	Property rights structure
PRC	Positive: initial success of *dabaogan*	Marxism: need to preserve socialist ownership	Low security threat, low war preparation	Initially low	Predominantly market socialism
Hungary	Positive: successful socialist market reform	Marxism: need to preserve socialist ownership	High security threat, low war preparation	High, resulting in response C, need to reform established industry through marketization	Market socialism
Soviet Union	Negative: grain crisis	Marxism: need to preserve socialist ownership	High security threat, high war preparation	Minimal	Command economy
ROC	Positive: successful state capitalist reform	*San-min chu-i:* non-constraining	High security threat, low war preparation	High, resulting in response A, austerity (state control); response B, privatization; response D, U.S.-imposed privatization	State capitalism

forced the Bolshevik regime to rely on price policy to direct peasant production. As more and more of the state's financial resources were devoted to industrial investment, the Bolsheviks found it extremely difficult to control agricultural production, hence the need to reconcentrate property rights. Here the failure of the dispersed rights structure in agriculture led to an overall concentration of property rights that included the extermination of the Nepmen in the cities and the total abolition of the market as an allocating mechanism in industry. In the case of the PRC, the early success of the agricultural reform (1978–84) prompted the state to introduce similar (though diluted) reform measures to the cities. Because the household responsibility system, or *dabaogan*, dispersed property rights in both the income and control realms, from 1984 to 1991 Chinese reformers alternately emphasized marketization and privatization in industry, though the overall direction of industrial reform was toward market socialism. Here a successful agricultural reform clearly had a positive impact on industrial reform.

Ideological Constraints

There are two ideologies in our four cases: Marxist socialism and Sun Yat-sen's *san-min chu-i* (Three Principles of the People). Marxist socialism is constraining with regard to ownership rights; *san-min chu-i* is not. As far as control power is concerned, both are non-constraining and compatible with market allocation as well as state planning.

Marxism is hostile to private property because it leads to the appropriation of the value that laborers contribute to the production process, that is, to the cardinal sin of exploitation. However, Marxism is not necessarily incompatible with market.[1] Market exchange does not in itself violate the principles of Marxism as long as the income accruing to such exchange can be fully appropriated by the laborers who are considered the sole providers of value. In terms of property rights reform, this means that marketization is a much more ideologically acceptable strategy than privatization. In addition to such value judgments, there is a second reason for ruling Communist parties to reject privatization as a means of economic reform, one that has to do with the belief system (not the value system) of the ideology. Marxism holds that any economic power (defined in terms of ownership of the means of production) translates

directly into political power. Privatization, as a transfer of ownership rights to private individuals, clearly means an immediate
weakening of the party-state's position vis-à-vis the society. Thus
the postrevolutionary elite in a Leninist regime may no longer be
committed to the values of Marxism but may still use Marx's materialist framework to analyze the distribution of political power.
They may object to privatization for purely political reasons and
use Marxism as a prism through which to view political reality,
rather than as a moral guide. In this sense, Marxism is constraining
with regard to the ownership issue even for postrevolutionary Leninist regimes.

San-min chu-i, on the other hand, is not constraining with regard to either ownership or the issue of the plan versus the market.
Sun Yat-sen assigned important roles to both the state and the private sector. The division between the two hinges on the nature of
the goods in question (which in turn determines the incentives for
private enterprises to produce them), the capital requirements of
the industry compared with the capacity of private entrepreneurs to
provide it, and the market structure for a particular industry, that is,
whether it is a natural monopoly. The state will directly participate
in production when the private sector lacks the motive or capacity
to do so, or when the market is noncompetitive. These are flexible
principles compatible with a wide range of ownership structures.
The same flexibility can be found in Sun's position with regard to
control power. He did not believe in state planning on a grand scale,
nor in a self-regulating market, but he did believe that the state
should intervene in market allocation when necessary. In short,
san-min chu-i is non-constraining with regard to both property
rights realms.

The NEM reformers in Hungary in the late 1960's were constrained by Marxist ideology, which limited their choices for increasing industrial efficiency through the dispersion of property
rights. This group of "naive reformers" thought that a limited socialist market was enough to invigorate the industrial sector. Their
attitude toward marginal privatization in the cities was very conservative because they followed the principle of market socialism
quite literally. In the Soviet Union, Stalin's revolution from above
was a direct reaction against the NEP, undertaken in part because
the NEP violated the principle of Marxism. The Bolsheviks of the

1920's were committed revolutionaries who believed in Marxism for both its value judgments and its political prescriptions. The sizable private areas of the economy allowed by the NEP aroused not only moral repugnance but also political anxiety. The command economy installed by the First Five-Year Plan was more compatible with Marxist ideology.[2] In the case of Taiwan, because *san-min chu-i* is non-constraining in both property rights realms, ROC technocrats could shift the island's quasi-command economy of the 1940's to state capitalism in the 1950's and 1960's without meeting much ideological resistance. Here economic pragmatism ruled supreme.

The PRC's 1984–91 economic reform basically followed the Hungarian model of market socialism. Both countries wanted to disperse property rights under the constraints of Marxism. It is true that the PRC took a more liberal attitude toward marginal privatization in the cities, in part because of the demonstration effect of the agricultural reform, in part because of the need to employ surplus labor from rural areas. However, this minor deviation from the market socialism model, as well as the lively debate on privatization, did not bring about significant modification of the basic reform framework. The main reform strategy of the PRC between 1984 and 1991 remained marketization and not privatization. Although the post-Mao elite lacked a deep commitment to the values of Marxism, they nevertheless adhered to Marx's political prescription by firmly controlling industrial ownership rights. Because it was this political factor that constrained the elite in the area of ownership reform, it comes as no surprise that the regime allowed more privatization in the countryside, where economic units were smaller and the possibility of a political challenge to the regime was considered less likely than in the cities.

External Security Threats

Whereas ideological constraints affect property rights mainly in the ownership realm, an external threat to a country's security has its major impact in the control realm. As the perception of such a threat increases, it is only natural for the state to take a more interventionist role and channel national resources to military fortification. If there is an overwhelming security threat, a country may need to replace market with plan as its major allocator, so that the economy can be geared to preparation for and fighting of a war. This concentration of economic control power in state hands, however, does not necessarily mean nationalization, as witnessed by the highly regimented yet predominantly private economies of Japan and Nazi Germany during World War II. In our four cases, the Bolsheviks had the most acute perception of a threat to their regime, which led directly to a draft industrialization and planned economy under the First Five-Year Plan. Both Hungary and Taiwan had serious security concerns, but their positions under the hegemony of superpowers prevented these concerns from leading to Soviet-style industrialization and the concentration of property rights necessitated by it. The PRC, on the other hand, enjoyed a relatively more secure position in the international arena and saw little need to regiment the economy for defense purposes. It was thus free to launch a marketizing reform in industry.

In the late 1960's, Hungary was securely cocooned in the Soviet bloc. After 1956, the Kadar regime loyally followed Moscow's line in international affairs, never trying to break away from the bloc (Nagy's attempt to do so had brought disaster to Hungary). Under the Soviet hegemony, Hungary as a Warsaw Pact country was shielded from unlikely Western attack, while at the same time deprived of an autonomous defense policy. When the NEM was launched, Soviet leaders did not perceive any need to push for rapid industrialization in Hungary for defense purposes. However, Hungary faced a serious security concern in the late 1960's, one unrelated to the East-West conflict. In view of the similar economic reform in Czechoslovakia (1965–68) and the suppression of the Prague Spring in 1968, the genuine security threat to Hungary actually came from the Soviet Union. However, this concern did not lead to serious attempts by the Kadar regime to build up its military capacity, because Kadar proved very skillful in convincing Soviet leaders that the non-political and well-prepared NEM was in their best interest, and because Hungary did not have an autonomous defense policy. The Bolsheviks, in contrast, had a strong sense of the insecurity of their position, and they had the capacity to pursue an independent defense policy. The regime was fully committed to its goal of world revolution and was aware of the inherent tension in its relations with the West. Fresh memories of the invasion by the West and Japan during the civil war, the "plots of Chamberlain and Poincaré," the breaking off of diplomatic relations by Britain in 1927, and the activities of the Japanese in the Far East all added to the regime's perception of external threat. The party as a whole believed that war against it would come before very long. But the NEP gave a sizable economic role to the market, which tended to allocate national resources to consumption-related production and not to heavy industry, which is the basis for national defense. A dramatic property rights restructuring was thus considered necessary to gear the Soviet economy to a draft heavy industrialization and a major military buildup.

In the 1950's and 1960's, Taiwan faced an overwhelming security threat from the mainland, which it tried to retake through military means. However, Taiwan was cocooned in the American bloc, and like Hungary did not have a fully autonomous defense policy. U.S. military and economic aid, American military advisors, and the presence of the Seventh Fleet cruising the Taiwan Strait protected as well as circumscribed the ROC. Though there were voices in the government pushing for rapid heavy industrialization and an independent defense policy (Wang Nai-chi 1987), the overwhelming American influence and the opinion of the technocrats favored the development of labor-intensive industries. Taiwan's perception of threat thus did not materialize into a drive to rapidly increase its heavy industry, hence it had no reason to concentrate property rights in the control realm for defense purposes. Finally, the PRC in the 1980's was as independent as the Soviet Union in the 1920's. However, the Chinese Communists faced an international environment much more favorable than the one the Bolsheviks had faced 60 years earlier. The PRC skillfully maneuvered to capture the pivot position in the U.S.-Soviet-Chinese triangle and received concessions from both superpowers. Its possession of nuclear weapons and long-range striking ability, the updating of the People's Liberation Army doctrine, and its quasi collaboration with the West all added to Beijing's confidence in a relaxing international environment. Defense was granted last priority among the Four Modernizations, and the military was forced to adjust to the economic reform, not the other way around. This meant that the regime could make marketization the major strategy of economic reform.

International Economic Pressure

The impact of international economic pressure on property rights is more complicated than that of the previous three factors. In our four cases, there are four types of response to balance-of-payments problems and growing foreign debt. The first and most obvious response (A) is the strategy in which the state directly cuts imports and promotes exports. Import certificates, foreign exchange controls, manipulation of the exchange rate to make imports expensive and exports cheap, tariff barriers, quota systems, direct subsidies for exporters, preferential loans, tax rebate schemes, and numerous other measures can be applied to reduce the trade imbalance and the country's indebtedness. The major property rights implication of this strategy is the concentration of control power in state hands in foreign trade–related areas. The second response (B) looks more closely at trade deficit problems and demands the establishment of import-substituting and export-expanding industries. The basis for this strategy is the absence of domestic industries that can produce substitutes for imported goods and competitive exports on the international market. This response is compatible with the first strategy in that the state must adopt a mercantilist policy in order to provide a protected market for nascent domestic industries and make the necessary technology, machinery, and other inputs available to domestic producers. This means tightened control of foreign trade. However, if the state faces a hard budget constraint and cannot afford to establish state enterprises in the targeted industries, the economic decision makers may be forced to resort to a privatization drive. A limited version of this response is one in which the state attracts export-oriented foreign investment with various concessions when it cannot finance such activities itself. The result is limited privatization.

The third type of response (C) assumes the existence of established industries in the country in question, probably because the balance-of-payments problems catch the economy when import substitution has already been completed. Here the primary prescription is to implement a marketizing reform in order to increase the efficiency of enterprises by assigning them greater control power and linking domestic prices with world-market prices. Finally, the last response (D) assumes that the trade deficit problem has reached crisis proportions, and that the survival of the economy hinges on massive foreign aid and/or credit, so that the donor/creditor's property rights preferences become the dominant factor in directing domestic economic reform. In the cases examined here, the West and international financial institutions dominated by Western countries (particularly the U.S.) acted as the donor/creditors, thus the external property rights preferences were generally for marketization and privatization. These four responses are not mutually exclusive, and more than one of them may be pursued simultaneously.

Of the four cases examined here, the Soviet Union in the 1920's was the least susceptible to international economic pressure. This was the case not only because the country was huge and rich in resources, but also because the Soviet regime in the 1920's was an international outcast: it suffered from isolation and had little trade with the outside world. As a result, the property rights structure of the Soviet economy was hardly affected by external economic factors. Hungary, on the other hand, was highly trade dependent, both in convertible currency trade and in ruble trade. The country's small size and poor resource endowment precluded the option of reducing its dependency on the international market. In the late 1960's, Hungary's major problem in its external economic relations was convertible currency trade deficit. When the Council for Mutual Economic Assistance suppliers could no longer meet many of Hungary's essential imports needs, there was increasing pressure to import more from the West, which translated into an increasing need to improve the quality of Hungary's exports. When the country was contemplating the NEM in the late 1960's, foreign trade considerations served to strengthen the case for economic reform along the marketizing line. Here response C prevailed. In order to make Hungary's exports more competitive on the Western markets, the NEM reduced the state's administrative control over enterprises and made them more sensitive to international competition. With an established industrial base created by the early import substitution drive, NEM reformers emphasized marketization as the major means for achieving economic efficiency.[3]

Like Hungary, Taiwan is also small and poor in resources. However, the trajectories of the two countries in trade-related property rights reform are quite different. Hungary started with a manageable trade imbalance that continued to grow despite the major economic reforms implemented in the late 1960's. The deficit/debt problems finally evolved into a major economic crisis, and Hungary brought in world capitalist forces to dictate its property rights reform. The ROC, on the other hand, started with a very serious trade imbalance and was totally dependent on U.S. aid for its economic survival. This made response D the dominant scenario in Taiwan in the 1950's. The U.S. clearly preferred privatization and directly linked its aid to the growth of Taiwan's private enterprises. However, the U.S. was willing to tolerate the ROC's mercantilist (i.e., response A) policies when the island's economy was extremely vulnerable. Thus Taiwan was able to use its industrial policies to protect its domestic market and promote exportation. Finally, Taiwan's economy was put under tremendous international economic pressure at a time when it lacked a basic industrial structure, a legacy of Japanese colonial policy. Hence the KMT state was forced to make establishing an import-substituting industry its first priority. Because the ROC government had adopted a hard budget constraint based on its mainland experience, it had to rely on privatization, rather than expansion of the state sector, to accomplish this. This is clearly an example of response B.

The PRC is a country as large and rich in resources as the former Soviet Union. Nevertheless, mainland China's open-door policy prior to 1984 had created a much greater trade dependence on the West than the Soviet Union experienced during the NEP period. Because the Chinese Communists faced a much more favorable international environment than the Bolsheviks did, they could orient the PRC's trade policy toward acquiring the technology and foreign investment needed to upgrade its obsolete industries. However, the country was not under great international economic pressure at the time that property rights reform was expanded into the cities. The PRC's first-wave industrial reform, launched in 1984, thus bore little relation to the country's foreign trade considerations (witness the PRC's trade surpluses of 1982–83). After 1984, China's balance-of-payments problems became much more severe, and the regime responded with an austerity cum export drive (response A) and an effort to attract export-oriented direct foreign investment (a limited response B). During the *zhili zhengdun* period, state control was strengthened and marginal privatization in areas related to export expanded. This development did not fundamentally alter the market socialism structure of Chinese industry, but it did inject more elements of private property into the coastal areas of the country.

The impact of agricultural reform, ideological constraints, external security threats, and international economic pressure are the four major factors behind the reform decisions made by the ruling elite in our four cases. In Hungary, those decisions were influenced by a successful agricultural reform and by the ideological constraints of Marxism. Hungary had no need to pursue rapid industrialization for defense purposes. Its increasing convertible currency trade deficit convinced the elite to marketize the Hungarian economy to make it more efficient, hence resulting in market socialism, or the transfer of control power to enterprises without a change in the ownership structure.

In the Soviet Union, the grain crisis doomed the liberal agricultural reform and had a negative effect on the industrial sector. The Bolsheviks were constrained by their ideology, and their perception of both internal and external threats to the regime demanded a national plan for rapid industrialization. The result was a command economy, or the concentration of both ownership rights and control power in state hands.

In the ROC, a successful land reform demonstrated the virtue of dispersed private ownership combined with overall state guidance. A non-constraining ideology gave ROC technocrats a free hand in reforming the economy. The ROC faced a serious external security threat but was circumscribed by the U.S. and unable to pursue an aggressive defense policy. International economic pressure resulted in a mercantilist policy that minimized imports and maximized exports, a privatization drive brought about by the combination of the state's hard budget constraint and the need to build an industrial base, and a push for privatization that resulted from strong U.S. influence. The result was state capitalism, or privatization with extensive state control.

In the PRC, *dabaogan* (privatization and marketization with limited tenure) was initially a great success and convinced reformers that similar measures should be applied to the cities. Marxist ideology made large-scale privatization of industry difficult but was compatible with the marketization reform. The international environment was generally favorable to the PRC, which saw no need to concentrate control power in state hands for national defense purposes. The result was a predominantly socialist market reform between 1984 and 1988, or marketization with only marginal privatization. This situation changed somewhat when China's balance-of-payments problems became more serious at the turn of the decade, and the regime responded to international pressure with an austerity cum export drive. The market was weakened and private property expanded in the export sector, but the basic structure of market socialism remained unchanged.

The PRC in the 1990's: Future Scenarios

In the 1990's, as well as in the 1980's, any change of economic policy in the PRC must be examined in a political context. In the wake of the Cultural Revolution and Deng Xiaoping's demystification of Marxism–Leninism–Mao Zedong Thought, the ideological legitimacy of the regime has been lost forever. The CCP has to rely on economic performance as its sole means of soliciting popular support. However, the authoritarian nature of the regime has not changed, which means it will show no reluctance to apply economic deprivation or blatant coercion to suppress any sign of opposition. The overriding concern of the elite will remain the preservation of the rule of the party. Any future property rights reform will be contemplated only if it serves that purpose. In this broad political context, we can examine the four factors that have proved critical in shaping the PRC's economic reform in the past and that will definitely have a profound impact on the country's economic future.

We will start with the factor that is least likely to change: the ideology of the regime. By ideology I mean not the value system of Marxism–Leninism–Mao Zedong Thought, which can no longer command the allegiance even of the old guard, but the belief system, or the political prescriptions derived from that system. The most important is the belief that for the party to continue holding political power, it must be the owner of the most important means of production. This is a principle derived from Marx's historical materialism that thus far has not been violated by any ruling Communist party. Because it is not moral repugnance but realpolitik that decides the party's attitude toward the ownership structure, it does not matter that the majority of the population, the peasants, have quasi ownership rights, hire labor, and transfer land, as long as the strategic means of production, large-scale industrial assets, are in state hands. This means that CCP ideology will not act against the continuation of *dabaogan* or the spread of *getihu* (or even *siying qiye*) as long their size is limited and their scope carefully circumscribed. However, the regime's ideology will surely prevent large-scale privatization of industry. This means that the PRC's industrial property rights reform, if continued in the 1990's, will be contained in the realm of marketization.

A second factor that is likely to remain stable in the 1990's is the external security threat to the PRC and any need to divert the bulk of national resources to a massive military buildup. The Soviet Union, in the past the major threat to mainland China's security, has disintegrated into fifteen bickering states, and this threat to Beijing has dipped to an all-time low. To be sure, this process may create ethnic conflicts along the Sino-Soviet border, which is straddled by many minority groups. In addition, the decline of Soviet power has reduced China's strategic importance and made it more vulnerable to Western pressure on human rights issues. However, these problems are generally not the kind that necessitate a rapid buildup of defense and a concentration of property rights for that purpose, as was the case in the Soviet Union at the end of the 1920's. It is only reasonable to expect the PRC's perception of external threat to remain low for another several years. That said, one cannot exclude the possibility that a rising Japan will touch off an arms race with the PRC in the 1990's, exactly the kind of situation that would require a massive concentration of national resources (Y. S. Wu 1993). This could happen if the current defense arrangement between the U.S. and Japan were broken off (e.g., because of the lack of a common enemy and because of U.S. unwillingness to continue paying the economic price for Japan's subordinate strategic role). A Japan left in charge of its own defense is a natural security threat to the PRC. This scenario, however, is unlikely in the near future, which means that the CCP regime will not soon be forced to dramatically increase the role of the plan versus the market in order to meet national defense needs.

The third factor is one that has great potential to change, and in a deteriorating manner. This is agricultural production, and grain production in particular. The rapidly growing population of mainland China, the shrinking amount of arable land, and the rapidly decreasing scale of farming make the prospects for agricultural growth very dim in the 1990's. By redirecting a portion of national resources to agriculture and reconcentrating property rights in many individual cases, the regime managed to prevent the grain crisis from exploding in 1989–91, though per capita grain production remained below the 1984 level. If a serious situation develops in large areas of the country, a rollback of *dabaogan* would be possible (a parallel to the Soviet scenario). Alternatively, the state may continue to vacillate between the often conflicting constraints of rural interests, urban demand, budget limits, and the current property rights structure without taking any decisive action, while the grain crisis continues and political disturbances become perennial. Of course, it is not totally unthinkable that the regime might eventually sell land to the peasants, thus creating another one-time boom in agricultural growth, but the fundamental problems of small-scale farming, lack of technology, and a large population would soon overtake the momentum unleashed by this move. The agricultural growth rate would again drop, and the need to control grain production and marketing would resurge. In all likelihood, agriculture will not be the engine of further economic reform in the 1990's, but rather a very probable cause for the reconcentration of property rights across the entire economy.

The fourth factor is one that will surely change, namely international economic pressure. The PRC has just emerged from a prolonged period of retrenchment, a direct result of the failure of the first-wave socialist market reform. A second reform aimed mainly at perfecting the market is now under way. The emphasis of this reform is to perfect "socialism with Chinese characteristics" by removing the perceived defects of the 1984–88 reform in order to create a "socialist market economy," as the party's Fourteenth Congress proclaimed in October 1992. The general trend remains one of marketization. The inner logic of this kind of reform suggests that a soft budget constraint will continue to coddle state enterprises and plague the economy, and that insatiable investment demand and widely fluctuating investment cycles will be perennial phenomena of the system. This will doubtless lead to serious balance-of-payments problems. Austerity will be the dominant policy of the regime for a while, but because it will not solve all of these problems, the regime will be forced to take more radical reform measures. Under great international economic pressure, the Marxist dictum of maintaining industrial ownership in state hands may lose force. The regime may be forced to dramatically expand private industrial assets in order to improve economic efficiency. It may also seek help from Western countries and international financial institutions and be forced to accept their conditions for such aid. The donor/creditor's property rights preferences would thus become dominant, meaning that a marketization cum privatization package (response D) would be imposed on mainland China.

However, this scenario, similar to that of Hungary in the 1980's, is based on the assumption that market socialism and state industry remain dominant. With *sanzi qiye*, private enterprise, and rural industry growing at a pace far exceeding that of state enterprises, it is possible that the PRC's non-state sector will take over more than 50 percent of its industry in the mid-1990's. This means that market socialism as practiced in large and medium-sized state enterprises will lose its dominant position. Non-state industry performed extremely well during the latter half of the *zhili zhengdun* period, in fact saving the regime from the post-Tiananmen economic crisis. A favorable trade balance was restored and international economic pressure was relieved. The expansion of the non-state sector thus goes hand in hand with the PRC's improved status on the world market.

A paradox is created here: the success of the non-state sector in solving balance-of-payments problems reduces the regime's need to tolerate it. Other things being equal, macro stability dampens the urge for reform, though it provides the economic environment necessary for structural changes. Here a critical decision has to be made. If accumulating foreign exchange and pursuing high export growth have become the paramount goals of the regime, such that they override other political considerations, we may see further development of the non-state sector. In a scenario similar to Taiwan's, coastal China may witness a great expansion of state capitalism, that is, of state-promoted and state-guided private or quasi-private enterprises geared to the world market. In this sense, the relative size of the state and non-state sectors actually determines which pattern the Chinese mainland will follow in the 1990's: that of Hungarian market socialism or state capitalism à la Taiwan. The Hungarian pattern points to great international economic pressure and increasingly radicalized reform measures that are forced on the regime. The Taiwan experience, on the other hand, suggests reduced international pressure, rising economic nationalism, and a gradual shift of industry from state ownership to mixed property rights and finally to private ownership. This development, however, would hinge on the ability of the world market to absorb the huge volume of exports that the Chinese mainland could produce.

In sum, the critical elements that militate for a concentration of property rights in the PRC in the 1990's are continuing ideological constraints, increasing security threats, deteriorating agricultural performance (especially in grain production), and limited international economic pressure. On the other hand, mainland China's liberalizing property rights reform will advance if official ideology is undermined, Japan is slow to replace the Soviet Union as a major security threat, agriculture can muddle through, and balance-of-payments problems and the state's debt burden mount. These scenarios are based on the comparisons we have made between the PRC in the 1980's and Hungary in the 1960's and 1970's, the Soviet Union in the 1920's, and the ROC in the 1950's and 1960's, and on the assumption that the authoritarian political system dominated by a Leninist-type party will endure in mainland China in the coming decade. It is possible that this assumption will not hold, and that a genuine people's revolution will triumph in the PRC. In that scenario, a rapid marketization cum privatization drive would be launched, limited only by the population's need for a suitable transition process, and the post-1989 Eastern European experience (including what is going on in Poland today) would become the most relevant case for comparison with the new China. However, that is a subject best dealt with in another study, one on property rights reform under democratizing post-Leninist regimes.

Reference Matter

Notes

Chapter 1

1. By "Leninist system," I mean a set of coherent social institutions centering on state control of the means of production and political monopoly by a Leninist party. The term "ultrareformist Dengism" requires some explanation here. The collapse of Leninist systems in Eastern Europe and the former Soviet Union after 1989, both in terms of privatization programs and the parties' loss of political monopoly, cannot be described as just another stage in the development of these systems. Rather, it is their destruction. Within the confines of a working Leninist system, i.e., one that is not collapsing, it is still appropriate to characterize Deng Xiaoping's policies as ultrareformist (even after the Tiananmen incident in 1989), for economic, if not political, reasons.

2. For a discussion of the statism behind the reform effort in the PRC, see Solinger 1993.

3. Zhao Suisheng (S. Zhao 1990) raises the issue of whether the post-Mao regime in the PRC is a strong one-party system with only a feeble political capacity to make and implement economic policies. The three areas he examines are the solution of political conflicts arising over policies at the top political elite level; the operation of the bureaucratic apparatus responsible for policy formulation at the central bureaucracy level; and control over local authorities responsible for policy implementation at the level of intermediate bureaucracies. He finds that the top power elite has not adopted a uniform set of rules and procedures; that the huge bureaucracy does not operate with a set of stable roles; and that relations between central and local authorities are ill defined. Zhao concludes that the regime lacks the capacity to turn its political will into policies and enforce them effectively through its institutions. In fact the three areas under Zhao's investigation are all within the state structure. The problems he detects demonstrate not the inability of the regime to restructure the economy, but rather its inability to discipline itself and come up with coherent plans and measures for implementing them. The regime in the post-Mao period remains highly autonomous and penetrating vis-à-vis the society.

4. Robert Tucker (1969b) discusses three levels of comparative com-

munist studies: artful juxtaposition, empirical comparison, and model building. This study opts for the third level.

5. This definition is adopted, with some modifications, from Pryor (1973).

6. Westerners' attitudes to property are rooted in their particular historical experience, i.e., the development of capitalism and the notion of commodity. Property is thus understood as private property, which the individual owner can use and dispose of. But this notion is far from universal and may blind Westerners to fundamental differences in the concept of property in other social groups (Hirschon 1984; Reeve 1986).

7. Even though there is a strong tradition for communist theorists to assert the existence of a primitive communism in which collective property rights prevailed, today communist and non-communist scholars agree that both personal and collective forms of property rights existed in the most primitive societies known to us. Their views differ, however, in that Marxist scholars consider personal property a marginal phenomenon in primitive societies, while Western scholars assume that even in those societies there existed a well-developed awareness of individuality and a corresponding sense of property. It is interesting to note how Soviet ethnologists differentiate between personal (*lichnaia*) and private (*chastnaia*) property, with the former devoid of connotations of surplus value and exploitation (Schott 1973: 71). This difference between two types of individual property is evident in Soviet law, which differentiates between "personal possessions" and "private property": personal possessions are homes, clothing, and so forth, which are acquired for personal use and which are not employed for the purpose of obtaining income; "private property" consists of items such as machines or land, which can be used for producing goods or services from which profit can be extracted (Pryor 1973: 377). Soviet law in regard to personal possessions is quite similar to such law in the West; on the other hand, Soviet law limits the amount of private property a person may possess.

8. In capitalism, income stemming from the ownership of the means of production accrues primarily to individuals; in socialism, such income accrues to the government (Pryor 1973: 11).

9. The *Communist Manifesto* maintains that "the theory of the Communists may be summed up in one sentence: Abolition of private property"; and "Communism deprives no man of the power to appropriate the products of society; all that it does is to deprive him of the power to subjugate the labor of others by means of such appropriation."

10. Codetermination—labor participation in the governing of businesses—is a major ongoing postwar social experiment in the former West Germany. The codetermination act of 1976 applies to all businesses in Germany with more than 2,000 employees. Six members of the board of directors represent the shareholders and six represent the employees. The chairman of the board is appointed by the shareholders and has a deciding vote. The law has changed the prevailing relationships among owners, managers, workers, and labor unions. These changes, in turn, affect the location of decision-making powers, the appropriability of rewards, and the relationship between risk taking and the bearing of costs (Pejovich 1989).

11. Since the devolution of power to the localities after the Great Leap Forward in 1958–59, the PRC's local governments have had more power vis-à-vis the center than their counterparts in other command economies (Wu and Reynolds 1987). This fact, as well as the strong egalitarian ethos and moral incentives that Mao Zedong grafted onto the original system, makes the pre-reform Chinese economy an imperfect example of a command economy (Goldstein 1988); however, one can still comfortably put it into this category.

12. The main protagonists in this debate were Oskar Lange, Ludwig von Mises, and Friedrich Hayek. The focus was whether efficient resource allocation could be achieved under socialism. Lange proposed a model of market socialism in which supply and demand are equilibrated through a trial and error method, in effect creating a simulated market. Lange's socialist enterprises are instructed to minimize production costs and to follow market signals in deciding outputs. Prices are determined by a central planning board, with the sole purpose of clearing the market. As surpluses arise here and shortages there, the board revises the pattern of prices and observes once again the effects. Through successive repetition of this procedure, an equilibrium price ultimately emerges, a result that is indistinguishable from competitive equilibrium. Hence all the allocative benefits of competition are gained without society suffering the distributive evils of capitalism (Nutter 1973). The Lange proposal was attacked by von Mises and Hayek, both of whom considered efficient outcomes impossible under socialism (Schroeder 1988). Frederic Pryor described a more complete form of market socialism, suggesting that "the government could have a high degree of ownership and yet completely delegate the exercise (or custody) of the property rights with regard to production to a third hired manager, as in an extreme form of market socialism" (Pryor 1973: 237), a possibility also recognized by Charles Lindblom (1977) and Alec Nove (1983).

13. Famous reform economists in this tradition include Evsey G. Liberman in the Soviet Union; Rezso Nyers in Hungary; Wlodzimierz Brus in Poland; and Ota Sik in Czechoslovakia (Kornai 1986b).

14. "State capitalism" was a term used by Nikolay Bukharin to refer to a capitalist economy centrally planned and regulated by the state. V. I. Lenin, however, used this term to refer to private industry in socialist Russia, which created some misunderstanding. My usage here is in line with Bukharin's, but does not include his Marxist assumptions, such as viewing the state as dominated by the bourgeoisie (Kolakowski 1981b: 28).

15. The most prominent include John Locke, Jean-Jacques Rousseau, Immanuel Kant, G. W. F. Hegel, and Karl Marx. Their theories on property laid the foundation for normative discussions in the field. The writings of John Rawls (1971), Robert Nozick (1974), Lawrence C. Becker (1977), and Alan Ryan (1984) are all in this tradition.

16. Prominent jurisprudents in this field include J. Austin, W. Blackstone, R. Pound, L. F. Vinding Kruse, H. Kelsen, and A. M. Honore.

17. Prominent ethnologists who have dealt with the subject of property include Lewis H. Morgan, Robert H. Lowie, Wilhelm Koppers, Wilhelm Schmidt, Richard Thurnwald, and Walter Nippold (Schott 1973). En-

gels accepted Morgan's major theme in his own writing, which was also in this ethnological tradition.

18. Political authoritarianism is here understood as a political system lacking regular mechanisms of popular control over the ruling elite.

19. The case of the Republic of China in Taiwan requires some explanation here. Literally speaking, the KMT has never been a Leninist party. Its official ideology—Sun Yat-sen's Three Principles of the People (nationalism, democracy, and the people's livelihood)—is explicitly opposed to Marxism-Leninism, and it has carried on a rivalry with the CCP for decades. But the KMT is organizationally Leninist, both in terms of internal structure (it has a party congress, central committee, central standing committee, secretariat, party chairman, etc.) and penetration into society (through party cells, specialized party organs targeting different groups of the population, regional branches, front organizations, etc.). Thus the KMT can be described as a Leninist-type party, particularly with regard to its organizational traits. That said, mainland China during the Republican period could not be described as having a centralized authoritarian political system dominated by a highly disciplined Leninist-type party. The KMT at that time was plagued by factionalism and was unable to successfully penetrate the society, as the rising influence of the CCP and the eventual defeat of the KMT in the civil war proved. However, following the civil war fiasco, a loose coalition of factions on the mainland was paradoxically transformed into a coherent party-state centered around the strong leadership of Chiang Kai-shek. Desperation, painstaking reflection, and the natural selection process during the retreat all contributed to the recuperation and rejuvenation of the KMT state. In addition, Taiwan society had not been activated politically. The power ratio between state and society guaranteed the state full autonomy and the capacity to extensively penetrate society (Y. S. Wu 1989). The ROC thus satisfies the requirements for comparability with the PRC (see Chap. 5).

20. The privatization of Taiwan's industry mainly took the form of government encouragement of the emergence of a large number of small and medium-sized private enterprises, rather than direct privatization of state enterprises, though the latter was also implemented throughout the 1950's.

Chapter 2

1. For a thorough discussion of the differences between agricultural and industrial reform in the PRC, see Shirk 1988.

2. Here we adopt the income definition of ownership because we are concerned with ownership of the means of production in a socialist system (see Chap. 1).

3. The capitalist enclaves included Special Economic Zones (SEZs), open cities, and certain delta areas. They were created in order to attract foreign investment and promote exports. The degree of openness to the outside world decreases as one moves from the SEZs to the open cities, the delta areas, and the inland. The first four SEZs, located in Shenzhen, Zhuhai, Shantou (in Guandong) and Xiamen (in Fujian), were created in 1979–80. In 1984, fourteen cities on or near the PRC's east coast were declared

open cities. In 1985, the Yangtze River, Pearl River, and southern Fujian deltas were added to the list of enclaves. In 1988, the province of Hainan became the fifth SEZ.

4. These included the Ten Regulations establishing the rights of enterprises (formally, the State Council's Decision on Further Expanding the Autonomy of State Industrial Enterprises) and reform of the planning and foreign trade systems.

5. Wu Jinglian's main position was to tighten monetary control before initiating price reform, in order to avoid inflation. He also proposed a two-step policy—"administrative adjustment first, free price formation second" (*xiantiao houfang*)—to reduce the shock of price reform. His position was criticized by more radical price reformers (Hua, Zhang, and Luo 1988: 17).

6. "Socialism with Chinese characteristics" is Deng Xiaoping's characterization of the reform. It is a catchword without clear definition. "The primary stage of socialism" is an ideological rationale for the unorthodox reform measures taken by the regime. The major task at this stage was to develop productivity by employing various forms of ownership. This doctrine was officially endorsed by the CCP at the Thirteenth Party Congress in early November 1987. Chinese market socialism is a clearer description of the major trends of the reform. Whatever the characterization of the reform, all CCP leaders agree on the need to insist on public ownership, a point made clear by Zhao Ziyang at the 1988 Beidaihe meeting (*World Journal*, Aug. 3, 1988).

7. The term *getihu* refers to small private businesses with fewer than eight employees. *Siying qiye* are private enterprises with eight or more employees (*Beijing Review*, July 18–24, 1988, pp. 10–11).

8. For a discussion of the politics behind the transition from profit retention and "tax for profit" in the early 1980's to the contract management responsibility system of the late 1980's, see White 1993: chap. 4.

9. There are numerous forms of QCJZ. They can be classified according to the contractor, the coverage and content of the contract, profit or loss sharing, the profit-sharing relations between state and enterprises, etc. (Sah 1991: 216–19). The basic spirit of the system is to maximize the production incentive of enterprises while guaranteeing state revenues (the same principle governs the household responsibility system in agriculture).

10. The exact connections between business cycles, reform cycles, and eruptions of social unrest are not the subject of this study. For a discussion of this subject, see Dittmer 1990; Dittmer and Wu 1993; Lin 1991; and Ch'en Te-Sheng 1992b.

11. Edward A. Hewett makes a clear distinction between economic reforms and policy changes. According to him, economic reforms refer to changes in the institutional arrangements constituting the system by which resources are allocated. Such reforms change the way economic decisions are made and deal with the fundamental causes of performance problems. Policy changes, on the other hand, use the existing system to implement new policies designed to improve performance. They are generally an ineffective substitute for genuine reforms (Hewett 1988: 12–19). From our point of view, economic reforms are reassignments of property rights,

whereas policy changes are decisions made under the same property rights structure. For a similar differentiation between "economic mechanism" and "economic policy," see Kornai 1989: 100.

12. I am following Sun Shangqing, vice director of the State Council's Research Center for Economic, Technological, and Social Development, in classifying Wu Jinglian and Zhou Xiaochuan as major representatives of the price reform school (see Sun 1988).

13. The two tasks set by the plenum were originally proposed by Liu Guoguang from the Chinese Academy of Social Sciences. Liu is a major economic advisor to Li Peng (*People's Daily*, Oct. 1, 1988; *World Journal*, Mar. 3, 1989).

14. For a thorough discussion of the causes of inflation in the PRC, see Holz 1992.

15. Extra-plan pricing had existed in the PRC before the 1984 industrial reform. There had always been a variety of transactions between regions and enterprises outside the planning system at prices higher than the planned level. There had also been a large number of small, inefficient industrial enterprises, set up to absorb surplus labor crowded out of farming due to the scarcity of arable land, that could sell their products at higher prices in order to cover higher costs. However, the dual pricing system was recognized, legalized, and expanded only after the 1984 reform. In May 1984, the State Council issued the Ten Regulations expanding the decision-making power of state enterprises. The Ten Regulations recognized the existence of a planned and a non-planned economy, state allocation of materials and free purchase by individual enterprises, and state-fixed and floating prices (ranging up to 20 percent higher or lower than state prices). In February 1985, the State Price Administration and the State Materials Administration jointly canceled the 20 percent limit and formally installed the dual pricing system (Wu and Zhao 1987).

16. The number of small private businesses, or *getihu*, dropped from 14.5 million at the end of 1988 to 12.4 million at the beginning of 1990, forcing the state to reconsider its policy toward this sector of the economy, which had a great deal of potential for absorbing the unemployment caused by the austerity program (*World Journal*, Mar. 12, 1990).

17. Two prominent entrepreneurs left the PRC after the June 4th crackdown, one for political, the other for economic, reasons. Wan Runnan, former general manager of the Sitong Group (Stone Corporation), based in Beijing, directly supported the students in the democracy movement and managed to flee mainland China after the massacre. Wan then became secretary general of the Front for a Democratic China (FDC), a Paris-based umbrella organization for Chinese democracy movements worldwide founded in September 1989. Deng Shaoshen, former general manager of the Guangzhou-based Wanbao Group, also left the PRC and settled in the U.S. in November 1989. Wan symbolizes the link between emerging entrepreneurs and the democracy movement. He is under political attack by the party. Deng represents the prosperous businesspeople in the south who can tolerate political suppression but are not willing to stand the squeeze put on private enterprises by the state. Sitong is the leading computer company in the PRC, and Wanbao is the top producer of household electronics. They

are two of four pilot enterprise groups (*shidian jituan*) approved by the State Council to spearhead the industrial reform.

18. For a discussion of the importance of the state sector in industry and the competition between it and the emerging non-state sector, and between their respective supporters in the central bureaucracies and in the provinces, see White 1993; Shirk 1985.

19. For the full text of the remarks on reform Deng made during his 1992 southern inspection tours, see Deng 1992.

20. For a thorough discussion of reformers' flexible approach as epitomized in Zhao Ziyang's strategy, see Shirk 1988.

21. Alec Nove is one of those economists studying socialist systems who are sensitive to the noneconomic factors the elite take into consideration when making major economic decisions. He points out political and social rationalities and suggests that an economically "optimum route" may prove counterproductive politically or socially. He recognizes that the party must somehow seek to reconcile its power functions with efficiency, which is essential if the aims of the party's own policies are to be effectively realized. He thus describes the party as having a split personality. Nove does not concern himself, as I do here, with seeking a common denominator for the various considerations and rationalities of the elite. See Nove 1964.

Chapter 3

1. There is a growing recent literature on comparative market reform in state socialism inspired by the similar experiences of Hungary and the PRC. See, for example, Balassa (1987), Hare (1988), Van Ness (1989), and especially Stark and Nee (1989), who provide a theoretical framework for comparing economic institutions in reforming state socialism.

2. The most systematic exposition of the stage theory of Leninist development is that made by Ken Jowitt (1975, 1983). Most scholars of comparative communism will at least agree that there is a historical shift from totalitarian to postrevolutionary regimes (Johnson 1970; Lowenthal 1970; Montias 1970).

3. Deng was CCP general secretary in 1957. At the Third Plenum of the Eighth Central Committee in September of that year, he gave a report in which he claimed that the thought transformation of Chinese intellectuals would take ten more years (Chang 1989: 31). His attitude toward the Campaign did not change after his second rehabilitation in 1977 (Deng 1984: 279).

4. The term "socialist enlightened absolutism" was coined by the famous Polish economic reformer Wlodzimierz Brus in his discussion of Kadarism (Brus 1980: 50).

5. The new electoral law of 1966 permitted multi-candidate elections and broadened the process of nominating candidates to include nominations from organizations other than local party cells. By 1971, 49 out of 352 electoral districts had two candidates on the ballot, giving 15 percent of the population a choice (Volgyes 1973: 217).

6. In 1972, Andras Hegedus, Agnes Heller, and Mihaly Vajda were expelled from the party and dismissed from their jobs at the Hungarian Acad-

emy of Sciences because their views on modernization were identified with
both "petty bourgeois revisionism" and the New Left. In 1973 and 1974,
writer Miklos Haraszti was tried on charges of slandering the state and fal-
sifying conditions in a tractor factory, the locale of his novel *Darabber*
(Piecework). In 1974, sociologists Gyorgy Konrad and Ivan Szelenyi were
arrested and harassed because of their views about the processes of development the state would follow in the future. As a result, Szelenyi was "advised" to emigrate to the West (Volgyes 1976: 107; Gati 1974: 24).

7. Hua resigned the premiership at the Third Session of the Fifth National People's Congress in September 1980, and resigned the party chairmanship as well as the chairmanship of the CCP Military Commission at
the Sixth Plenum of the Eleventh Central Committee in June 1981.

8. The document was the "Resolution on Certain Questions in the
History of Our Party Since the Founding of the People's Republic of China."
It severely attacked Mao's theory of "continued revolution under the dictatorship of the proletariat," claimed that there were no grounds at all for
defining the cultural revolution as "a struggle against the revisionist line or
the capitalist road," urged "emancipating the mind" and "seeking truth
from facts," and upheld the Four Insistences: "the socialist road, the people's democratic dictatorship, the leadership of the Communist Party, and
Marxism-Leninism and Mao Zedong Thought." It declared that "after socialist transformation was fundamentally completed, the principal contradiction our country has had to resolve is that between the growing material
and cultural needs of the people and the backwardness of social production," and "all our Party work must be subordinated to and serve this central task—economic construction" (*Beijing Review*, July 6, 1981, pp. 10–
39).

9. A difference between the economic difficulties the two countries
faced before reform began was that Hungary, a small and trade-dependent
country, had developed balance-of-payments problems that had to be re-
solved, whereas China, after decades of economic autarky, was much less
vulnerable to trade imbalances (Hare 1988; Nyers 1983).

10. Similar distinctions are made by Morris Bornstein (1977), Tamas
Bauer (1987–88), and Jan Prybyla (1990). The forerunner of marketization
reform was Yugoslavia in the 1950's. Then came a redistribution of resources to the consumption sector (not to the extent of overtaking heavy
industry) in the immediate post-Stalin period in all of Eastern Europe, followed by administrative reforms in the German Democratic Republic
(GDR), the Soviet Union, and Bulgaria in the 1960's. In the late 1960's,
Czechoslovakia and Hungary launched similar marketization reforms. The
Prague Spring ended abruptly because the Czechoslovak reform spread to
the political realm and went beyond what the Soviet Union would tolerate.
The 1970's witnessed more administrative and technical reforms, such as
the GDR's *Kombinate* (Koziolek 1987–88), but were primarily characterized by heavy borrowing by Eastern European countries, as a substitute for
domestic reform, and the accumulation of huge foreign debts, though marketization gained an additional stronghold in the PRC at the end of the decade. The international financial crises of the early 1980's engulfed all the
debt-ridden countries in Eastern Europe and forced them into austerity,

without changing the established patterns of perfecting versus marketizing that these countries had been following. Finally, the democracy movement that swept the Soviet Union and Eastern Europe in 1989 set in motion radical economic reforms that aim not only at marketization, but privatization.

11. Hungarian agriculture was collectivized during the First Five-Year Plan period (1949–53). The following two Nagy governments (1953–55, 1956) reversed the trend by making membership in agricultural cooperatives voluntary. The 1956 uprising and its aftermath produced severe setbacks for collectivized agriculture, with 63 percent of the cooperatives dissolved in November and December of that year. A recollectivization campaign was launched between 1958 and 1961. By 1962, 92.5 percent of Hungary's arable land was in the socialist sector (Marrese 1983; Toma and Volgyes 1977: 17).

12. As a result of successful agricultural reform, a prosperous kulak class emerged in both countries. In the mid-1970's, more than 30 percent of the active and working peasantry in Hungary earned more than 10,000 forints per month per household, entitling them to membership in the new "middle class" (Volgyes 1976). Similarly, a group of *wanyuanhu* (ten-thousand-yuan households) emerged in the PRC.

13. The Hungarians did not decollectivize their agriculture, but modified its property rights structure and invested heavily in it (Marrese 1983). Their Chinese counterparts, however, dramatically cut state investment in agriculture and depended on a more radical property rights reform to stimulate agricultural production. The one-time stimulus provided by this radical institutional change peaked in 1984, when a record grain harvest was registered. This was followed by years of drops in grain production as the state failed to provide sufficient factors of production for agriculture (Fewsmith 1988).

14. The more liberal attitude of the Chinese reformers in this respect may be traced back to the fact that the totalitarian period in mainland China was quite protracted as compared with the Hungarians' much shorter experience with high totalitarianism. The artificially sustained revolution under Mao intensified the alienation of the population, the victimization of the elite, and the urgent need to save the economy through radical reform measures. As a result, agricultural reform gained momentum right after Deng Xiaoping's political ascendancy in 1978, and it took the form of both marketization and privatization. In contrast, Hungarian agricultural reform was not initiated until three years after the defeat of the dogmatists, and it took the form of market socialism, i.e., marketization without privatization.

15. What the Hungarians called "regulators" the Chinese referred to as "levers" (*ganggan*). State ownership suggests limits on the industrial reform in categories A and B in Table 3. Circumscribed markets show an incomplete reform in category C. Monopolies are defects in category D. Economic regulators or levers are the reserved powers at the state's hands in the four categories.

16. For the Hungarian incentive system, see Portes 1970. For the Chinese "tax for profit" formula, see Naughton 1985.

17. The overdue ownership reform in Hungary in the 1980's produced an array of ownership forms for which one can easily find counterparts in the PRC. There were small-scale private enterprises in the service industry and in manufacturing, and retail shops were leased or contracted out to private individuals. But one can also find uniquely Hungarian phenomena, such as the Enterprise Business Work Partnerships (EBWPs). The EBWPs are groups of workers subcontracting a part of the operations of their parent enterprises. They use enterprise assets and materials, pay a fee for them, and keep what remains as profit (Prybyla 1986). This innovation co-opts the widespread illegal practices of workers who use enterprise facilities during regular work hours for private benefit. It also bypasses wage restrictions designed by the state to prevent the extravagant use of wage increases and bonuses that is associated with a soft budget constraint. Most important of all, however, is the fact that the EBWPs create a part-time contract responsibility system (to use the Chinese term) within the socialist enterprises. The EBWP members are normal workers during regular hours and subcontractors after work. This suggests a more cautious move toward ownership reform than that observed in the PRC.

18. In 1968, about 30 percent of the total interenterprise turnover of raw materials and unfinished goods was transacted at fixed prices, 40 percent at prices subject to maxima or other limits, and 30 percent at free-market prices. The corresponding figures for purchase prices paid by producers for finished goods were 3 percent, 19 percent, and 78 percent; for consumer prices, 20 percent, 57 percent, and 23 percent (the latter rose to 30 percent in 1969) (Portes 1970: 308).

19. In the Hungarian case, part of these remaining state controls were considered "brakes" that permitted central authorities to intervene in the economy in order to stave off economic and political upheaval and that then could be released as the reform progressed. In fact, the brakes were not released in 1971 as promised. On the contrary, central intervention was increased toward the end of the first NEM reform.

20. Janos Kornai called mandatory planning (direct bureaucratic control) "coordination Mechanism 1A," guidance planning (indirect bureaucratic control) "Mechanism 1B," and the self-regulating market "Mechanism 2." The Hungarian reform shifted the dominant mode of coordination from Mechanism 1A to Mechanism 1B. The proposed shift to Mechanism 2 never materialized. This set of concepts corresponds with the usage here, except that for Kornai Mechanism 1B is not market coordination, and that market socialism applies pure market coordination of Mechanism 2 (Kornai 1989: 78). I agree with Peter Van Ness (1989: 6), who feels that Kornai's definition is too restrictive.

21. That inflation and income differentiation are the two major reasons for opposition to market reform is clearly indicated by Kornai in "Some Lessons from the Hungarian Experience for Chinese Reformers" (Kornai 1989).

22. Between 1959 and 1965, several piecemeal measures were introduced that included the creation of a four-tier pricing system, a shift of power from the ministries to the trusts, a reordering of industrial priorities,

the adoption of quality norms, and the introduction of a new profit-sharing system. They were policy changes and were not comparable to the structural reform of 1968.

23. The NEM created a complicated incentive system. From gross revenues were deducted costs, which included materials, wages, depreciation, payroll tax, capital charges (in 1968, paid only on assets owned by the enterprise, i.e., not financed by credit), and interest on short- and long-term credit. The enterprise then paid a further tax on gross revenues or subsidies received. The resulting amount was taxable profit. This was divided into development and sharing portions in proportion to the capital/labor ratio of the enterprise. The former was taxed at 60 percent, the latter progressively, leaving the development and sharing funds. A small part of each went into a reserve fund. The enterprise could use the remainder of the development fund (plus 60 percent of depreciation allowances, on average) to expand fixed and working capital, while the sharing fund financed welfare expenditures and cash distributions to workers and staff. The rules governing these distributions made them a very substantial part of the income of executives (including directors and deputies) and higher-level technical employees, but a much smaller part of manual worker income, since wages were taken off revenues as costs before the sharing fund was created. The average wage control system deducted wage increases above the 1967 level from the sharing fund, thus forcing managers to keep the average wage level low and seek cheap labor: a measure to combat cost inflation and unemployment, since managerial rewards were tied to the sharing fund (Portes 1970).

24. In 1970, wages paid to newly hired workers were deducted from the sharing fund. In 1971, the sharing fund was cut back by increased taxes on profits and a new levy on wage increases. In 1976, a 35 percent wage tax and a steep progressive tax on the sharing fund were imposed to prevent rapid increases in personal income. Also in 1976, four forms of wage control were institutionalized: relative wage level control, relative wage bill control, central wage level control, and central wage bill control. In 1985, progressive taxation on the levels of individual employee earnings, rather than on the increases in average earnings, was introduced, allowing enterprises to decide on earnings levels and increases on a worker-by-worker basis, without worrying about the effects of these choices on the overall increase in earnings. Only if the overall increase exceeded the increase in value added would another tax be paid in addition to the taxes based on earnings (Buky 1972: 35; Hewett 1980: 511; Marrese 1981: 68–69).

25. The increase in the inflation rate following the first-wave industrial reform mainly had to do with the regime's attempt to use price increases to suppress domestic consumption for the purpose of imposing austerity. It did not suggest any ineffectiveness of the wage control mechanism.

26. The annual growth rate of labor productivity in industry immediately after the introduction of the NEM was 0.9 percent for 1968 and 0.3 percent for 1969, compared with an average growth rate of 4.6 percent for the pre-reform years 1960–67 (Marrese 1981).

27. This has become conventional wisdom among reformers in the 1990's; witness the unsuccessful move by the Soviet government in early 1991 to soak up excess rubles before introducing a price reform.

28. Under *caizheng baogan*, provinces are responsible for collecting a tax quota to be delivered to the center, and they enjoy free disposition of any above-quota tax revenues. This system not only fueled inflation by encouraging provincial governments to prompt the enterprises within their jurisdictions to expand, it also made the provinces more financially independent and exacerbated regionalism. At the Fifth Plenum of the Thirteenth Central Committee in November 1989, central planners tried to replace *caizheng baogan* with a new "tax sharing" system that would strengthen Beijing's financial control over the provinces. This plan was strongly opposed by the provinces and was not put into effect then.

29. The extra-budget portion of state enterprises' total investment had been increasing since the 1960's. The reform accelerated this trend. Also, there was investment made by the non-state sector, especially rural industry, that completely escaped state budgetary control (Perkins 1988: 617).

30. A bonus system was introduced after 1978 to replace the egalitarian practice of "eating from the same big pot" (providing practically equal wages to every worker regardless of productivity). However, bonuses were often provided indiscriminately to all workers, even in the absence of profits, thereby contributing to general wage increases. In May 1984, the government imposed a special tax on enterprises for excess bonuses (30 percent on bonuses equal to two and a half to four months' wages; 100 percent on bonuses equal to four to six months' wages; and 300 percent on bonuses equal to more than 6 months' wages). Also, the government announced a tax on future increases in wages and bonuses beyond their 1984 levels. As a result, enterprises began to raise base wages to escape the bonus tax and to establish a high base for 1984. The total wage bill of enterprises rose by 21.3 percent in 1984 and 22 percent in 1985, compared with 6 percent in 1983 (Balassa 1987: 422; Y. Li 1989: 657).

31. Although the income position of Chinese manual laborers relative to other social strata did not constitute the primary reason for reversal of the reform, as was the case in Hungary in the early 1970's, inequality brought about by economic reform did create social tension in two areas: the income differentiation between eastern and western provinces, and the relative deprivation of administrative employees and intellectual workers. Historically, the coastal provinces of China had been much more developed than the inland, a trend artificially suppressed by Mao's egalitarian policies and economic autarky. Shanghai was a typical case of development in coastal China: until 1949 it was the country's largest and most developed metropolitan area; later it took a diametrically opposite role as the base for ultraleftist radicals during the Cultural Revolution period, when its development stagnated. The open-door policies of the late 1970's and the "golden coast" strategy in the late 1980's dramatically changed this situation and widened the east-west gap by granting more autonomy to the coastal provinces that enjoyed proximity to the world market, superiority in infrastructure, higher levels of education, and links to overseas Chinese.

Under the policy of "permitting a part of the people to become prosperous before the rest," two Chinas emerged. The eleven western provinces and territories, with 300 million of the country's 1.1 billion people, produced only 17 percent of the 1987 GNP of US$293 billion. The ten provinces and municipalities in the east, with 360 million people, accounted for a remarkable 53 percent. In order to redress this interregional imbalance, central planners attempted to shift from an industrial policy that favored particular regions to one favoring specific industries during the Eighth Five-Year Plan period (1991–95). Another prominent income disparity was that between urban residents with fixed incomes and those actively involved in economic activities. The state's policy, with its loose wage control and large bonuses, favored production workers over administrative employees and intellectual workers, who received no bonuses to offset price increases and saw their income position deteriorating not only against that of production workers, but against those of rich peasants and private entrepreneurs (Naughton 1986). In 1978, state workers in knowledge-intensive occupations earned an average of 2 percent more than manual workers; by 1986, manual workers earned an average of 10 percent more than administrative or intellectual workers (Prybyla 1989: 6). However, this economically underprivileged group, particularly those in academic positions, enjoyed a relaxed intellectual climate in which they could easily find outlets for their dissatisfaction. The student demonstrations in 1986–87 and 1989 were directly related to this economic condition.

32. Low import levels reduce competition on the domestic market and deprive developing companies of needed inputs, while the stress on exports makes officials reluctant to allow any firm that exports to the West to close, no matter how inefficient its production. Many of these exporting companies are producers of raw materials and semi-finished goods that account for almost 50 percent of hard-currency earnings and are heavily subsidized by the state, which in turn not only taxes other companies more heavily, but also borrows from abroad to finance its budget deficit.

Chapter 4

1. A comparison of the Soviet Union in the 1920's and the PRC in the latter half of the 1980's, distant as the two cases are from each other in terms of time, actually enjoys advantages that comparisons involving either with other socialist countries cannot provide. Both countries are large in size and have a comparable degree of local complexity. Their regimes are highly autonomous, with leaders' decisions based on their values, perceptions, and the balance of internal forces. No one can dictate to a Stalin or a Deng. Finally, and most important, the degrees of development of the two countries in terms of employment distribution are highly comparable. Both are huge developing countries where peasants constitute 80 percent of the population. Size, autonomy, and the degree of development add to the original similarities in the political and economic structures of the two countries (a Leninist party, private agriculture, state control of the economic "commanding heights") to make a meaningful framework for the comparison undertaken here.

2. On the question of whether War Communism started right after the October Revolution or was preceded by a hiatus from November 1917 to the middle of 1918, see Meyer 1972: 192; Nove 1982: 46.

3. Many of these measures were forced on the Bolsheviks by the civil war and were modeled on the wartime planning experiences of imperial Germany (Silverman 1972: 20). In this sense, they were merely temporary policies and had nothing to do with the realization of the ultimate goals of the revolution. But the Russian term *voennyi kommunizm* was also understood as "militant communism," which implies that the regime was sincere in its professed intention to introduce communism with one stroke through militant radicalism (Meyer 1972: 193). In a reflection of the ambiguity of the term, opinions among the Bolsheviks on the proper strategy for the party at the time were divided, with Lenin on the practical side (but not without a utopian fervor) and Bukharin carried away by the spirit of civil war (Moore 1965). For a discussion of to what degree War Communism was due to the drive to remake society and to what degree to improvisations provoked by the demands of civil war, see Roberts 1970.

4. The value system of an ideology is different from its belief system. In this study, ideology is defined as a behavior-oriented thought system composed of a set of interrelated belief system, value system, and operational program, the purpose of which is to sustain or undermine the established order of the society. Ideology thus has cognitive, evaluative, and prescriptive functions (Mullins 1972: 510). A belief system is made up of idea units that contain factual judgments. A value system is composed of idea units carrying value judgments. Different degrees of intensity are assigned to different idea units (Kelly and Fleron 1971: 57–59), making them more or less resistant to conflicting ideas. One can speak of the "openness" of a system, the readiness with which new messages can be processed and integrated into it (Lane 1970: 66). The distinction between belief and value systems is not consciously observed by an individual, though it serves an important analytical purpose. An operational program is composed of a series of instructions designed to achieve certain goals under specific conditions. It is derived from the interaction between the belief and value systems. The belief system, value system, and operational program are universal psychological constructs that are necessary in order for individuals to take goal-oriented action. The uniqueness of ideology is that it provides a coherent set of the three systems in an effort to preoccupy the mind of a believer. The function of an ideology is to direct the behavior of individuals either to support or to destroy the established social order. Because of its internal coherence and lack of openness to new messages, an ideology sometimes has to change, as when the empirical world produces overwhelming evidence against its most treasured beliefs. But the value commitments in the ideology do not have to change correspondingly. This situation leads to the designing of a new operational program that aims at the same goal under the new set of circumstances. An ideology can also change if its main goal deteriorates, as can happen when the experience of putting the ideology into practice proves disillusioning. In this case, the value system is undermined, but the belief system remains intact. People may still rely on the image of the world provided by the old doctrine to guide their

actions, albeit toward a different set of goals. One may observe different rates of deterioration for the beliefs and values contained in an ideology (the operational program, as a derivative of the interaction between the belief and value systems, changes with the two). There is a huge body of literature on ideology. For the historical root of the concept, see Duverger 1977: 74; Baradat 1979; and Cox 1969: 10, 14. For Marx's definition of ideology, see Marx in Tucker 1978: 4, 149, 172; see also Kelsen 1955 and McCarney 1980. For Mannheim and his science of ideology, or sociology of knowledge, see Mannheim 1936: 1970; Connolly 1967; and Feuer 1975: 184. For the Communist concept of ideology, see Lenin 1953: 355; *Bol'shaya Sovetskaya Entsiklopedia*, 1952, 17: 333–34 and 1973, 17: 39–41; Yakhot 1979; Scanlan 1981; and *Jianming Zhexue Cidan*, 1955, p. 331. For Western definitions of the concept and its relation to cognitive psychology, see Lane 1962; Shils 1968; H. Johnson 1968; Mullins 1972; Rokeach 1960: 33; Converse 1967; Kelly and Fleron 1971; and Geertz 1967. For the function of ideology, see Lasswell and Kaplan 1961: 76; Plamenatz 1970: 72; Macridis 1980: 69; Schurmann 1968: 18; Gyorgy and Blackwood 1967: 6; and Lane 1970: 62.

5. For a discussion of the literature on the postrevolutionary stage, see Meaney 1987.

6. "Democratic centralism" was proposed by Lenin in 1906 as the organizational principle of the Social Democratic Labor Party (later the Communist Party of the Soviet Union). The Fourth Congress of the party adopted that principle in the same year. Since then "democratic centralism" has been hailed as the party's guiding principle. In practice, under Lenin this meant full discussions among top party leaders (in which Lenin usually prevailed) and maximum discipline once decisions had been made (not without exceptions, e.g., the actions taken by Grigorii Zinoviev and Lev Kamenev against the Central Committee's November 1917 decision to establish one-party rule). The result was an oligarchy with a *prima inter pares*.

7. One can use a conceptual continuum to locate the desired degree of concentration of power proposed or practiced by major actors in the international socialist movement. The "revisionists" of the Second International, such as Eduard Bernstein, envisioned democratic socialism and supported the democratic institutions of their time as vehicles with which to introduce socialist measures (Kolakowski 1981a: 101). They were in favor of democracy for all political parties and classes. The deeds, if not the words, of the "centrists," notably Karl Kautsky, coincided with the "revisionist" stance (Kolakowski 1981a: 46). The true believers in Marx's "dictatorship of the proletariat," such as Rosa Luxemburg, believed in multiple socialist parties competing in a democratic way, to the exclusion of capitalist parties (Luxemburg in Silverman 1972: 140). Lenin argued for a further concentration of political power by equating dictatorship of the proletariat with one-party rule by the Bolsheviks. In practice, he excluded other socialist parties, such as the Socialist Revolutionaries and the Mensheviks, from the political scene as early as 1918 (Hough and Fainsod 1979: 84). Finally, Stalin put himself above the party and established absolute personal rule. Thus, one can see a steady increase in the concentration of political power from "bourgeois" democracy to dictatorship of the proletariat, one-party

rule, and finally one-man rule. During the NEP period, the Soviet Union was gradually moving from one-party rule (a principle endorsed by all Bolsheviks) to one-man rule. China under Deng, on the other hand, was moving in the opposite direction, from one-man rule to one-party rule (i.e., to an oligarchy with a *prima inter pares*).

8. Lenin and the Central Committee were attacked by the Military Opposition (which opposed employing former tsarist officers and restoring military discipline) at the Eighth Party Congress in 1919; by the Democratic Centralists (who were against the practice of concentrating power in the center and dispatching oppositionists to distant places) at the Ninth Congress in 1920; and by the Workers' Opposition (which supported autonomy for the trade unions and opposed one-man management) at the Tenth Congress in 1921.

9. The disillusionment of Western observers with CCP leaders' professed interest in and efforts at establishing socialist legality was expressed by Anthony Dicks in his postscript to "The Chinese Legal System: Reforms in Balance," which was written before the Tiananmen massacre. There he noted that "the foregoing article can only serve as a high water mark, indicating the level which the legal developments reached before the tide of reform so rapidly ran out" (Dicks 1989: 576). However, one might argue that it was never the intention of the Chinese leadership to constrain its own actions against political challenges to its authoritarian rule with established legal procedures. It is worth noting that right before the crackdown, there was an appeal to replace the category of "counterrevolutionary crimes" in the Criminal Law (adopted in June 1979, 30 years after the revolution) with "the crime of violating the interests of the state" (Dicks 1989: 573). After the crackdown, "counterrevolution" as a crime regained prominence.

10. At the Third Annual Meeting of the Seventh People's Congress in March 1990, Deng resigned from his last important position, that of chairman of the State Military Commission, a move corresponding to his resignation from the chairmanship of the party's Military Commission at the Fifth Plenum of the Thirteenth Central Committee in November 1989.

11. A good example of this is Deng's attitude toward the Central Advisory Commission, a party organ created at the Twelfth Party Congress in 1982. Deng's original intention was to use this commission to retire old cadres. However, he found the conservatives there useful when he decided to purge Hu Yaobang (in 1987) and Zhao Ziyang (in 1989). The ranking members of the Advisory Commission were then invited to attend the enlarged politburo meetings at which critical decisions were made. After Jiang Zemin was designated successor to Deng following the June Fourth Incident, the Central Advisory Commission became a potential threat to Jiang's position. Deng therefore maneuvered to abolish the Advisory Commission at the Fourteenth Party Congress in October 1992.

12. The system of class designation was artificially maintained under Mao after the material basis of the classes had disappeared, i.e., with socialization of the means of production in the 1950's. Class status accompanied each individual in every aspect of life, providing advantages and disadvantages that had a leveling effect on the society as a whole. The system was abolished only in 1979 (Dicks 1989: 547).

13. Hua Guofeng continues to be a member of the Central Committee despite his purge. Hu Yaobang remained a member of the politburo until his death. Zhao Ziyang was charged with "supporting the riot and dividing the party," but as of the Fourteenth Party Congress in 1992, his fate was not yet sealed. Many old cadres, such as Ye Jianying and Peng Zhen, were forced to retire unwillingly, although the latter managed to participate in central decision making without any official position during and after the 1989 Tiananmen incident.

14. On the way in which the 1983 Campaign Against Spiritual Pollution was kept out of agriculture, industry, and technology, and conservatives, notably Hu Qiaomu (then director of the party's Propaganda Department), were forced to compromise under pressure from Deng and Hu Yaobang, see Chang 1989: 28; Merle Goldman 1985: 22. On the way in which the Anti–Bourgeois Liberalization Movement was diverted from its initial struggle against the right to one against the left after Zhao Ziyang's talk on May 13, 1987, and on how Zhao had received Deng's endorsement for his talk beforehand, see *World Journal*, Mar. 22, 1990.

15. For example, the expulsion of Fang Lizhi, Liu Binyan, and Wang Ruowang from the party during the Anti–Bourgeois Liberalization Movement in 1987 was aimed at satisfying conservatives in the cultural field while reformers were allowed to recapture the initiative on the economic and political fronts, as witnessed by the reform-oriented Thirteenth Party Congress held later that year.

16. The regime attached great importance to agriculture, as evidenced by the resolution of the Twelfth Party Congress, held in April 1923, which stated: "Agriculture, although it is still on a low technical level, plays the dominant role in the economy of the U.S.S.R. . . . Our party must not forget . . . the virtual preponderance of the peasant economy. . . . Agriculture will for a long time remain the basis of the economy of the U.S.S.R." (Jasny 1972: 19).

17. From 1923 on, the government expanded the state and cooperative network at an increasing rate, and its share of the trade turnover rose continuously at the expense of the Nepmen. In 1922–23, private enterprises' share of all retail trade was 78 percent. This share fell to 57.7 percent in 1923–24, 42.5 percent in 1924–25, 42.3 percent in 1925–26, and 36.9 percent in 1926–27 (Nove 1982: 103).

18. Lenin's attempt during War Communism to abolish money is called "authority without prices" by Charles Lindblom in his six-category classification of nonmarket and market systems. "Authority without prices" is the extreme form of authoritarian organization that makes physical allocations without prices, money, and markets (Lindblom 1977: 105).

19. Several measures have been taken to reform the banking system. In 1982, the Bank of Agriculture and the Bank of China were freed from direct subordination to the State Council. In 1983, the PBC was designated the central bank of China, and the mechanisms of central banking were gradually installed. Power over personnel in local branches has been transferred from local governments to the banks. For all these reform measures, the PBC is still directly under the control of the State Council and is obligated to fund state deficits, and local branches are still under pressure from local governments to extend soft credit to enterprises within their jurisdictions.

20. The significance of the PRC's openness to the outside world will be discussed fully when we move to the comparison between mainland China and Taiwan in Chapter 5.

21. The heads of the households in the *mir* decided how to allot the land—for example, by periodically redistributing strips of land within a three-field system—and collectively bore the responsibility for paying taxes and redemption dues.

22. The KMT did, however, carry out a successful land reform in Taiwan at about the time the Communists were redistributing land on the mainland.

23. There are three theories about how the household responsibility system came to dominate the agricultural reform. The first stresses the role of central reformers in employing the usual mechanisms of control to make a reluctant peasantry accept the system. The second emphasizes the spontaneity of peasants in influencing high-level authorities to endorse the system the peasants desired. The third theory is a synthetic one that differentiates between the initiation and implementation stages of the reform: local people initiated, the state implemented. This theory recognizes that different ecological settings, cropping patterns, procurement quotas, and commercial opportunities all made a difference in peasants' response to reform. Thus, for example, the rice farmers in the south were enthusiastic about family farming, while the peasants in the North China Plain and Manchuria were more committed to collectivism and were reluctant to adopt the household responsibility system. The reform-minded farmers initiated the change from below. The state then recognized the utility of the new pattern, and a national policy to install the system was implemented, in many cases against the will of those peasants not attracted by the reform. For the theory of state-led reform, see Unger 1986; Hartford 1985. For the peasant-led version, see Tang 1988. For the synthetic theory, see Kelliher 1992.

24. The hardening of the budget constraint is, of course, only one aspect of the link between performance and retained profits (see Table 3). It suggests that economic units are taking financial responsibility for their performance on the market and the state is refraining from benevolent intervention. The other aspect is the absence of excessive and precarious taxation. Rich Chinese peasants, the ten-thousand-yuan households, were harassed by jealous rural cadres and suffered encroachments on their income power (*People's Daily*, Aug. 17, 1985). The dampening effect this had on their profit motive is obvious, but its severity is hard to gauge. Nevertheless, under the new system the link between performance and reward was strengthened enough that motivational efficiency increased dramatically. It was estimated that the incentives provided by the transfer of income power to individual households accounted for three-quarters of all the gains in agricultural productivity between 1978 and 1984. The higher procurement prices paid by the state explained the rest of those gains.

25. Central Document No. 1 of 1984 stipulated the length of the land tenure. In most cases, lands were allocated for household responsibility for a period of fifteen years. When a large initial investment is required to bring the land into production—as in the case of wasteland—contracts stipulate longer terms.

26. By 1983, procurement prices for grains exceeded their 1977 levels by 15 to 20 percent, those for oilseeds by 27 percent, for sugar by 26 percent, for cotton by 30 percent, and for hogs by 27 percent (Sicular 1991: 347). In 1981, state subsidies for agricultural products were 25 billion yuan, nearly one-quarter of annual state revenues (Harding 1987: 103).

27. The abolition of the compulsory procurement system was considered by some to be only a gesture, not an actuality, because later declines in production and deliveries led the regime to back away from the 1985 reform and turned voluntary contracts for grain into mandatory obligations. On the other hand, some hailed the 1985 initiatives as a decisive step toward liberalization in agriculture. For the first opinion, see Sicular 1992; for the second, see Shirk 1988.

28. Lands were allotted to households on a per capita or per laborer basis (Croll 1988a). In order to ensure fairness, each production team first ranked all of its fields according to fertility. Plots of different grades were then distributed equally among the households (the specific plots allocated to each household were determined by lottery). As a result, every family received several small scattered plots of different grades.

29. Leon Trotsky, Evgeni Preobrazhensky, and (later) Kamenev and Zinoviev took the Leftist stance in the 1920's. Among the top Bolshevik leaders, Bukharin, Mikhail Tomsky, and Aleksei Rykov took the Rightist position. Bukharin was the main theorist of the NEP. He developed the themes of Lenin's last writings and did an about-face in his own position, going from being an extreme Leftist who opposed the Treaty of Brest-Litovsk and pressed for thorough nationalization and total state control of the economy, to being the most fervent advocate of Lenin's concessions to the peasants, the Nepmen, and foreign capitalists. From 1925 to 1927, Bukharin was Stalin's chief ideological supporter against the Leftist opposition. He parted with Stalin when the latter took an anti-peasant position toward the end of the NEP. Stephen Cohen and Moshe Lewin, both of whom reject the traditional interpretation of Soviet history (represented by, for example, Zbigniew Brzezinski, Adam B. Ulam, Merle Fainsod, and Leszek Kolakowski), which sees continuity between Bolshevism and Stalinism, consider Bukharin's program—one-party rule, cultural pluralism, and a mixed economy—to have been more in tune with the original doctrine of Bolshevism. For the revisionist school that Cohen and Lewin represent, Bukharinism was a viable long-term alternative for the Bolsheviks in the 1920's, while Stalinism was a deviation from the path that Lenin chose for the party. For the academic debate on continuity in Soviet history, see Cohen 1985; Tucker 1977.

30. The expectation of lower growth rates based on expanding fixed capital, rather than exploitation of the residue of resources left over from the previous phase, was expressed in the "diminishing curve" theory, an idea accepted by the Fifteenth Party Congress in 1927.

31. Hannah Arendt held the opposite opinion, namely that intervention from abroad was no longer a danger when, by 1930, the Soviet regime had been recognized by a majority of the world's governments and concluded commercial and other international agreements with many countries (Arendt 1968: 21). However, what matters was not whether there was a true immediate threat, but whether the regime that ultimately deter-

mined defense needs and the pace and direction of industrialization perceived such a threat.

32. During the 1920's, the Bolsheviks' perception of a threat and their defense needs were immediately related to defending the socialist revolution. Nationalist feelings were initially obscured—the regime's cosmopolitan outlook predominated during the early years of the Soviet Union—but they were to receive increasing emphasis as Stalin ascended to power. Stalin's ideas of "socialism in one country," formulated in 1924–25, already contained nationalist elements, but he did not openly stir nationalist feelings until his position was secure. Six years later, he explicitly stated:

To slacken the pace [of industrialization] would mean to lag behind; and those who lag behind are beaten. We do not want to be beaten . . . [Russia] was ceaselessly beaten for her backwardness. She was beaten by the Mongol Khans, she was beaten by Turkish Beys, she was beaten by Swedish feudal lords, she was beaten by Polish-Lithuanian Pans, she was beaten by Anglo-French capitalists, she was beaten by Japanese barons, she was beaten by all—for her backwardness. For military backwardness, for cultural backwardness, for political backwardness, for industrial backwardness, for agricultural backwardness. She was beaten because to beat her was profitable and went unpunished. You remember the words of the pre-revolutionary poet: "Thou art poor and thou art plentiful, thou art mighty and thou art helpless, Mother Russia." . . . We are fifty or a hundred years behind the advanced countries. We must make good this lag in ten years. Either we do it or they crush us. (Quoted in Deutscher 1949: 328)

This shift to a nationalist appeal to defend the motherland was evident during the First Five-Year Plan period, when the regime demanded tremendous sacrifices from the population.

33. The basic attitude of the regime in this regard was expressed clearly by Zhao Ziyang: "We are going to strengthen our national defense. However, we are not going to increase our military expenditure." Defense was given last priority in the Four Modernizations, and Li Peng listed as number ten in his ten priority tasks "the building of national defense as China's economy develops." See Kreisberg 1988.

34. General Secretary Jiang Zemin pointed out the danger of "peaceful evolution" on September 29, 1989, in his speech marking the 40th anniversary of the PRC:

Beginning in the late 1950s, after the failure of their military interventions, they [international reactionary forces] shifted the focus of their policy to "peaceful evolution." They adopt political, economic and cultural means to infiltrate and influence socialist countries, exploiting their temporary difficulties and reforms. They support and buy over so-called "dissidents" through whom they foster blind worship of the Western world and propagate the political and economic patterns, sense of values, decadent ideas and life-style of the Western capitalist world. When they feel there is an opportunity to be seized, they fabricate rumors, provoke incidents, plot turmoil, and engage in subversive activities against socialist countries. . . . The struggle between infiltration and counter-infiltration, subversion and counter-subversion, "peaceful evolution" and "counter–peaceful evolution" will last a long time. In this connection, people of all nationalities, and all Party members, especially leaders, must maintain a high degree of vigilance.

For Jiang's speech and a comparison between "peaceful evolution" and the regime's perception of a threat to "peaceful transformation" in the late 1950's and early 1960's, see Chang 1990.

35. For example, from 1958 to 1978, investment in heavy industry was ten times as high as in light industry (Lee 1983).

36. In his report to the Thirteenth Party Congress in 1987, Zhao Ziyang made this point crystal clear: "Today's world is characterized by a rapidly growing revolution in technology, increasingly intense market competition and a volatile political situation. We are faced with formidable and pressing challenges. If we do not recognize this and redouble our efforts, our country and our people may fall further behind in the world. History requires our generation and the next few generations of Chinese—Communist Party members first of all—to rouse themselves, unite as one, and do all they can to catch up" (Z. Zhao 1987).

37. Lenin himself offered this vision in his last article, "Better Fewer But Better": "If we shall see to it that the working class retains the leadership of the peasantry, we shall be able, by exercising the greatest possible parsimony in the economy of our state, to use everything we save to develop our large-scale machine industry, to develop electrification, the hydraulic extraction of peat, to finish the construction of Volkhovstroi, etc. In this, and in this alone lies our hope" (Lenin in Erlich 1967: 7).

38. Thus for Deng, "Whether the Party's line is conducive to the development of the productive forces . . . is the only arbiter of the correctiveness of this line" (Deng in Sullivan 1985: 77). And for Zhao, "Whatever measures are conducive to the development of our productive forces are what we want, which will be encouraged and permitted; whatever actions are necessary for developing our commodity economy will be adopted" (the "new two whatevers"; *Central Daily News*, Apr. 22, 1990). Deng's theory on the primacy of the productive forces (*wei shengchanli lun*) was heavily criticized by the Gang of Four in 1975 and contributed to his purge in 1976. Deng's political ascendance led to the adoption of *wei shengchanli lun* as an official doctrine. It was emphasized in Zhao's report to the Thirteenth Party Congress in October 1987 and in his "new two whatevers" (versus Hua's "two whatevers," which supported Mao's theories), proposed in February 1988. The retrenchment that began in the fall of 1988 and the political regimentation following the June Fourth Incident of 1989 diluted the regime's emphasis on the primacy of the productive forces. However, on Apr. 20, 1990, the *People's Daily* again advocated Zhao's "new two whatevers" (with only slight modifications in wording), thus reaffirming the regime's basic orientation. Finally, on Feb. 23, 1992, the *People's Daily* advised the nation to take advantage of useful capitalist practices and to recognize the fact that some form of exploitation will exist for a long period of time to come in socialist China.

39. After 1925, Bukharin recognized the danger of a resurgence of capitalism in the countryside and spoke of the need for changing the production relations of the economy. He said: "If there were a fall in the relative weight of the working class in its political and its social and class power . . . this would subvert the basis of the proletarian dictatorship, the basis of our government" (see Nove 1964: 21).

40. According to Lowenthal (1970: 45), in 1927, kulaks made up only 3.9 percent of the village population and accounted for 13 percent of the grain production.

41. The ten-thousand-yuan households are almost without exception

households headed by cadres or ex-cadres from production brigades or communes or young educated peasants and ex-servicemen who have developed managerial or technical skills, marketing ability, or personal networks (Croll 1988a: 89).

42. In the *Communist Manifesto*, Marx described peasants as conservative and reactionary because they wanted to turn back the clock of history. The father of Russian Marxism, Georgy Plekhanov, also characterized peasants as defenders of oriental despotism for thousands of years and as the political opposite to the revolutionary proletariat (Cheng Hsueh-chia 1976: 42). Karl Kautsky, the leading theorist of the Second International, analyzed the different roles played by peasants and industrial workers. For him, both classes wanted to move upward to the position of owners of the means of production. However, the industrial organization created by modern technology was such that the seizure of the means of production by workers in industry could only take a collective form, thus conforming to the ideal of socialism. On the other hand, it was physically possible for peasants to divide up the land and make themselves petty producers and small proprietors, hence perpetuating private property in the countryside. The result of a peasant revolution, if allowed to take its own course, would be simply a redistribution of land, not socialization of the means of production (Kautsky 1980). Herein lies the fundamental difference between the proletariat and the peasantry. Nevertheless, as Stalin later pointed out in *The Foundations of Leninism*, it was possible for peasants to become allies of the proletariat as long as their hunger for land disposed them against the old regime that the proletariat targeted as its major enemy at a particular historical juncture. But the basis of this alliance was destined to erode once peasants rose to the status of petty proprietors and the proletariat wanted to realize its socialist ideals.

43. For a different point of view on the calculations of the post-Mao leadership, see Friedman 1990.

44. The notion that economic power breeds political power is not a uniquely Marxist idea. For a typical Western theory on how money affects politics, see Charles Lindblom's theory of "circularity in polyarchy" (Lindblom 1977).

45. Preobrazhensky, the leading theorist of the Left, thus argued for rapid industrialization. For him, the principal task of a socialist state in its initial phase is to create a strong industrial base and ensure the necessary degree of capital accumulation. All other economic aims must be subordinate to this goal (Kolakowski 1981b). However, because Russia was still a "backward" country, capital accumulation could only be achieved by expropriation of the surplus production of the society, as under capitalism. This is Preobrazhensky's famous theory of "primitive socialist accumulation," in which he proposed to extract the maximum amount of surplus value from peasant labor in order to increase investment in industry.

46. The state's position in the countryside after the reform has been assessed in various ways. Some scholars (e.g., Croll [1988b]) emphasize that the Chinese peasantry is reemerging and its bargaining position against the state has been strengthened. Others (e.g., Kelliher [1986]) concede that the state has given up some of its power, but they believe it still firmly controls

the areas in which it has strategic interests. Finally, some scholars (e.g., Shue [1988]) argue that the state has ultimately gained more control as a result of the reform. I believe that state power has been eroded, not in the political field, but in the economic arena, and not because the state has been directly challenged by emerging forces in rural society, but because it has lost its efficacy in achieving particular state goals, such as controlling migration to the cities.

47. Gordon White (1987a) pictures three scenarios for China's future. The first is the triumph of rural capitalism and the disintegration of the socialist state. The second is recollectivization provoked by a heightened perception of threat to the regime. The third is what he calls "social capitalism," in which elements of a socialist state and a private rural economy complement each other. White asserts that the third scenario is the most likely. Put in a strictly political context, social capitalism is indeed more probable than the triumph of rural capitalism and recollectivization, given that up to the end of the 1980's there had not been a concrete political threat to the regime from rural capitalist forces, nor had there been a sense of crisis acute enough to plunge the regime into recollectivization to head off a political challenge. However, the lack of a political threat from the countryside does not guarantee that the regime will not roll back the reforms for nonpolitical reasons, a point that will be made clear in the following discussion.

48. The widening price divergence was only partly the result of the state's policy to lower the procurement price of grain. Other contributing factors included a much slower recovery rate for industry than for agriculture, the monopolistic position and lack of efficiency of state industry, and a costly distribution system (Nove 1982).

49. The ratio of the price index of industrial goods to that of farm produce was 1.61 in October 1922. It rose to 2.97 in October 1923, then dropped to 1.41 in October 1924 (Jasny 1972: 18).

50. The year 1926 witnessed an excellent grain harvest and marketing. From 1926 to 1928, the output of grain stagnated. This was clearly due to the unfavorable terms of trade of the Left price policy. In 1926–27, grain production was 76.6 million tons; it then declined slightly, to 73.3 million tons in 1927–28 and 71.7 million tons in 1928–29 (Lewin 1965: 163). Not only did production stagnate, the amount of grain brought to market also dropped. Whereas before the war more than 25 percent of the crop was marketed, in 1926–27 peasants disposed of only 13 percent of the crop in this way (Jasny 1972: 26).

51. Before the revolution, Russia had 16 million farms. By 1925, the number had risen to 25 million (Deutscher 1949: 303).

52. In the latter half of the 1980's, China's goal for grain production was 500 million tons annually. In 1984, actual production was only 407 million tons. It dropped to 379 million tons in 1985, rose to 391 in 1986 and 402 in 1987, then dropped again to 394 in 1988.

53. China's first baby boom occurred in the early and mid-1950's, when the birth rate reached 30 per 1,000 inhabitants. The second peak was in 1963, when the rate rose to 43 per 1,000. The current one started in 1985, as a natural extension of the second boom. The number of women between

the ages of 20 and 29 (the prime childbearing years) was 96 million in 1986. It reached 123 million by 1992. Despite harsh birth control measures and the one-child-per-couple policy, the birth rate reached 21.2 per 1,000 in 1987, and the population grew by more than 15 million in 1988 alone. The government has predicted that the population will reach 1.2 billion by the end of the century, but the present rate of increase puts the figure at 1.3 billion (the 1.1 billion mark was reached in April 1989). In general, this population growth presents a huge challenge to China's production capacity, one felt most immediately in grain production. China already supports 22 percent of the world's population on 7 percent of the world's arable land, and this ratio will continue to deteriorate into the next century (Hou 1990).

54. In order to stimulate agricultural production, the regime raised procurement prices considerably in the late 1970's. This act, together with the incentives provided by the household responsibility system, greatly improved the income position of peasants vis-à-vis industrial workers, who did not benefit from industrial reform until 1984. From 1985 on, however, with industrial reform taking effect in the cities and terms of trade deteriorating for the peasants, rural/urban income disparity widened again. In 1980, the average rural income was 44 percent of the average urban income. It rose to 54 percent in 1984 and then dropped to 46 percent in 1988.

55. It was estimated that at the beginning of 1984, 13 to 14 percent of all peasant households specialized in activities other than crop growing.

56. The infrastructure problem was caused by the drop in state and collective investment in agriculture and the inability and unwillingness of peasants to increase their investment. Peasants were unable to spend money on fixed assets because of the dispersion of capital that accompanied decollectivization. As small producers, they lacked the means to invest significantly in the agricultural infrastructure, and they were unwilling to invest what little they did have because the return prospects were slim. Not only did the time limits imposed on their property rights restrict their horizon, the unappropriable nature of public property also deterred them from investing in certain areas (notably irrigation).

57. A price reform was tried in May 1988, only to repeat the 1985 scenario on a larger scale. The disastrous result effectively excluded the market mechanism as a solution to the agricultural crisis. The state did manage to increase slightly the procurement prices for grain in 1989. However, because subsidies for agricultural products had reached 40 billion rmb in 1989, or roughly 13 percent of total state revenue, the ability of the government to continue absorbing the difference between procurement prices and urban consumer prices was limited. In 1990, some of the costs of agricultural subsidies were to be passed on to enterprises and administrative units in order to reduce the burden on the state treasury (*World Journal*, Mar. 29, 1990).

58. The average official grain purchase price increased by 21.9 percent in 1989, compared with 15.1 percent the previous year and 8 percent in 1987. Agriculture's share in state capital construction rose from 3.0 percent in 1988 to 3.3 percent in 1989 and 3.9 percent in 1990.

59. These arguments were seldom expressed openly, because they directly contradicted the cardinal principle of the Dengist reform. However,

the fact that reformers felt the need to express intensive criticism of such views indicates that restorationists remained influential (Fewsmith 1988).

60. The PRC's own experience demonstrates the connection between grain crisis and agricultural collectivization. In the 1950's, the CCP originally hoped for gradual and voluntary collectivization, and its policy called for the socialist transformation of agriculture to be completed in the course of three five-year plans. The process was accelerated during the winter of 1954–55, after heavy flood damage reduced the harvest and caused a grain crisis. The regime responded to this crisis first by sending cadres from house to house to appraise peasants' needs and to expose hoarders (i.e., to undertake requisitioning à la *prodrazverstka*). The party then sped up collectivization, and the number of agricultural producers' cooperatives soared from 90,000 to 670,000 during that single winter (Lowenthal 1970).

61. The percentage of the rural labor force engaged in agricultural activities increased from 78.5 percent in 1988 to 79.2 percent in 1989 (*World Journal*, Apr. 11, 1990).

62. For the importance of the *xiang* government and its bureaucratic nature, see White 1987b.

63. The losers include, among others, heavy industry, inland provinces, central planning agencies, and industrial ministries, or the "Communist coalition," as Susan Shirk calls it (Shirk 1985).

64. The NEP dilemma, i.e., that of a financially constrained state caught between private rural interests and state urban interests in agricultural prices, is shared by both Leninist and non-Leninist developing countries (Gray 1988). The major difference between them is that non-Leninist states do not attempt to solve the dilemma through collectivization. In view of the lack of state capacity in Poland, one can treat the PUWP regime as a borderline case.

Chapter 5

1. This chapter offers a partial answer to the question of whether mainland China will be able to follow in the footsteps of the East Asian NICs—Taiwan, South Korea, Hong Kong, and Singapore—and turn itself into a huge NIC. The success stories of these four countries have been told in different ways, with some versions emphasizing traditional culture and human resources (Berger and Hsiao 1988; Hofheinz and Calder 1982), some focusing on the international context and historical contingencies (Evans 1987), and still others stressing institutional innovations and government policies. In the last category, there are at least three schools of thought. The first considers the underlying authoritarian political structure a crucial factor in bringing about East Asian economic miracles (C. Johnson 1985). The second singles out the grand policy shift from import-substituting industrialization to export-led expansion as the single most important reason behind the rise of the East Asian NICs (Cheng and Haggard 1987b). The third provides a neoclassical explanation and attributes the performance of the four countries to their liberal and open economic policies (E. Chen 1979). Though the grand shift and neoclassical theories put a similar emphasis on East Asia's openness to the international market, the former stresses the importance of the state in implementing and sustaining an export-promo-

tion policy that may be highly interventionist, whereas the neoclassical explanation concentrates on the NICs' conformity with the prescriptions of the liberal trade theory. Many of the factors considered critical by these theories have been present in mainland China since 1949, including a population heavily influenced by Confucianism and an authoritarian state that is capable of initiating autonomous economic policies. Clearly, the lack of sustained productivity growth that separates the track record of the PRC from those of the East Asian NICs is not attributable to these shared elements, but to something that is unique in mainland China. Here the centrally controlled command economy immediately stands out as the most prominent difference between the PRC and the NICs. This chapter concentrates on this property rights issue and targets Taiwan, at its turning point in the 1950's and 1960's, as the referent case. It does not argue that the ROC's state capitalism is a necessary condition for economic success. The case of Hong Kong clearly suggests that there are alternatives to this property rights structure that may also lead to sustained high growth. However, the Taiwan experience in particular and state capitalism in general do prove highly conducive to rapid economic development based on continuous productivity growth in the East Asian context.

2. The mainlanders who came to Taiwan with the KMT and the native Taiwanese were alien to each other when the island was returned to China in 1945. The native Taiwanese were descendants of early Chinese settlers from Fukien (especially from Chang-cho and Ch'uan-cho [the Hoklo group]) and Canton (mainly from Ch'ao-cho [the Hakka group]). During Japanese rule (1895–1945), Taiwan was transformed from a Chinese province into a model colony of the Japanese empire. The island provided rice, sugar, and other agricultural products for Japan. The colonizers promoted primary education and provided infrastructure for Taiwan's early industrialization while brutally suppressing political dissent. The Taiwanese population thus experienced marginal social mobilization and formed its identity mainly as a result of economic development under an authoritarian and efficient colonial regime (Tsurumi 1984; Mendel 1974). The mainlanders, on the other hand, were political refugees heavily mobilized by decades of turbulent events in mainland China. Nationalist sentiment was at its height among the mainlanders, and the social mobilization process that created their identity was political and anti-Japanese. Thus, although there were no ethnic differences between the mainlanders and Taiwanese, they had different collective memories and different identities when they encountered each other in 1945. This identity conflict, combined with mismanagement of economic affairs by General Ch'en Yi, agitation by local activists, and the economic repercussions of the civil war on the mainland resulted in the Taiwanese uprisings known as the Erh Erh Pa Incident (Y. S. Wu 1989; Gold 1986b; Y. Wei 1974; Kerr 1965).

3. During the *kai-tsao* period, Nationalist Party members were required to reregister, and those considered disloyal or corrupt were purged. The KMT was defined as a revolutionary democratic party that adhered to democratic centralism. There were membership drives aimed at recruiting more farmers, workers, intellectuals, and soldiers and indoctrinating them with Sun Yat-sen's Three Principles of the People (Tien 1989: 66–69).

4. Sun Yat-sen, the founder of the KMT, accepted the advice of the Comintern to reform his party after Ch'en Chiung-ming, one of his favorite disciples, revolted and drove him from the presidential residence in Canton in June 1922. In 1923, Mikhail Borodin was sent to China as the major Comintern advisor to Sun. Borodin drafted a new constitution for the KMT that modeled its structure on that of the Russian Communist Party/Bolshevik (Wilbur 1983: 534). This draft constitution was adopted by the KMT National Congress of January 1924. Since then the KMT has had a Leninist party structure, though party discipline has never been as strict as in a Marxist-Leninist party like the CCP. Following Borodin's design, the KMT was hierarchically organized and equipped with a Central Executive Committee (CEC) and a Central Supervising Committee (CSC). Both were elected by the annual National Congress. The CEC assumed full power in running the party between congresses. There were also a Secretariat and a number of functional departments targeting various sectors of the society (youth, women, etc.), through which the party hoped to create a genuine mass movement in support of its goals. Borodin and Soviet military advisors also urged Sun to create a revolutionary military force thoroughly indoctrinated with the nationalist ideology of the KMT. The result was the establishment of the military academy at Whampoa that later produced the officer corps of the KMT's National Revolutionary Army. There was also an organizational parallel between the party and state, with party organs monitoring and controlling government policies. The state, the military, and all social organizations were to be integrated through the party. The basic structure of this party-state remained unchanged after 1924, though it did not function well because many warlords and other heterogeneous elements were co-opted into the system. The KMT's defeat on the mainland and its move to Taiwan paradoxically invigorated the organization by making it more "Leninist." However, the organizational features of the KMT only made it a "Leninist-type" party, not a Marxist-Leninist party. There were great differences between the two: for one thing, the KMT did not subscribe to Marxist-Leninist ideology; for another, the economic programs of the two were entirely different. For a characterization of the ROC's political system, see Tai 1970; Winckler 1984; Myers 1987; Y. S. Wu 1989; Tien 1989; and Chen 1989.

5. One famous example of the KMT's authoritarian political control was the suppression of a critical political magazine, *Free China Fortnightly*, and of the abortive China Democratic Party in 1960. Lei Chen, a well-known mainlander journalist, was jailed for his attempt to form an opposition organization with the indigenous Taiwanese elite. It was obvious that the KMT would tolerate individual locally oriented opponents, but not nationally organized political groups (Crozier 1976: 376; Y. Chen 1989).

6. The economic fiascoes and political disturbances on the mainland in the 1950's and 1960's did rekindle Chiang's hopes of retaking the lost land. However, nothing significant came of these opportunities except occasional commando raids on the coast and guerrilla activities in the mainland's southeastern provinces (Crozier 1976).

7. One rare incident of popular unrest was the anti-American rioting that took place in Taipei on May 23, 1957. It was touched off by the acquit-

tal of Robert Reynolds, a master sergeant in the U.S. Army who had been charged with manslaughter in the death of a 30-year-old Chinese. As it turned out, the explosion of popular anger was an isolated incident, never to be repeated.

8. Among the supporters of "new authoritarianism" were Chen Yizi and Wang Xiaoqiang of the Research Institute on China's Economic Structure, Wu Jiaxiang of the Central Office of the CCP, and Dai Qing of the *Guangming Daily* (*World Journal*, Mar. 13, 1989). Wu's article in the *World Economic Herald* (the most liberal newspaper in the PRC, which was closed down by the authorities in March 1990, after being forced to suspend publication for ten months) of January 16, 1989, offered the most complete presentation of the theory.

9. At the time, the American-educated Wu Kuo-chen, governor of Taiwan in the early 1950's, and General Sun Li-jen were favored by the U.S. However, they were unable to mount a strong challenge to Chiang's leadership.

10. In the 1950's and early 1960's, transnational corporations showed little interest in investing in the small, poor, and insecure island of Taiwan. As a result, U.S. policy toward the ROC was dominated by strategic considerations (Pang 1990).

11. Taiwan's land reform was strikingly similar in almost every detail to South Korea's. Both were patterned after the previous land reform carried out in Japan under the auspices of the Supreme Commander for the Allied Powers. The strong influence of American experts, noticeably of Wolf Ladejinsky, who served as land-reform advisor to all three countries, is quite obvious in Taiwan (Scitovsky 1986). Ladejinsky was placed at Ch'en Ch'eng's service by General Douglas MacArthur. Though the reform in Taiwan was more carefully prepared and executed than its Japanese predecessor, certain very important methods of implementing it were carried over from the Japanese case (see Kindermann 1987: 395).

12. The "land to the tiller" (*keng-che yu ch'i t'ien*) tenet was an important doctrine in Sun Yat-sen's *min-sheng chu-i*. It evolved from his ideas about equalization of land ownership (*p'ing-chun ti-ch'uan*), which were first adopted in 1905 in the Manifesto of Chung-kuo T'ung-meng-hui, predecessor of the KMT. In 1926, one year after Sun's death, the KMT's Canton headquarters passed a resolution calling for a 25 percent rent reduction, the first move toward land reform based on Sun's ideas. However, there was little implementation of reform measures except for a rent reduction in western Hupeh and Szechwan (Kindermann 1987: 389). This failure was due to the central government's lack of political control over provincial and local authorities, KMT recruitment policies that emphasized the landowning class (North 1954), and the inability of the ruling elite to appreciate the importance of land reform.

13. Other measures taken at the same time included the setting up of local farm tenancy committees, which made decisions on further rent reductions in case of crop failures; the abolition of the practice of paying rent in advance; the mandatory registration of written contracts with fixed leases of three to six years; and the granting to tenants of first option to purchase land from its owners (Kuo, Ranis, and Fei 1981: 50).

14. The Land to the Tiller Act allowed landlords to retain a maximum

of three chia (1 chia = 0.97 hectares) of seventh- to twelfth-grade paddy field (Gold 1986b: 65).

15. In 1957, part-owner farmers and owner-cultivators owned more than 83 percent of total farmland. The proportion of owner-cultivators to total farm families increased from 36 percent in 1949 to 60 percent in 1957, while the proportion of tenant farmers fell from 39 percent to 17 percent (Kuo, Ranis, and Fei 1981: 57).

16. Their land was undervalued (by roughly 50 percent) when the government purchased it, and the bonds used to reimburse them paid an interest rate well below market level (4 percent per annum, compared to a prevailing market rate of 30 to 50 percent). As for the stocks of the four public companies, only the largest landowners were capable of taking advantage of these assets and turning themselves into new industrialists (e.g., the Koo family, which became the largest shareholder of Taiwan Cement). The smaller landowners, because of their lack of experience in and knowledge of industry, promptly sold their stocks at below-market prices, thus failing to capture the opportunities offered by the nascent industrial boom.

17. Mainland agriculture plunged into a period of much lower growth in 1985. It grew 3.4 percent in 1985, another 3.4 percent in 1986, 5.8 percent in 1987, and 1.6 percent in 1988 (International Financial Statistics 1990: 166).

18. As late as 1966–68, Taiwan's Provincial Food Bureau still disposed of 42 percent of the rice it collected as rations to members of the armed forces, military dependents, government employees, and teachers (i.e., the chun-kung-chiao jen-yuan). Another 25 percent was earmarked for market stabilization sales.

19. The growth rate of the retail price index on the mainland was 250 percent in 1946, 1,650 percent in 1947, and 2,780 percent in 1948 (Feuerwerker 1983: 114).

20. Between 1948 and 1959, the income of the average tenant farmer in Taiwan would have increased by only 16 percent had there been no land reform, as compared to the 107 percent increase achieved under the reform (Thorbecke 1979: 176).

21. The reorganization of the farmers' associations in 1953 eliminated the remaining influence of landlords and local gentry, incorporated lending into the associations' activities, and strengthened state control. The reorganized farmers' associations provided credit services, training opportunities, and marketing assistance. They were also entrusted with supervising the rice/fertilizer barter program and collecting land taxes and land purchase payments.

22. Chiang Mon-lin, chairman of the JCRR from 1948 to 1964, stated that "land reform will not have its full effect, unless it is followed by an increase of production with the aid of modern technology" (Kindermann 1987: 391). He described land reform and agricultural technology as the two wings of a bird. There are many examples of countries in which a land redistribution scheme was not accompanied by complementary measures such as those provided by the JCRR, a shortcoming that led to serious reductions in production and consequent failure of the reform (Thorbecke 1979: 210).

23. Before 1937, Japanese spending on capital formation in Taiwan con-

centrated on agriculture, especially on the construction of irrigation facilities (such as the Chianan Reservoir in the Tainan district). The only industry that existed was food processing, particularly sugar refining, which accounted for 50 percent of total factory production during the 1930's (Fei, Ranis, and Kuo 1979: 24). Thus direct and indirect investment by Taiwan's government-general in nonagricultural industries averaged only 2.9 percent of total government investment spending between 1901 and 1935. This jumped to 6.56 percent between 1936 and 1938, reflecting the shift of government policy in wartime (Toshiyuki and Yuzo 1984: 416).

24. Another sign of the Japanese-dominated industrialization of Taiwan was the disparity between the increasing proportion of male industrial workers among total working males and the nearly constant proportion of Taiwanese industrial workers among total Taiwanese working males throughout the colonial period. Many of the newly created urban-industrial jobs were filled by Japanese immigrants brought in by the major Japanese *zaibatsu* and expatriate firms. As a result, industrial development in the colonial period had more impact on the economy than on the Taiwanese population (Ho 1975: 424).

25. In all, the Taiwanese owned less than 10 percent of the joint stock in larger scale operations and 22 percent of the capital in industry (Fei, Ranis, and Kuo 1979: 25).

26. In 1939, firms owned by Japanese accounted for 15.1 percent of all firms employing 5 to 49 workers. The percentage of Japanese-owned firms rose with the scale of employment, from 46.0 percent (50 to 99 workers) to 61.8 percent (100–199 workers) to 96.5 percent (200 workers and above) (Toshiyuki and Yuzo 1984: 419). One thus finds a dualistic economy: a small handful of large, modern, heavily capitalized enterprises owned by Japanese dominated a manufacturing sector composed mostly of small traditional Taiwanese establishments.

27. For the importance of the economic pilot agency, see C. Johnson 1982.

28. The Resistance War greatly expanded the Nationalist government's control of the economy. Before the war, the government held only 11 percent of the capital in Chinese-owned industrial enterprises. By 1942, state enterprises accounted for 70 percent of the capital, 32 percent of the workers, and 42 percent of the industrial horsepower in the Nationalist-controlled area. The Nationalist Resources Commission was set up in 1935 to develop industry in the interior and to supervise the heavy and technical industries. The Industrial and Mining Adjustment Administration was created just after the outbreak of the war to facilitate the removal of privately owned factories to the interior. However, it grew into a major participant in light industry, producing consumer goods in competition with private enterprises. The four government banks also increased their direct participation in and ownership of industry and business, in an effort to acquire tangible assets in order to protect the real value of their capital (Eastman 1986: 600). The Resources Commission attracted the best talents in wartime China. K. Y. Yin, K. T. Li, and Sun Yun-suan, the most important economic technocrats of the ROC in the 1950's, 1960's, and 1970's, respectively, were recruited into the Commission in the 1930's and 1940's on the mainland (Shen 1972: 37; Li Kwoh-Ting 1987: 305; Yang 1989: 102). For the

continuity in institutions and personnel in the economic bureaucracy throughout the 1940's and 1950's, see Wang Nai-chi 1987.

29. The private sector in the PRC fared much better in retail trade than in industry. In 1980, private enterprises generated only 0.7 percent of all retail trade. This share jumped to 9.6 percent in 1984, not including peasants' sales of agricultural products to the cities (another 5.0 percent) (Sah 1986: 13).

30. According to Kornai, there was a whole generation of "naive reformers" in the Soviet Union and Eastern Europe, including Evsey G. Liberman in the Soviet Union; Gyorgy Peter, Sandor Balazsy, Peter Erdos, Tamas Nagy, Istvan Varga, and Rezso Nyers in Hungary; Wlodzimierz Brus in Poland; and Ota Sik in Czechoslovakia (Kornai 1986b: 1728).

31. The similarity between the industrial reforms in Hungary and the PRC is hardly surprising. The Chinese consciously looked to Hungary for economic lessons and invited prominent reform economists like Janos Kornai to prescribe solutions to the PRC's economic problems (Stark and Nee 1989: 2).

32. Some conceptual clarification is in order here. We have observed that pure market socialism and state capitalism are diametric opposites: the former is defined as state ownership without state control, the latter as private ownership with state control. However, market socialism as practiced by Hungary and the PRC still preserved a large role for the state (as exemplified by the use of economic levers and guidance planning), while Taiwan's state capitalism went through limited marketization even in the 1950's and 1960's. This similarity in the state's selective use of market prompted Gordon White and Robert Wade to talk about the partial convergence toward guided markets of the capitalist and socialist countries in East Asia (White and Wade 1988: 25). As indicated in Chapter 1, I fully recognize the distance between the ideal economic types and the empirical cases. But this recognition should not deter us from applying the two-by-two model to the empirical cases, mainly because the thrust of property rights restructuring can be neatly captured by the typology employed here. Thus, for example, by locating the starting points of Taiwan and mainland China in the same property rights quadrant (state ownership cum state control), and ascertaining their ending points in state capitalism (private ownership and state control) and market socialism (state ownership without state control), respectively, we can clearly delineate the main direction of their property rights reforms: privatization for Taiwan and marketization for mainland China. This conclusion holds true even if we treat state ownership and state control as continuous, instead of dichotomous, variables: in this case, the different slopes of the developmental curves of Taiwan and mainland China also indicate that the major movement for Taiwan was toward privatization, while that of mainland China was toward marketization.

33. Total trade was about 90 percent of the net national product in 1935–37. Trade with Japan accounted for around 90 percent of total trade (Scott 1979).

34. Up until 1957, the imports financed by U.S. aid exceeded 40 percent of total imports every year.

35. At the end of 1950, the net foreign assets of Taiwan's banking sys-

tem were estimated at only US$15 million, equal to one or two months' imports.

36. In many less-developed countries where the central bank is not autonomous, there is always the temptation for the government to increase spending and order the central bank to create money to cover its budget deficit. In this way, the state can acquire any amount of goods and services from the market without going through the normal legislative process. The government faces no budget constraint. The major cost, of course, is the danger of generating inflation. When it was on the mainland, the ROC government would order the central bank to purchase government bonds. This strategy was facilitated by the fact that the positions of governor of the central bank and finance minister were usually held by the same person, who in both capacities was subject to dismissal (Li Kwoh-Ting 1988: 22).

37. A similar case of financial constraints forcing the state to shift its strategy from direct participation in industrial production to encouragement of private enterprises can be found in the 1880 Matsukata reform in Japan. There the policy shift was imposed on the government by the need to bring imports and exports under control and to keep the government solvent. Under the "Outline of Regulations for the Sale of Government-Operated Factories," the government sold its pilot plants and provided private entrepreneurs with exclusive licenses and some capital. The beneficiaries of this policy were big merchant houses such as Mitsui, Mitsubishi, and Sumitomo, which later became the *zaibatsu* (C. Johnson 1982: 85). As it turned out, the Matsukata reform was the beginning of Japanese state capitalism, which was characterized by strong government control and the near absence of state ownership in production (Samuels 1987: 2).

38. In some rare cases where its ideology proved incompatible with the requirements of economic development, the government found it very difficult to override the outdated tenet. The debate over a population growth policy is a good example. With the sudden influx of over 2 million mainlanders and a high birth rate in 1953–58, Taiwan was desperately in need of a policy aimed at slowing the rate of population increase. However, there was strong opposition to such a policy, based on the argument that it would reduce the ROC's military strength vis-à-vis the mainland, that it was not necessary given rising food production, and that it was directly against Sun Yat-sen's teachings. The last reservation proved the most recalcitrant. In 1924, Sun had raised his concern about the future possibility of China being swallowed up by imperialist powers with high population growth rates. He considered China's huge population the guarantee for its survival. As a result, in the 1950's, ROC programs for family planning and birth control could only be sponsored by the semi-autonomous JCRR, with American help, and conducted at the provincial level. The top leadership did not endorse the population policy until 1966, after Sun Fo, Sun Yat-sen's son, reinterpreted his father's teachings by emphasizing the threat from the "red imperialists" (the Communists) based on poverty that was closely linked with high population growth in a backward society (Li Kwoh-Ting 1988). It was fortunate for the technocrats that conflicts between ideology and their economic programs were relatively few.

39. For a discussion of the function of *san-min chu-i*, see Pang 1988: 79; Myers 1986: 44.

40. For the concept of industrial policy in general, see C. Johnson 1982, 1984a. For the whole "package" of Taiwanese industrial policy and its similarities with the Japanese and Korean policies, see C. Johnson 1984b, 1985.

41. These imports were encouraged by the overvalued New Taiwan dollar, a device used by the government to promote import substitution (Ho 1978: 194).

42. The production index of the textile industry (with 1954 = 100), after rising rapidly and steadily from 3 in 1946 to 100 in 1954, was 105 in 1955, 99 in 1956, 109 in 1957, and 106 in 1958 (Ho 1978: 195).

43. It was not until the 1970's, when the Ten Major Constructions were implemented, that the government shifted to the second phase of import substitution. Steel, shipbuilding, heavy machinery, and petrochemical refining were among the priority industries developed by the government (Cheng and Haggard 1987a: 31).

44. The fact that deepening was not an economically appropriate strategy certainly does not mean that the state could not adopt it for political reasons. Stephen Haggard (1986) argues that a strong labor movement and the lack of state autonomy from the short-term interests of the private sector made deepening a natural strategy in Latin America. These elements clearly did not exist in Taiwan in the late 1950's and early 1960's, when it had an authoritarian political system dominated by a Leninist-type party.

45. There was a similar case involving K. T. Li, the successor to Yin, in 1966 (Chou 1982: 21).

46. Yin's philosophy was state capitalism, or the state encouragement and guidance of private enterprises in pursuance of its developmental goals. He was extremely flexible in designing economic policies to fit this broad goal. Yin's shift from major proponent of primary import substitution to champion of export expansion was based on his perception of the needs of the time and his lack of allegiance to any specific economic theory (Pang 1988: 65).

47. The U.S. was interested in accelerating Taiwan's economic development at this juncture in order to phase out U.S. aid, create a model for other aid recipients, and demonstrate the superiority of a free economy.

48. Sugar accounted for 85.2 percent of the value of total exports by the food processing industry in 1961. Its share had dropped to 36.2 percent by 1971. During the same period, the share of canned food jumped from 4.9 percent to 32.0 percent.

49. The food processing industry's share in total manufacturing expansion declined from 25.4 percent in 1954–61 to 14.6 percent in 1961–66 and 8.9 percent in 1966–71. In the same period, that of textiles and footwear grew from 7.3 percent to 14.2 percent and 27.3 percent. That of electronics increased from 2.8 percent to 8.8 percent and 12.8 percent (Kuo, Ranis, and Fei 1981: 10).

50. Of the four, the most important was "readjustment" (*tiaozheng*), which demanded shifting national resources from heavy industry toward agriculture, energy, and transportation. This major retreat from the Ten-Year Plan was announced by Hua himself at the Second Meeting of the Fifth People's Congress in June 1979 (Walsh 1984; Ying 1982).

51. In 1973, Japan imported one million tons of crude oil from China's Daqing oil field. This marked the beginning of the PRC's export of large

quantities of petroleum to the West. From 1978 to 1983, mainland China increased its exports to Japan by 150 percent, with petroleum and petroleum products accounting for 55 percent of the increase (Wu Yuan-li 1987: 72). In 1983, crude and refined petroleum made up 50.1 percent of the PRC's exports to Japan and 19.1 percent of the country's exports to the U.S. However, crude oil production stagnated and even decreased at the beginning of the 1980's. At the same time, domestic consumption increased. Petroleum exports peaked in 1985, in terms of both volume and value. Other factors working against the mainland's petroleum exports included the high wax content of its crude oil and slackening demand on the international market through most of the 1980's (Wei Ai 1983: 371).

52. Textile agreements were signed between all of the major industrialized countries and the PRC. An agreement was reached in 1980 that imposed quotas on the PRC's textile exports to the U.S. (Wei Ai 1983: 372). In 1983, when the original agreement expired, the two countries had a serious dispute over whether the PRC's textile exports to the U.S. through the entrepôt of Hong Kong should be considered direct exports and thus subject to quota regulations. This dispute led to U.S. imposition of additional quotas on PRC textiles, to which the PRC retaliated by suspending its purchases of American cotton, synthetic fibers, and soybeans. New agreements were signed in August 1983 and December 1987 that contained further restrictions on mainland China's textile exports to the U.S. (Wei Ai 1990: 80). Limits were also imposed by the 1986 Multifiber Arrangement. However, unlike petroleum exports, PRC exports of textiles and apparel continued to grow in the latter part of the 1980's, making the textile industry the largest exporter in mainland China and the PRC the number one textile exporter on the U.S. market.

53. The PRC's stronger export position can be demonstrated in an international perspective. It is true that the PRC's export composition in the early 1980's was in many respects quite similar to that of other low-income economies in its emphasis on primary products and textile exports. However, mainland China, like India, had a high percentage of exports of manufactured goods compared with other low-income economies and was highly self-sufficient when it came to industrial machinery. Furthermore, it was an exporter, not an importer, of petroleum (World Bank 1985: 102).

54. In 1981, the PRC canceled half of the Baoshan steelworks project undertaken with the Japanese, in order to slash investment and suppress imports. The resulting "Baoshan shock" strongly affected Japanese confidence in the investment environment in the PRC (C. Johnson 1986a: 119).

55. The PRC enjoyed surpluses in its current account balance from 1981 to 1984 (World Bank 1985: 107). In the 1950's, Taiwan's imports exceeded exports by more than 60 percent (Ho 1978: 115).

56. Thus, three years after the CCP had taken control of the mainland, light industry's share of GNP was 27.8 percent, while heavy industry accounted for only 15.3 percent.

57. During the First Five-Year period, production of iron, steel, and electricity grew by more than 300 percent. By comparison, production of cotton cloth grew by only 32 percent, and grain production rose only 20 percent (Lee 1983: 65).

geted Taiwan as the "goal market" (*mubiao shichang*) of the entire Fujian area and has made various special concessions to *taishang*, including granting them tax exemptions and deductions, allowing them to transfer real estate property rights, and providing prompt administration, all of which are usually furnished on terms better than those granted to non-Taiwanese foreign investors. As a result, *taishang* investment in Xiamen increased by 485 percent in 1989 and accounted for 70 percent of Xiamen's total DFI that year (Fang Shan 1990).

76. The enterprises funded by Taiwanese capital are typically medium- or small-sized companies (with an average investment of US$1.09 million) that process or assemble labor-intensive products. Most (about 56 percent) are wholly owned by the Taiwanese, and most are export oriented (on average, more than 70 percent of their products are for export).

Chapter 6

1. This is why, when Yugoslav Communists sought an alternative to the Soviet model of Marxism during their ideological strife with Moscow in the 1950's, they came up with a version of market socialism.

2. Stalin did not opt for market socialism because of the urgent need to concentrate control power in state hands for national defense purposes, a point discussed in the following section.

3. The NEM brought about a trade balance between 1968 and 1973. Then the deteriorating terms of trade, worldwide recession, and unchecked investment growth that accompanied the retrenchment policies of the mid-1970's created a considerable trade imbalance. As a result, the country was forced back to reform (Nyers 1983). Once again, marketization, or response C, was stressed. One of the most important measures in this second-wave reform was a price reform that linked domestic prices with world-market prices in an attempt to achieve greater allocative efficiency. However, response A, including centralized policies to slash imports and promote an export drive, was also present (Kornai 1986b: 1721). Because austerity measures (response A) and marketization (response C) are often contradictory, the net effect of Hungary's second-wave reform in reducing its trade imbalance in the 1980's was not impressive. When the international financial situation continued to deteriorate into the decade, Hungary's deficit/debt problems reached crisis proportions, and response D became dominant. As in the case of Poland, the IMF tried to impose a reform package on Hungary that stressed both marketization and privatization. Though there has been stronger resistance to this pressure in Hungary than in Poland, the influence exerted by international financial institutions has proved overwhelming. Their preferences for marketization and privatization of property rights have thus carried great weight in Hungary's economic reform (*Report on Eastern Europe*, Jan. 26, 1990, p. 45).

58. The PRC's 400,000 state enterprises were mostly equipped with Soviet machinery from the 1950's. They were characterized by "three olds" and "two lows": old technology, old products, and old equipment; and low quality and low efficiency (C. Y. Cheng 1990: 18).

59. In 1979, it was decided that the PRC would selectively import only technology and equipment that could modernize existing enterprises. This policy was reaffirmed by Zhao Ziyang in his report at the Fourth Meeting of the Fifth People's Congress in 1981 (Lee 1983: 78).

60. For example, government investment in state enterprises was 41.2 percent of total investment in that sector in 1971–79. This share dropped to 27.5 percent in 1980–84. At the same time, enterprise self-financing and bank loans played an increasingly important role. This change in the funding pattern, however, should not be overemphasized, since funds from the banking system are actually another means of state investment.

61. In 1978, 1.56 million people from Hong Kong and Macao visited the mainland. The number rose to 8.56 million in 1983.

62. Even before the reform, the mainland economy could satisfy the basic need for nondurable consumer goods; it was production of consumer durables that was extremely underdeveloped. For example, in 1979 the country produced only 180,000 washing machines and 42,000 refrigerators for a population approaching one billion (C. Y. Cheng 1990: 21).

63. A good example can be found in the process through which a nineteen-point program of economic and financial reform was adopted by the ROC government at the urging of AID. The program was initially drawn up by AID to accelerate Taiwan's economic development and create a self-generated growth pattern. At the end of 1959, AID mission director Wesley C. Haraldson urged Ch'en Ch'eng and his economic team (K. Y. Yin, C. K. Yen, and K. T. Li) to convey the importance of such reform to Chiang Kai-shek, which they did successfully. The U.S. plan was then expanded into a nineteen-point program that included measures proposed by the Chinese side, and was approved by the ROC's Executive Yuan Council and the KMT's Central Standing Committee in early 1960 (Pang 1988).

64. In 1965, when U.S. aid was terminated, K. T. Li managed to secure a US$150 million loan from Japan and a US$30 million loan from the Exim Bank of the U.S. (Li Kwoh-Ting 1987: 309). This was the beginning of an inflow of international capital based on profit considerations.

65. Japan offered the largest government loans to the PRC in the 1980's. The first package of yen loans was issued in 1979–83 for 330 billion yen (US$1.5 billion in 1979 dollars). The second package, for 1984–90, amounted to 540 billion yen (US$2.3 billion in 1984 dollars). The third package, for 1990–95, totaled 810 billion yen (US$6.3 billion in 1988 dollars) (Okita 1990: 135). None of the packages was attached to conditions for privatization in mainland China.

66. For example, there was an overall endorsement of the PRC's market socialist reform by the World Bank in its comprehensive 1985 report on China. The Bank's major suggestions for the PRC were "a greater use of market regulation to stimulate innovation and efficiency," "strong planning combining indirect with direct economic control," and "modification and extension of social institutions to maintain the fairness in distribution

that is fundamental to socialism." This report also congratulated the PRC on having combined state and market regulation in such a way as to produce rapid and efficient growth, and on having managed to avoid intolerable poverty among substantial segments of its population. It was emphasized that "there is thus a vital need to guard against losing the strengths of the existing system—its capacity to mobilize resources, as well as to help the poor—in the course of overcoming its weaknesses" (World Bank 1985: 19).

67. Ch'en was Chiang's chief military lieutenant on the mainland and served as chief of the general staff from 1946 to 1948. In 1949, he was appointed governor of Taiwan and given the task of preparing the island for the massive retreat from the mainland. From 1949 to 1965, Ch'en had full power to restructure the ROC economy. It was under him that land reform was implemented. He also chaired the Taiwan Production Board (TPB), the earliest economic general staff in Taiwan, in 1949. He headed the powerful Council for U.S. Aid (CUSA) from 1950 to 1954, and after its merger with the Economic Stabilization Board (ESB)—the successor to the TPB—headed CUSA again from 1958 to 1963, a turning point in Taiwan's economic development. Ch'en took part in the *kai-tsao* campaign as a member of the Central Reform Committee (1950–52). He was also premier from 1950 to 1954 and from 1958 to 1963; vice *tsungtsai* of the KMT (1957–65); and vice president of the Republic of China (1954–65). Until his death in 1965, Ch'en was widely considered Chiang's successor. His power, prestige, and popularity among the people were unprecedented among Chiang's followers. Tension did exist between the two men; however, Ch'en definitely had the full support of and enjoyed complete delegation of authority from the supreme leader in managing the economy (Pang 1988: 59). Ch'en came from a military background, but he respected the opinions of the technocrats who designed the transformation of Taiwan's economy in the 1950's and 1960's. Zhao Ziyang, on the other hand, began his career as a local CCP leader before the 1949 defeat of the KMT. He was the first party secretary of Guandong in the early 1960's. Like many of his colleagues, Zhao was purged when the Cultural Revolution began, sent to work in a factory, and eventually rehabilitated. His performance in Sichuan earned him a seat on the Central Committee at the Tenth Party Congress in 1973. In 1980, by successfully implementing Deng's reform program, Zhao assumed the premiership, replacing Hua Guofeng. In 1982, he was elected to the Standing Committee of the politburo. After 1983, Zhao replaced Chen Yun as the most powerful economic policymaker in mainland China. He then headed the newly established State Commission on Reform of China's Economic Structure (Tigaiwei) and its Research Institute (Tigaisuo). A group of economic reformers worked under Zhao, but they were quite different from the technocrat-privatizers that worked under Ch'en in the 1950's and 1960's.

68. In July 1980, the Economic Research Center headed by Xue Muqiao was established under the State Council. In May 1981, the Economic-Technical Research Center headed by Ma Hong was also set up under the State Council. The two merged to become the new Economic-Technical-Social Development Research Center in 1985 (Chiang Chen-ch'ang 1989). Be-

cause this institute was directly under the State Council, unlike the Research Institute on Reform of China's Economic Structure and the Research Institute on Rural Development, it exercised greater influence, at least during the early 1980's.

69. The young reformers shared the background of having lived in rural areas during the Cultural Revolution. They became undergraduate students and graduate students at Peking University, People's University, the Chinese Academy of Social Sciences (CASS), etc., in the late 1970's, and organized study groups to exchange ideas on reforming China's agriculture. Many of them were recruited into Tigaisuo and Fazhansuo in 1984–85. In Tigaisuo were Chen Yizi, Zhou Xiaochuan, Wang Xiaoqiang, etc. In Fazhansuo, under veteran reformer Du Runsheng, were Zhou Qiren, Chen Xiwen, Luo Xiaopeng, etc. The years 1985 and 1986 witnessed the heyday of the two institutes' influence, when Tigaisuo drafted industrial reform policies and Fazhansuo prepared the annual Central Document No. 1. During the same period, Wu Jinglian of the State Council's Economic-Technical-Social Development Research Center and Hua Sheng and Zhang Xuejun of the CASS exercised some influence on the government's reform policies. In 1987–88, with economic reform facing mounting difficulties and Zhao Ziyang shifting from prime minister to secretary-general of the CCP, more conservative reformers, such as Wang Mengkui of the State Planning Commission and Zhang Yanning of the reshuffled Tigaiwei, gained influence. Universities had much less influence than these government agencies and institutes. Thus even though Li Yining and the Beida Xuepai ("Beijing University school") enjoyed much popularity overseas, their influence at home was limited.

70. *Getihu* were treated as individual laborers (*geti laodongzhe*) rather than businesses and protected by the 1982 Constitution. The rapid development of the private sector subsequently created many larger private enterprises. In 1988, *siying qiye* were officially recognized and their rights protected by law.

71. The first Export Processing Zone in Taiwan was established in Kaohsiung in 1966. In 1971, it was joined by the zones in Nantze and Taichung.

72. Of course the goals of the SEZs included aspects of earning hard currency, and the EPZs were designed in part to acquire foreign technology. But these were secondary to the purposes for which the SEZs and EPZs were established (Prybyla 1984; Li Kwoh-Ting 1988).

73. This rule was later partially relaxed to allow limited local sales upon approval and after payment of a customs duty.

74. In 1979–86, sole foreign ownerships accounted for a negligible 1.6 percent of DFI in the PRC. Joint and contractual joint ventures accounted for 35 percent and cooperative development ventures for 25.9 percent (Yeh 1989: 61).

75. Generally speaking, production costs in Xiamen are around 75 percent of production costs in Taiwan. In addition to its economic attractiveness, Xiamen offers geographical proximity, language compatibility (Taiwanese is a southern Fujian dialect), and the many other advantages that a common cultural background provides. At the same time, Beijing has tar-

Bibliography

Adelman, Irma, and David Sunding. 1987. "Economic Policy and Income Distribution in China." *Journal of Comparative Economics* 11 (3): 444–61.

Almond, Gabriel A., and G. Bingham Powell. 1978. *Comparative Politics.* Boston: Little, Brown.

Arendt, Hannah. 1968. *Totalitarianism.* New York: Harcourt Brace Jovanovich.

Balassa, Bela. 1978. "The Economic Reform in Hungary." *European Economic Review* 11 (3): 245–68.

———. 1987. "China's Economic Reforms in a Comparative Perspective." *Journal of Comparative Economics* 11 (3): 410–26.

Ball, Alan. 1985. "NEP's Second Wind: The New Trade Practice." *Soviet Studies* 37 (3): 371–85.

Baradat, Leon P. 1979. *Political Ideologies: Their Origins and Impact.* Englewood Cliffs, N.J.: Prentice-Hall.

Bauer, Tamas. 1983. "The Hungarian Alternative to Soviet-Type Planning." *Journal of Comparative Economics* 7 (3): 304–16.

———. 1987–88. "Perfecting or Reforming the Economic Mechanism?" *Eastern European Economics* 26 (2): 5–34.

Becker, Lawrence C. 1977. *Property Rights.* London: Routledge and Kegan Paul.

Berger, Peter L., and Hsin-Huang Michael Hsiao. 1988. *In Search of an East Asian Development Model.* New Brunswick, N.J.: Transaction.

Bernstein, Thomas. 1967. "Leadership and Mass Mobilization in the Soviet and Chinese Collectivization Campaigns of 1929–30 and 1955–56: A Comparison." *China Quarterly* 31: 1–47.

Bertsch, Gary, and Thomas Ganchow, eds. 1976. *Comparative Communism: The Soviet, Chinese, and Yugoslav Models.* San Francisco: W. H. Freeman.

Bhalla, R. S. 1984. *The Institution of Property: Legally, Historically, and Philosophically Regarded.* Lucknow, India: Eastern Book.

Bognar, Jozsef. 1984. "Further Developments in Economic Reform." *New Hungarian Quarterly* 25 (95): 45–54.

Bornstein, Morris. 1977. "Economic Reform in Eastern Europe." In U.S. Congress, Joint Economic Committee, ed., *East European Economies Post-Helsinki*. Washington, D.C.: Government Printing Office.

Brugger, Bill, ed. 1985. *Chinese Marxism in Flux, 1979–84*. Armonk, N.Y.: M. E. Sharpe.

Brus, Wlodzimierz. 1980. "Political System and Economic Efficiency: The East European Context." *Journal of Comparative Economics* 4 (1): 40–55.

Brzezinski, Zbigniew. 1967. *Ideology and Power in Soviet Politics*. New York: Praeger.

Buky, Barnabas. 1972. "Hungary's NEM on a Treadmill." *Problems of Communism* 21 (5): 31–39.

Chalmers, Douglas A. 1985. "Corporatism and Comparative Politics." In Howard Wiarda, ed., *New Directions in Comparative Politics*. Boulder, Colo.: Westview Press.

Chang Chen-pang. 1989. "Teng Hsiao-p'ing si-hsiang te liang-ch'ung hsing" (The duality of Deng Xiaoping's thoughts). *Mainland China Studies* 32 (2): 25–31.

————. 1990. "'Peaceful Evolution' Strikes Fear into the Hearts of the Chinese Communists." *Issues and Studies* 26 (6): 43–53.

Chen, Edward. 1979. *Hyper-growth in Asian Economies: A Comparative Study of Hong Kong, Japan, Korea, Singapore and Taiwan*. London: Macmillan.

Ch'en Te-Sheng. 1992a. "Chung-kung 'shih-san chieh pa-chung ch'uen hui' cheng-ching fa-chan fen-hsi" (An analysis of political and economic developments at the Eighth Plenum of the Thirteenth Central Committee of the CCP). *Studies in Communism* 18 (2): 1–10.

————. 1992b. *Chung-nan-hai cheng-ching tung-hsiang* (Peking's recent political and economic trends). Taipei: Yung-yeh.

————. 1993. "'Shih-szu-ta' hou te ta-lu ching-chi ch'ing-shih" (The economic situation in mainland China after the CCP's Fourteenth Party Congress). *Mainland China Studies* 36 (1): 27–41.

Chen, Yaobang. 1989. "China's Agriculture: After Ten Years of Reform." *China Reconstructs* 38 (2): 8–11.

Ch'en Yu-Ch'en. 1988. "Chung-kung ching-chi kai-ke shih-nien" (A decade of economic reform in the PRC). *Mainland China Studies* 31 (6): 28–31.

Cheng, Chu-Yuan. 1990. *Behind the Tiananmen Massacre: Social, Political, and Economic Ferment in China*. Boulder, Colo.: Westview Press.

Cheng Hsueh-chia. 1976. *Lien Ning chu-i kuo-chia-lun chih p'i-p'an* (Critique of the state theory in Leninism). Taipei: Institute for the Study of International Communism.

Cheng, Tun-jen. 1989. "Democratizing the Quasi-Leninist Regime in Taiwan." *World Politics* 41 (4): 471–99.

Cheng, Tun-jen, and Stephen Haggard. 1987a. *Newly Industrializing Asia in Transition*. Berkeley, Calif.: Institute of International Studies.

————. 1987b. "State and Foreign Capital in the East Asian NICs." In Frederic C. Deyo, ed., *The Political Economy of East Asian Industrialism*. Ithaca, N.Y.: Cornell University Press.

Chevrier, Yves. 1988. "NEP and Beyond: The Transition to 'Modernization' in China (1978–1985)." In Stephan Feuchtwang, Athar Hussain, and Thierry Pairault, eds., *Transforming China's Economy in the Eighties*. Vol. 1. Boulder, Colo.: Westview Press.

Chiang Chen-ch'ang. 1982. *Chung-kuo ta-lu ch'ing-nien min-chu yun-tung chih t'an-t'ao* (An exploration into the young democratic movement in mainland China). Taipei: Yiu Shih.

——. 1989. "Chung-kung cheng-ching kai-ke te chih-nang-t'uan" (The think tanks for the CCP's political and economic reforms). *Mainland China Studies* 31 (10): 29–40.

Chiang Chi-feng. 1989. *Wang-p'ai ch'u-chin te chung-nan-hai ch'iao-chu* (Tiananmen countdown). Taipei: Central Daily News.

Chilcote, Ronald H. 1985. "Alternative Approaches to Comparative Politics." In Howard Wiarda, ed., *New Directions in Comparative Politics*. Boulder, Colo.: Westview Press.

Chou Yu-K'ou. 1982. "Hsi-shu ts'ai-ching shou-chang te pei-ching" (Examining the backgrounds of economic officials). In *Ch'eng-chang te t'ung-k'u* (Growing pains). Taipei: Commonwealth.

Clark, Cal. 1987. "The Taiwan Exception: Implications for Contending Political Economy Paradigms." *International Studies Quarterly* 31: 327–56.

Cohen, Stephen F. 1985. *Rethinking the Soviet Experience: Politics and History Since 1917*. Oxford: Oxford University Press.

Connolly, William E. 1967. *Political Science and Ideology*. New York: Atherton Press.

Converse, Philip E. 1967. "The Nature of Belief Systems in Mass Politics." In David Apter, ed., *Ideology and Discontent*. New York: Free Press.

Cox, Richard, ed. 1969. *Ideology, Politics and Political Theory*. Belmont, Calif.: Wadsworth.

Croll, Elisabeth. 1988a. "The New Peasant Economy in China." In Stephan Feuchtwang, Athar Hussain, and Thierry Pairault, eds., *Transforming China's Economy in the Eighties*. Vol. 2. Boulder, Colo.: Westview Press.

——. 1988b. "Reform, Local Political Institutions and the Village Economy in China." In David S. G. Goodman, ed., *Communism and Reform in East Asia*. London: Frank Cass.

Crozier, Brian. 1976. *The Man Who Lost China*. New York: Scribner's.

Csaki, Csaba. 1983. "Economic Management and Organization of Hungarian Agriculture." *Journal of Comparative Economics* 7 (3): 317–28.

Deng Xiaoping. 1984. *Selected Works of Deng Xiaoping*. Beijing: Foreign Languages Press.

——. 1992. "Deng Xiaoping tongzhi zai Wuchang, Shenzhen, Zhuhai, Shanghai dengdi de tanhua yaodian" (The main points of Comrade Deng Xiaoping's talks in Wuchang, Shenzhen, Zhuhai, and Shanghai). In Zhonggong Shenzhen shiwei xuanchuanbu, ed., *Yijiujiuer nian chun: Deng Xiaoping yu Shenzhen* (The spring of 1992: Deng Xiaoping and Shenzhen). Shenzhen: Haitian chubanshe.

Deutscher, Isaac. 1949. *Stalin: A Political Biography*. Oxford: Oxford University Press.

Deyo, Frederic C., ed. 1987. *The Political Economy of East Asian Industrialism*. Ithaca, N.Y.: Cornell University Press.

Di Ying. 1988. "Tsou-kuo ts'ung-ch'ien, hui-tao wei-lai" (Revisit the past, return to the future). *Commonwealth* 81: 14–54.

Dicks, Anthony. 1989. "The Chinese Legal System: Reforms in the Balance." *China Quarterly* 119: 540–76.

Dittmer, Lowell. 1980. "Chinese Communist Revisionism in Comparative Perspective." *Studies in Comparative Communism* 13 (1): 3–40.

———. 1981. "The Strategic Triangle: An Elementary Game—Theoretical Analysis." *World Politics* 33 (4): 485–515.

———. 1983. "Comparative Communist Political Culture." *Studies in Comparative Communism* 16 (1/2): 9–24.

———. 1987. "Mao and the Politics of Revolutionary Mortality." *Asian Survey* 27 (3): 316–39.

———. 1990. "Patterns of Elite Strife and Succession in Chinese Politics." *China Quarterly* 123: 405–30.

———. 1992. "Mainland China's Position in the Pacific Strategic Balance: Looking Toward the Year 2000." *Issues and Studies* 28 (1): 1–17.

Dittmer, Lowell, and Yu-Shan Wu. 1993. "The Political Economy of Leadership in Reform China: Macro and Micro Informal Politics Linkages." Paper presented at the 45th Annual Meeting of the Association for Asian Studies, Los Angeles.

Djilas, Milovan. 1953. *The New Class*. New York: Praeger.

do Rosario, Louise. 1989. "An Uneasy Calm." *Far Eastern Economic Review* (Aug. 10).

Duverger, Maurice. 1977. *The Idea of Politics: The Use of Power in Society*, trans. Robert North and Hugh Murphy. London: Methuen.

Eastman, Lloyd E. 1986. "Nationalist China During the Sino-Japanese War, 1937–1945." In John K. Fairbank and Albert Feuerwerker, eds., *The Cambridge History of China*. Vol. 13. Cambridge, Eng.: Cambridge University Press.

Easton, David. 1965. *A Systems Analysis of Political Life*. New York: Wiley.

Ehrlich, Eva. 1985. "The Size Structure of Manufacturing Establishments and Enterprises: An International Comparison." *Journal of Comparative Economics* 9 (3): 267–95.

Erlich, Alexander. 1967. *The Soviet Industrialization Debate*. Cambridge, Mass.: Harvard University Press.

———. 1977. "Stalinism and Marxian Growth Models." In Robert Tucker, ed., *Stalinism: Essays in Historical Interpretation*. New York: W. W. Norton.

Evans, Peter. 1979. *Dependent Development: The Alliance of Multinational, State, and Local Capital in Brazil*. Princeton, N.J.: Princeton University Press.

———. 1987. "Class, State, and Dependence in East Asia: Lessons for Latin Americanists." In Frederic Deyo, ed., *The Political Economy of East Asian Industrialism*. Ithaca, N.Y.: Cornell University Press.

Fainsod, Merle. 1958. *Smolensk Under Soviet Rule*. Cambridge, Mass.: Harvard University Press.

Fang Shan. 1990. "T'ai-shang tui-min t'ou-tzu chih kai-k'uang" (Taiwanese investment in Fukien). *Mainland China Studies* 33 (4): 39–47.
Fang Shue-ch'uen. 1987. "Chung-kung shih-san-ta jen-shih pu-shu fen-hsi" (An analysis of the personnel arrangements made at the CCP's Thirteenth Party Congress). *Mainland China Studies* 30 (5): 12–28.
Fei, John C. H. 1988. "A Bird's Eye View of Policy Evolution on Taiwan: An Introductory Essay." In K. T. Li, *The Evolution of Policy Behind Taiwan's Development Success*. New Haven, Conn.: Yale University Press.
Fei, John C. H., Gustav Ranis, and Shirley W. Y. Kuo. 1979. *Growth with Equity: The Taiwan Case*. Oxford: Oxford University Press.
Feuer, Lewis. 1975. *Ideology and the Ideologists*. New York: Harper & Row.
Feuerwerker, Albert. 1983. "Economic Trends, 1912–49." In John K. Fairbank, ed., *The Cambridge History of China*. Vol. 12. Cambridge, Eng.: Cambridge University Press.
Fewsmith, Joseph. 1988. "Agricultural Crisis in China." *Problems of Communism* 37 (6): 78–93.
Fischer, George. 1968. *The Soviet System and Modern Society*. New York: Atherton Press.
Fischer, Stanley, and Alan Gelb. 1991. "The Process of Socialist Economic Transformation." *Journal of Economic Perspectives* 5 (4): 91–105.
Fitting, George. 1982. "Export Processing Zones in Taiwan and the People's Republic of China." *Asian Survey* 22 (8): 732–44.
Flakierski, Henryk. 1979. "Economic Reform and Income Distribution in Hungary." *Cambridge Journal of Economics* 3 (1): 15–32.
Fleron, Frederic. 1969. "Toward a Reconceptualization of Political Change in the Soviet Union: The Political Leadership System." In Frederic Fleron, ed., *Communist Studies and the Social Sciences*. Chicago: Rand McNally.
Friedman, Edward. 1990. "Deng Versus the Peasantry: Recollectivization in the Countryside." *Problems of Communism* 39 (5): 30–43.
Friedrich, Carl J., and Zbigniew K. Brzezinski. 1956. *Totalitarian Dictatorship and Autocracy*. New York: Praeger.
Furubotn, Eirik G., and Svetozar Pejovich, eds. 1973. *The Economics of Property Rights*. Cambridge, Mass.: Ballinger.
Gati, Charles. 1974. "The Kadar Mystique." *Problems of Communism* 23 (3): 23–35.
Geertz, Charles. 1967. "Ideology as a Cultural System." In David Apter, ed., *Ideology and Discontent*. New York: Free Press.
Gerschenkron, Alexander. 1962. *Economic Backwardness in Historical Perspective*. Cambridge, Mass.: Harvard University Press.
Gilpin, Robert. 1987. *The Political Economy of International Relations*. Princeton, N.J.: Princeton University Press.
Gold, David A., Y. H. Lo, and Erik Olin Wright. 1975. "Recent Developments in Marxist Theories of the Capitalist State." *Monthly Review* 26: 29–43; 27: 36–51.
Gold, Thomas. 1986a. "Multilateral Lending Agencies in East Asia." In Robert A. Scalapino and Chen Qimao, eds., *Pacific-Asian Issues: Amer-*

ican and Chinese Views. Berkeley, Calif.: Institute of East Asian Studies.

―――. 1986b. *State and Society in the Taiwan Miracle*. Armonk, N.Y.: M. E. Sharpe.

Goldman, Marshall. 1987. *Gorbachev's Challenge: Economic Reform in the Age of High Technology*. New York: W. W. Norton.

Goldman, Merle. 1985. "Culture." In Steven M. Goldstein, ed., *China Briefing, 1984*. Boulder, Colo.: Westview Press.

Goldstein, Steven M. 1988. "Reforming Socialist Systems: Some Lessons of the Chinese Experience." *Studies in Comparative Communism* 21 (2): 221–37.

Goodman, David S. G. 1988. "Communism in East Asia: The Production Imperative, Legitimacy and Reform." In David S. G. Goodman, ed., *Communism and Reform in East Asia*. London: Frank Cass.

Gray, Jack. 1988. "The State and the Rural Economy in the Chinese People's Republic." In Gordon White, ed., *Developmental States in East Asia*. New York: St. Martin's Press.

Griffith, William E. 1985. "Sino-Soviet Relations and the Asian Quadrangle, 1984." *Issues and Studies* 21 (1): 113–25.

Gyorgy, Andrew, and George D. Blackwood, eds. 1967. *Ideologies in World Affairs*. Waltham, Mass.: Blaisdell.

Haberstroh, John R. 1978. "The Case of Hungary: Liberal Socialism Under Stress." *Journal of Comparative Economics* 2 (2): 111–25.

Haggard, Stephen. 1986. "The Newly Industrializing Countries in the International System." *World Politics* 38 (2): 343–70.

Harding, Harry. 1984a. "Competing Models of the Chinese Communist Policy Process: Toward a Sorting and Evaluation." *Issues and Studies* 20 (2): 13–36.

―――. 1984b. "The Study of Chinese Politics: Toward a Third Generation of Scholarship." *World Politics* 36 (2): 284–307.

―――. 1984c. "The Transformation of China." *The Brookings Review* 2 (3): 3–7.

―――. 1987. *China's Second Revolution*. Washington, D.C.: Brookings Institution.

Hare, Paul. 1977. "Economic Reform in Hungary: Problems and Prospects." *Cambridge Journal of Economics* 1 (4): 317–33.

―――. 1988. "What Can China Learn from the Hungarian Economic Reforms?" In Stephan Feuchtwang, Athar Hussain, and Thierry Pairault, eds., *Transforming China's Economy in the Eighties*. Vol. 2. Boulder, Colo.: Westview Press.

Hartford, Kathleen. 1985. "Socialist Agriculture is Dead; Long Live Socialist Agriculture! Organizational Transformations in Rural China." In Elizabeth J. Perry and Christine Wong, eds., *The Political Economy of Reform in Post-Mao China*. Cambridge, Mass.: Harvard University Press.

Held, Virginia, ed. 1980. *Property, Profits, and Economic Justice*. Belmont, Calif.: Wadsworth.

Hewett, Edward A. 1980. "Lessons of the 1970's and Prospects for the 1980's." In U.S. Congress, Joint Economic Committee, ed., *East Euro-*

pean Economic Assessment: Part I, Country Studies. Washington, D.C.: Government Printing Office.

—. 1988. *Reforming the Soviet Economy: Equality Versus Efficiency.* Washington, D.C.: Brookings Institution.

Hirschon, Renee, ed. 1984. *Women and Property—Women as Property.* London: Croom Helm.

Ho, Samuel P. S. 1975. "The Economic Development of Colonial Taiwan: Evidence and Interpretation." *Journal of Asian Studies* 34 (2): 417–39.

—. 1978. *Economic Development of Taiwan, 1860–1970.* New Haven, Conn.: Yale University Press.

Hofheinz, Roy, and Kent E. Calder. 1982. *The Eastasia Edge.* New York: Basic Books.

Holz, Carsten. 1992. *The Role of Central Banking in China's Economic Reform.* Ithaca, N.Y.: Cornell University East Asia Program.

Hou, Ruili. 1990. "Population Problems on the Eve of the 1990 Census." *China Today* 34 (3): 26–29.

Hough, Jerry F. 1974. "The Soviet System: Petrification or Pluralism?" In Lenard J. Cohen and Jane P. Shapiro, eds., *Communist System in Comparative Perspective.* New York: Anchor.

Hough, Jerry F., and Merle Fainsod. 1979. *How the Soviet Union Is Governed.* Cambridge, Mass.: Harvard University Press.

Hua Sheng, Zhang Xuejun, and Luo Xiaopeng. 1988. "Zhongguo gaige shinian: huigu, fansi he qianjing" (Ten years in China's reform: Looking back, reflection and prospect). *Jingji Yanjiu* 1988 (9): 13–37.

Huang, Yasheng. 1990. "The Origins of the Pro-Democracy Movement." *The Fletcher Forum* 14 (1): 30–39.

Huntington, Samuel P. 1970. "Social and Institutional Dynamics of One-Party Systems." In S. Huntington and C. Moore, eds., *Authoritarian Politics in Modern Society: The Dynamics of Established One-Party Systems.* New York: Basic Books.

—. 1971. "The Change to Change: Modernization, Development, and Politics." *Journal of Comparative Politics* 3 (3): 283–322.

Janos, Andrew C. 1986. *Politics and Paradigms: Changing Theories of Change in Social Science.* Stanford, Calif.: Stanford University Press.

Jasny, Naum. 1972. *Soviet Economists in the Twenties.* Cambridge, Eng.: Cambridge University Press.

Johnson, Chalmers. 1962. *Peasant Nationalism and Communist Power.* Stanford, Calif.: Stanford University Press.

—. 1970. "Comparing Communist Nations." In Chalmers Johnson, ed., *Change in Communist Systems.* Stanford, Calif.: Stanford University Press.

—. 1982. *MITI and the Japanese Miracle.* Stanford, Calif.: Stanford University Press.

—. 1984a. "Introduction: The Idea of Industrial Policy." In Chalmers Johnson, ed., *The Industrial Policy Debate.* San Francisco: ICS Press.

—. 1984b. "*La Serenissima* of the East." *Asian and African Studies* 18 (1): 57–73.

—. 1985. "Political Institutions and Economic Performance: The Government-Business Relations in Japan, South Korea, and Taiwan." In

Robert Scalapino, Seizaburo Sato, and Jusuf Wanandi, eds., *Asian Economic Development: Present and Future.* Berkeley: University of California Press.

——. 1986a. "Japan's Role in Asia and the Pacific." In Robert A. Scalapino and Chen Qimao, eds., *Pacific Asian Issues: American and Chinese Views.* Berkeley, Calif.: Institute of East Asian Studies.

——. 1986b. "The Nonsocialist NICs: East Asia." *International Organization* 40 (2): 557–65.

Johnson, Harry. 1968. "Ideology and the Social System." In *International Encyclopedia of Social Sciences.* Vol. 7. New York: Crowell Collier and Macmillan.

Jowitt, Ken. 1975. "Inclusion and Mobilization in European Leninist Regimes." *World Politics* 28 (1): 69–96.

——. 1983. "Soviet Neotraditionalism: The Political Corruption of a Leninist Regime." *Soviet Studies* 35 (3): 275–97.

Kao Ch'ang and Wang Tung-ying. 1991. "Ta-lu tsung-t'i ching-chi ch'ingshih fen-hsi" (An analysis of the macroeconomic situation in mainland China). Paper presented at the Conference on the Current Mainland Economic Situation, Chung-Hua Institution for Economic Research, Taipei.

Kassof, Allen. 1964. "The Administered Society." *World Politics* 16 (4): 558–75.

Kautsky, Karl. 1980. *Die Diktatur des Proletariats* (The dictatorship of the proletariat), trans. Cheng Hsueh-chia. Taipei: Li Ming.

Kelliher, Daniel. 1986. "The Political Consequences of China's Reforms." *Comparative Politics* 18 (4): 479–93.

——. 1990. "Privatization and Politics in Rural China." In Gordon White, ed., *The Chinese State in the Era of Economic Reform: The Road to Crisis.* London: Macmillan.

——. 1992. *Peasant Power in China: The Era of Rural Reform, 1979–1989.* New Haven, Conn.: Yale University Press.

Kelly, Rita Mae, and Frederic J. Fleron. 1971. "Motivation, Methodology and Communist Ideology." In Roger Kanet, ed., *The Behavioral Revolution and Communist Studies.* New York: Free Press.

Kelsen, Hans. 1955. *The Communist Theory of Law.* New York: Praeger.

Kerr, George. 1965. *Formosa Betrayed.* Boston: Houghton Mifflin.

Kindermann, Gottfried-Karl. 1987. "Agrarian Revolution and Land Reform in Divided China: The Political Dimensions." In Yu-ming Shaw, ed., *Reform and Revolution in Twentieth-Century China.* Taipei: Institute of International Relations.

Kolakowski, Leszek. 1981a. *Main Currents of Marxism: Its Origins, Growth and Dissolution.* Vol. 2, *The Golden Age,* trans. P. S. Falla. Oxford: Oxford University Press.

——. 1981b. *Main Currents of Marxism: Its Origins, Growth and Dissolution.* Vol. 3, *The Breakdown,* trans. P. S. Falla. Oxford: Oxford University Press.

Kornai, Janos. 1986a. *Contradictions and Dilemmas.* Cambridge, Mass.: MIT Press.

——. 1986b. "The Hungarian Reform Process: Visions, Hopes, and Reality." *Journal of Economic Literature* 24 (4): 1687–1734.

———. 1989. "Some Lessons from the Hungarian Experience for Chinese Reformers." In Peter Van Ness, ed., *Market Reforms in Socialist Societies: Comparing China and Hungary*. Boulder, Colo.: Lynne Rienner.

Kovrig, Bennett. 1984. "Hungary." In Teresa Rakowska-Harmstone, ed., *Communism in Eastern Europe*. Bloomington: Indiana University Press.

———. 1987. "Hungarian Socialism: The Deceptive Hybrid." *Eastern European Politics and Societies* 1 (1): 113–34.

Kowalewski, David. 1981. "China and the Soviet Union: A Comparative Model for Analysis." *Studies in Comparative Communism* 14 (4): 279–306.

Koziolek, Helmut. 1987–88. "The Economic Strategy of the Eleventh Party Congress of the SED and the New Stage in Science-Production Relations." *Eastern European Economics* 26 (2): 64–83.

Kreisberg, Paul H. 1988. "PRC Foreign Policy After the Thirteenth Party Congress." Paper presented at the Seventeenth Sino-American Conference on Mainland China, Institute of International Relations, Taipei.

Kuo, Shirley W. Y., Gustav Ranis, and John C. H. Fei. 1981. *The Taiwan Success Story: Rapid Growth with Improved Distribution in the Republic of China, 1952–1979*. Boulder, Colo.: Westview Press.

Lampton, Michael D., ed. 1987. *Policy Implementation in Post-Mao China*. Berkeley: University of California Press.

Lane, Robert. 1962. *Political Ideology*. New York: Free Press of Glencoe.

———. 1970. *Political Thinking and Consciousness*. Chicago: Markham.

Lange, Peter, and Hudson Meadwell. 1985. "Typologies of Democratic Systems: From Political Inputs to Political Economy." In Howard Wiarda, ed., *New Directions in Comparative Politics*. Boulder, Colo.: Westview Press.

Laswell, Harold D., and Abraham Kaplan. 1961. *Power and Society: A Framework for Political Inquiry*. New Haven, Conn.: Yale University Press.

Lee Chin-Shin. 1983. "Chung-kung hsien-chieh-tuan kung-yeh cheng-ts'e" (The CCP's industrial policy at the present stage). In King-yu Chang, ed., *Chung-kung hsien-chieh-tuan ching-chi cheng-ts'e* (The CCP's economic policy at the present stage). Taipei: Institute of International Relations.

Lenin, V. I. 1953. *Sochineniya* (Collected works). Vol. 5. Moscow: Gosudarstvennoe Izdatel'stvo Politicheskoi Literatury.

Lewin, Moshe. 1965. "The Immediate Background of Soviet Collectivization." *Soviet Studies* 17 (2): 162–79.

———. 1968. *Russian Peasants and Soviet Power*. Evanston, Ill.: Northwestern University Press.

Li Kwoh-Ting. 1987. *Kung-tso yu hsin-yang* (Vision and devotion: Witnessing economic and social development on Taiwan, ROC). Taipei: Commonwealth.

———. 1988. *The Evolution of Policy Behind Taiwan's Development Success*. New Haven, Conn.: Yale University Press.

Li, Yunqi. 1989. "China's Inflation: Causes, Effects, and Solutions." *Asian Survey* 24 (7): 655–68.

Lieberthal, Kenneth, and Michel Oksenberg. 1988. *Policy Making in* ·

China: Leaders, Structures, and Processes. Princeton, N.J.: Princeton University Press.

Lijphart, Arend. 1971. "Comparative Politics and the Comparative Methods." *American Political Science Review* 65: 682–93.

Lin, Chong-Pin. 1991. "China: The Coming Changes." *American Enterprise* 2 (1): 18–25.

Lindblom, Charles. 1977. *Politics and Markets.* New York: Basic Books.

Liu, P. L. 1976. *Political Culture and Group Conflict in Communist China.* Santa Barbara, Calif.: ABC-Clio.

Lowenthal, Richard. 1970. "Development Versus Utopia in Communist Policy." In Chalmers Johnson, ed., *Change in Communist Systems.* Stanford, Calif.: Stanford University Press.

———. 1983. "The Post-Revolutionary Phase in China and Russia." *Studies in Comparative Communism* 16 (3): 191–201.

Lundberg, Erik. 1979. "Fiscal and Monetary Policies." In Walter Galenson, ed., *Economic Growth and Sturctural Change in Taiwan.* Ithaca, N.Y.: Cornell University Press.

Luo Rujia. 1986. "Zhonggong zhengti gaige de beijing yu qianjing" (The background and prospects of the CCP's political structural reform). *Cheng Ming,* October, pp. 23–25.

McCarney, Joe. 1980. *The Real World of Ideology.* Sussex, Eng.: Harvester.

Macpherson, C. B. 1973. *Democratic Theory.* Oxford: Clarendon Press.

Macridis, Roy C. 1980. *Contemporary Political Ideologies.* Cambridge, Mass.: Winthrop.

Mannheim, Karl. 1936. *Ideology and Utopia: An Introduction to the Sociology of Knowledge,* trans. Louis Wirth and Edward Shils. New York: Harcourt, Brace & World.

———. 1970. "Marxism: The Last Ideology." In Judith N. Shklar, ed., *Political Theory and Ideology.* London: Macmillan.

Marrese, Michael. 1981. "The Evolution of Wage Regulation in Hungary." In P. G. Hare, H. K. Radice, and N. Swain, eds., *Hungary: A Decade of Economic Reform.* London: George Allen & Unwin.

———. 1983. "Agricultural Policy and Performance in Hungary." *Journal of Comparative Economics* 7 (3): 329–45.

Meaney, Constance Squires. 1987. "Is the Soviet Present China's Future?" *World Politics* 39 (2): 203–30.

Mendel, Douglas H. 1974. "The Formosan Nationalist Movement in Crisis." In Yung-Hwan Jo, ed., *Taiwan's Future.* Tempe: Arizona State University Press.

Meyer, Alfred G. 1970. "Theories of Convergence." In Chalmers Johnson, ed., *Change in Communist Systems.* Stanford, Calif.: Stanford University Press.

———. 1972. *Leninism.* New York: Praeger.

Millar, James R., and Alec Nove. 1976. "Was Stalin Really Necessary? A Debate on Collectivization." *Problems of Communism* 25 (4): 49–62.

Montias, John. 1970. "Types of Communist Economic Systems." In Chalmers Johnson, ed., *Change in Communist Systems.* Stanford, Calif.: Stanford University Press.

Moore, Barrington, Jr. 1965. *Soviet Politics—The Dilemma of Power: The Role of Ideas in Social Change*. New York: Harper & Row.

Mullins, Willard A. 1972. "On the Concept of Ideology in Political Science." *American Political Science Review* 66 (2): 498–510.

Myers, Ramon H. 1987. "Political Theory and Recent Political Developments in the Republic of China." *Asian Survey* 27 (9): 1003–1022.

Myers, Ramon H., and Yamada Saburo. 1984. "Agricultural Development in the Empire." In Ramon H. Myers and Mark R. Peattie, eds., *The Japanese Colonial Empire, 1895–1945*. Princeton, N.J.: Princeton University Press.

Nathan, Andrew J. 1973. "A Factionalism Model for CCP Politics." *China Quarterly* 53: 34–66.

————. 1990. *China's Crisis*. New York: Columbia University Press.

Naughton, Barry. 1985. "False Starts and Second Wind: Financial Reforms in China's Industrial System." In Elizabeth J. Perry and Christine Wong, eds., *The Political Economy of Reform in Post-Mao China*. Cambridge, Mass.: Harvard University Press.

————. 1986. "How Much Have Urban Dwellers Benefited from China's Economic Reforms?" Paper presented at the Berkeley Regional China Conference, University of California, Berkeley.

————. 1992. "Implications of the State Monopoly over Industry and Its Relaxation." *Modern China* 18 (1): 14–41.

North, Douglass. 1981. *Structure and Change in Economic History*. New York: W. W. Norton.

North, Robert C. 1954. *Kuomintang and Chinese Communist Elites*. Stanford, Calif.: Stanford University Press.

Nove, Alec. 1964. *Economic Rationality and Soviet Politics*. New York: Praeger.

————. 1982. *An Economic History of the U.S.S.R.* New York: Penguin Books.

————. 1983. *The Economics of Feasible Socialism*. London: George Allen and Unwin.

Nozick, Robert. 1974. *Anarchy, State, and Utopia*. New York: Basic Books.

Nutter, G. Warren. 1973. "Market Without Property: A Grand Illusion." In Eirik G. Furubotn and Svetozar Pejovich, eds., *The Economics of Property Rights*. Cambridge, Mass.: Ballinger.

Nyers, Rezso. 1983. "Interrelations Between Policy and the Economic Reform in Hungary." *Journal of Comparative Economics* 7 (3): 211–24.

Okita, Saburo. 1990. "Japan's Quiet Strength." *Foreign Policy* 75: 128–45.

Oksenberg, Michel. 1982. "Economic Policy-Making in China." *China Quarterly* 90: 165–94.

Oksenberg, Michel, and Steven Goldstein. 1974. "The Chinese Political Spectrum." *Problems of Communism* 23: 1–13.

Olsen, Richard. 1983. "Interaction Between Law and Society: An Interpretation of Law in Action and the Function of Property Rights." Ph.D. diss., University of Zurich.

Pang, Chien-kuo. 1988. "The State and Economic Transformation: The Taiwan Case." Ph.D. diss., Brown University.

———. 1990. "The State and Socioeconomic Development in Taiwan Since 1949." *Issues and Studies* 26 (5): 11–36.

Parsons, Talcott. 1964a. "Communism and the West: The Sociology of the Conflict." In Amitai and Eva Etzioni, eds., *Social Change*. New York: Basic Books.

———. 1964b. "Evolutionary Universals in Society." *American Sociological Review* 3: 338–57.

Pejovich, Steve. 1989. "Liberty, Property Rights, and Innovation in Eastern Europe." *CATO Journal* 9 (1): 57–70.

Perkins, Dwight. 1986. *China: Asia's Next Economic Giant?* Seattle: University of Washington Press.

———. 1988. "Reforming China's Economic System." *Journal of Economic Literature* 26: 601–45.

Piettre, Andre. 1973. "Property: Part II, Property from the Judicial Standpoint." In C. D. Kernig, ed., *Marxism, Communism and Western Society: A Comparative Encyclopedia*. New York: Herder & Herder.

Plamenatz, John. 1970. *Ideology*. London: Pall Mall Press.

Portes, Richard D. 1970. "Economic Reforms in Hungary." *American Economic Review: Papers and Proceedings* 60 (2): 307–13.

———. 1977. "Hungary: Economic Performance, Policy and Prospects." In U.S. Congress, Joint Economic Committee, ed., *East European Economies Post-Helsinki*. Washington, D.C.: Government Printing Office.

Poulantzas, Nicos. 1973. *Political Power and Social Classes*. London: New Left Books.

Prybyla, Jan S. 1984. "Mainland China's Special Economic Zones." Paper presented at the Thirteenth Sino-American Conference on Mainland China, Institute of International Relations, Taipei.

———. 1986. "Mainland China and Hungary: To Market, To Market." Paper presented at the Fifteenth Sino-American Conference on Mainland China, Institute of International Relations, Taipei.

———. 1989. "China's Economic Experiment: Back from the Market?" *Problems of Communism* 38 (1): 1–18.

———. 1990. "Economic Reform of Socialism: The Dengist Course in China." *Annals* 507: 113–22.

Pryor, Frederic L. 1973. *Property and Industrial Organization in Communist and Capitalist Nations*. Bloomington: Indiana University Press.

Pye, Lucian W. 1981. *The Dynamics of Chinese Politics*. Cambridge, Mass.: Oelgeschlager, Gunn and Hain.

———. 1988a. "The Asian Capitalism: A Political Portrait." In Peter L. Berger and Hsin-Huang Michael Hsiao, eds., *In Search of an East Asian Development Model*. New Brunswick, N.J.: Transaction.

———. 1988b. "China: Economics as Engine of Political Change?" *The Fletcher Forum* 12 (2): 221–30.

Ranis, Gustav. 1979. "Industrial Development." In Walter Galenson, ed., *Economic Growth and Structural Change in Taiwan*. Ithaca, N.Y.: Cornell University Press.

Ranney, Austin, ed. 1968. *Political Science and Public Policy*. Chicago: Markham.

Rariden, Robert Lee. 1983. "The Right to Property: Its Source and Its Limits." Ph.D. diss., University of Miami.

Rawls, John A. 1971. *Theory of Justice.* Cambridge, Mass.: Harvard University Press.
Reeve, Andrew. 1986. *Property.* Atlantic Highlands, N.J.: Humanities Press International.
Reynolds, Bruce L. 1987. "Trade, Employment, and Inequality in Postreform China." *Journal of Comparative Economics* 11 (3): 479–89.
Rigby, T. H. 1964. "Organizational, Traditional, and Market Societies." *World Politics* 16 (4): 539–57.
———. 1976. "Politics of Mono-Organizational Society." In Andrew Janos, ed., *Authoritarian Politics in Communist Europe.* Berkeley, Calif.: Institute of International Studies.
———. 1977. "Stalinism and the Mono-Organizational Society." In Robert Tucker, ed., *Stalinism: Essays in Historical Interpretation.* New York: W. W. Norton.
Roberts, Paul Craig. 1970. "War Communism: A Re-examination." *Slavic Review* 29 (2): 238–61.
Robinson, William F. 1973. *The Pattern of Reform in Hungary: A Political, Economic and Cultural Analysis.* New York: Praeger.
Rokeach, Milton. 1960. *The Open and Closed Mind.* New York: Basic Books.
Ryan, Alan. 1984. *Property and Political Theory.* New York: Basil Blackwell.
Sah, Edward K. 1986. "Major Contradictions in Peiking's Economic Reforms." Paper presented at the Fifteenth Sino-American Conference on Mainland China, Institute of International Relations, Taipei.
———. 1990. "Chung-kung ch'i-yeh ling-tao t'i-chih te kai-ke" (The reform of the leadership structure in mainland China's enterprises). *Mainland China Studies* 32 (10): 32–40.
———. 1991. *Chung-kung shih-nien ching-kai ti li-lun yu shih-chien* (Theory and practice of the decade-old economic reform in mainland China). Taipei: Institute of International Relations.
Samuels, Richard J. 1987. *The Business of the Japanese State.* Ithaca, N.Y.: Cornell University Press.
Sartori, Giovannio. 1976. *Parties and Party Systems.* Cambridge, Eng.: Cambridge University Press.
Scanlan, James P. 1981. "Yakhot and Ojzerman on Ideology." *Studies in Soviet Thought* 22 (3): 193–95.
Schmitter, Philippe. 1974. "Still the Century of Corporatism?" In B. Pike and Thomas Stritch, eds., *The New Corporatism: Social and Political Structures in the Iberian World.* Notre Dame, Ind.: University of Notre Dame Press.
Schott, Rudiger. 1973. "Property: Part I, Property from the Ethnological Standpoint." In C. D. Kernig, ed., *Marxism, Communism and Western Society: A Comparative Encyclopedia.* New York: Herder & Herder.
Schroeder, Gertrude E. 1988. "Property Rights Issues in Economic Reforms in Socialist Countries." *Studies in Comparative Communism* 21 (2): 175–88.
Schurmann, Franz. 1968. *Ideology and Organization in Communist China.* Berkeley: University of California Press.
Scitovsky, Tibor. 1986. "Economic Development in Taiwan and South Ko-

rea." In Lawrence J. Lau, *Models of Development: A Comparative Study of Economic Growth in South Korea and Taiwan.* San Francisco: ICS Press.

Scott, Maurice. 1979. "Foreign Trade." In Walter Galenson, ed., *Economic Growth and Structural Change in Taiwan.* Ithaca, N.Y.: Cornell University Press.

Shen Yun-Lung. 1972. *Yin Chung-jun hsien-sheng nien-p'u ch'u kao* (Biography of K. Y. Yin). Taipei: Chuan-chi wen-hsueh.

Shils, Edward. 1968. "The Concept and Function of Ideology." In *International Encyclopedia of Social Sciences.* Vol. 7. New York: Crowell Collier and Macmillan.

Shirk, Susan. 1985. "The Politics of Industrial Reform." In Elizabeth J. Perry and Christine Wong, eds., *The Political Economy of Reform in Post-Mao China.* Cambridge, Mass.: Harvard University Press.

———. 1988. "The Political Economy of Chinese Industrial Reform." In David Stark and Victor Nee, eds., *Remaking the Economic Institutions of Socialism: China and Eastern Europe.* Stanford, Calif.: Stanford University Press.

Shue, Vivienne. 1988. *The Reach of the State: Sketches of the Chinese Body Politic.* Stanford, Calif.: Stanford University Press.

Sicular, Terry. 1992. "China's Agricultural Policy During the Reform Period." In U.S. Congress, Joint Economic Committee, ed., *China's Economic Dilemmas in the 1990's: The Problems of Reforms, Modernization, and Interdependence.* Armonk, N.Y.: M. E. Sharpe.

Silverman, Saul N., ed. 1972. *Lenin.* Englewood Cliffs, N.J.: Prentice-Hall.

Simonton, James W. 1926. "Austin's Classification of Proprietary Rights." *Cornell Law Quarterly* 11 (3): 277–99.

Skilling, H. Gordon. 1966. "Interest Groups and Communist Politics." *World Politics* 18 (3): 435–51.

Skilling, H. Gordon, and Franklyn J. C. Griffiths, eds. 1971. *Interest Groups in Soviet Politics.* Princeton, N.J.: Princeton University Press.

Skocpol, Theda. 1979. *States and Social Revolutions.* Cambridge, Eng.: Cambridge University Press.

———. 1982. "Bringing the State Back In." *SSRC Items* 36 (1/2): 1–8.

Solinger, Dorothy. 1985. "Economic Reform." In Steven M. Goldstein, ed., *China Briefing, 1984.* Boulder, Colo.: Westview Press.

———. 1993. *China's Transition from Socialism.* Armonk, N.Y.: M. E. Sharpe.

Stark, David, and Victor Nee. 1989. "Toward an Institutional Analysis of State Socialism." In Victor Nee and David Stark, eds., *Remaking the Economic Institutions of Socialism: China and Eastern Europe.* Stanford, Calif.: Stanford University Press.

Sullivan, Michael. 1985. "The Ideology of the Chinese Communist Party Since the Third Plenum." In Bill Brugger, ed., *Chinese Marxism in Flux, 1978–84.* Armonk, N.Y.: M. E. Sharpe.

Sun Shangqing. 1988. "Dui ruogan shenhua gaige silu de jianyao pingjie" (Brief comments on several trends of thought on deepening reform). Paper presented at the Fourth Economic Symposium of Chinese Young Economists, University of California, Berkeley.

Szurek, Jean-Charles. 1987. "Family Farms in Polish Agricultural Policy: 1945–1985." *Eastern European Politics and Societies* 1 (2): 225–54.
Tai, Hung-chao. 1970. "The Kuomintang and Modernization in Taiwan." In Samuel P. Huntington and Clement H. Moore, eds., *Authoritarian Politics in Modern Society: The Dynamics of Established One-Party Systems*. New York: Basic Books.
Tang Xin. 1988. "Dui zhongguo jingji tizhi gaige zhanlue de yanjiu" (Studies on the economic reform strategy). Paper presented at the Fourth Economic Symposium of Chinese Young Economists, University of California, Berkeley.
Teiwes, Frederick C. 1974. "Chinese Politics, 1949–1965: A Changing Mao." *Current Scene* 12 (1): 1–15.
———. 1979. "The 'Rules of Game' in Chinese Politics." *Problems of Communism* 28 (5/6): 67–76.
Thorbecke, Erik. 1979. "Agricultural Development." In Walter Galenson, ed., *Economic Growth and Structural Change in Taiwan*. Ithaca, N.Y.: Cornell University Press.
Tien, Hung-mao. 1989. *The Great Transition: Political and Social Change in the Republic of China*. Stanford, Calif.: Hoover Institution Press.
Toma, Peter A., and Ivan Volgyes. 1977. *Politics in Hungary*. San Francisco: W. H. Freeman.
Toshiyuki, Mizoguchi, and Yamamoto Yuzo. 1984. "Capital Formation in Taiwan and Korea." In Ramon H. Myers and Mark R. Peattie, eds., *The Japanese Colonial Empire, 1895–1945*. Princeton, N.J.: Princeton University Press.
Treadgold, Donald W., ed. 1967. *Soviet and Chinese Communism: Similarities and Differences*. Seattle: University of Washington Press.
Trotsky, Leon. 1970. *The Revolution Betrayed*. New York: Pathfinder Press.
Tsurumi, E. Patricia. 1984. "Colonial Education in Korea and Taiwan." In Ramon H. Myers and Mark R. Peattie, eds., *The Japanese Colonial Empire, 1895–1945*. Princeton, N.J.: Princeton University Press.
Tucker, Robert C. 1969a. *The Marxian Revolutionary Idea*. New York: W. W. Norton.
———. 1969b. "On the Comparative Study of Communism." In Frederic Fleron, ed., *Communist Studies and the Social Sciences*. Chicago: Rand McNally.
———, ed. 1978. *The Marx-Engels Reader*. New York: W. W. Norton.
Tung, An-Chi. 1988. "Taiwan's Adjustment After the Oil Shocks: 1973–1985." Ph.D. diss., University of California, Berkeley.
Ulam, Adam B. 1968. *Expansion and Coexistence*. New York: Praeger.
———. 1974. *Stalin: The Man and His Era*. New York: Viking Press.
Unger, Jonathan. 1986. "The Decollectivization of the Chinese Countryside: A Survey of Twenty-eight Villages." *Pacific Affairs* 58 (4): 585–606.
Van Ness, Peter. 1970. *Revolution and Chinese Foreign Policy*. Berkeley: University of California Press.
———, ed. 1989. *Market Reforms in Socialist Societies: Comparing China and Hungary*. Boulder, Colo.: Lynne Rienner.

Volgyes, Ivan. 1973. "Hungary in the Seventies: The Era of Reform." *Current History*, May, pp. 216–19.
———. 1976. "Limited Liberalization in Hungary." *Current History*, March 1976: 107–10.
Von Laue, Theodore H. 1964. *Why Lenin? Why Stalin?* Philadelphia: Lippincott.
Walder, Andrew G. 1986. *Communist Neo-Traditionalism: Work and Authority in Chinese Industry*. Berkeley: University of California Press.
Walsh, J. Richard. 1984. "Eight Characters in Search of a Strategy: Political Economic Reform in Post-Mao China." *Asian Affairs* 11 (1): 25–44.
Wang Nai-chi. 1987. "Taiwan ching-chi fa-chan yu k'ang-chan ch'i-chien ching-chi chien-she" (Economic development on Taiwan and economic construction during the resistance war). *Central Daily News*, September 11.
Wang Ruoshui. 1983. "Lun yihua wenti" (On the question of alienation). *Cheng Ming* 74: 68–72.
Wei Ai. 1983. "Chung-kung hsien-chieh-tuan te wai-mao cheng-ts'e he wai-tzu li-yung" (Current trade policy and foreign capital utilization of the PRC). In Chang King-yu, ed., *Chung-kung hsien-chieh-tuan ching-chi cheng-ts'e* (The CCP's economic policy at the present stage). Taipei: Institute of International Relations.
———. 1990. "Economic and Trade Relations Between the United States and Mainland China in the Past Decade." *Issues and Studies* 26 (4): 63–82.
Wei, Yun. 1974. "Political Development in the Republic of China on Taiwan: Analysis and Projections." In Yung-Hwan Jo, ed., *Taiwan's Future*. Tempe: Arizona State University Press.
Wen Hsien-shen. 1984. "Ching-chien-hui te kuo-ch'u hsien-tsai yu wei-lai" (The Council for Economic Planning and Development: Its past, present, and future). *Commonwealth* 42: 12–25.
White, Gordon. 1987a. "The Impact of Economic Reforms in the Chinese Countryside." *Modern China* 13 (4): 411–40.
———. 1987b. "Riding the Tiger: Grass-Roots Rural Politics in the Wake of the Chinese Economic Reforms." In Ashwani Saith, ed., *The Re-emergence of the Chinese Peasantry: Aspects of Rural Decollectivization*. London: Croom Helm.
———. 1993. *Riding the Tiger: The Politics of Economic Reform in Post-Mao China*. Stanford, Calif.: Stanford University Press.
White, Gordon, and Robert Wade. 1988. "Developmental States and Markets in East Asia: An Introduction." In Gordon White, ed., *Developmental States in East Asia*. New York: St. Martin's Press.
Whiting, Allen. 1983. "Assertive Nationalism in Chinese Foreign Policy." *Asian Survey* 23 (8): 913–33.
Wilbur, C. Martin. 1983. "The Nationalist Revolution: From Canton to Nanking, 1923–28." In John K. Fairbank, ed., *The Cambridge History of China*. Vol. 12. Cambridge, Eng.: Cambridge University Press.
Wiles, Peter. 1974. "The Control of Inflation in Hungary, January 1968–June 1973." *Economic Appliquee* 27: 119–48.
Winckler, Edwin A. 1984. "Institutionalization and Participation on Tai-

wan: From Hard to Soft Authoritarianism?" *China Quarterly* 99: 481–99.

Wong, Christine. 1985. "Economic Performance." In Steven M. Goldstein, ed., *China Briefing, 1984*. Boulder, Colo.: Westview Press.

Wong, John. 1992. "Implications of the Growth Trends in Mainland China's Grain Production." *Issues and Studies* 28 (1): 39–52.

World Bank. 1985. *China: Long-Term Development Issues and Options*. Baltimore, Md.: Johns Hopkins University Press.

Wu An-chia. 1990. "Chung-kung shih-san-chieh wu-chung ch'uen-hui hou te cheng-chih hsing-shih" (The political situation after the CCP's Fifth Plenum of the Thirteenth Central Committee). *Mainland China Studies* 32 (7): 5–10.

Wu, Jinglian, and Bruce L. Reynolds. 1987. "Choosing a Strategy for China's Economic Reform." Paper presented at the annual meeting of the American Economic Association, Chicago.

Wu, Jinglian, and Zhao Renwei. 1987. "The Dual Pricing System in China's Industry." *Journal of Comparative Economics* 11 (3): 309–18.

Wu Yuan-li. 1987. *Chung-kung kuo-chi ching-chi cheng-ts'e* (The PRC's international economic policy). Taipei: Yu-Shih.

Wu, Yu-Shan. 1989. "Marketization of Politics: The Taiwan Experience." *Asian Survey* 24 (4): 382–400.

———. 1990. "The Linkage Between Economic and Political Reform in the Socialist Countries: A Supply-Side Explanation." *Annals* 507: 91–102.

———. 1993. "Liang-chi t'i-hsi te peng-chieh yu chung-kung te wai-chiao cheng-ts'e" (The collapse of the bipolar system and the PRC's foreign policy). Paper presented at the Twentieth Sino-Japanese Conference on Mainland China, Tokyo.

Yahuda, Michael. 1979. "Political Generations in China." *China Quarterly* 80: 793–805.

Yakhot, I. 1979. "The Marxian Notion of Ideology." *Studies in Soviet Thought* 20 (1): 43–49.

Yan, Hongchang. 1989. "Masters of the Land." *China Reconstructs* 38 (2): 11–13.

Yang Ai-Li. 1989. "Sun Yun-Suan chuan" (The biography of Sun Yun-Suan). *Commonwealth* 92: 86–132.

Ye, Meng-Hua. 1991. "The Privatization of State-Owned Enterprises in Eastern European Countries." *Papers of the Center for Modern China*, no. 14.

Yeh, Chang-mei. 1989. "The Three Kinds of Foreign-Invested Enterprises in Mainland China." *Issues and Studies* 25 (3): 58–79.

Ying I-Chang. 1982. "Ts'ung li-shih kuan-tien k'an ching-chi t'iao-cheng" (Economic readjustment in a historical perspective). Paper presented at the Eleventh Sino-American Conference on Mainland China, Institute of International Relations, Taipei.

Young, G. David. 1989. "Hungary: Debt Versus Reform." *The World Today* 45 (10): 171–75.

Yu, Yu-lin. 1988. "Why Should Chao Emphasize Coastal Economic Development?" *Issues and Studies* 24 (12): 1–4.

Zhao, Renwei. 1988. "On the Current Economic Structural Reform in

China." Paper presented at the Conference on Chinese Economic Relations, University of California, Berkeley.

Zhao, Suisheng. 1990. "The Feeble Political Capacity of a Strong One-Party Regime: An Institutional Approach Toward the Formulation and Implementation of Economic Policy in Post-Mao Mainland China (Part One)." *Issues and Studies* 26 (1): 47–80.

Zhao, Ziyang. 1987. "Advance Along the Road of Socialism with Chinese Characteristics." In *Thirteenth National Congress of the Communist Party of China*. Beijing: *Beijing Review*.

Zhou, Xiaochuan. 1988. "The Price Reform in China: Solved and Unsolved Problems." Paper presented at the Fourth Economic Symposium of Chinese Young Economists, University of California, Berkeley.

Zweig, David. 1990. "Evaluating China's Rural Policies: 1949–1989." *The Fletcher Forum* 14 (1): 18–29.

Index

In this index an "f" after a number indicates a separate reference on the next page, and an "ff" indicates separate references on the next two pages. A continuous discussion over two or more pages is indicated by a span of page numbers, e.g., "57–59." *Passim* is used for a cluster of references in close but not consecutive sequence.

Aczel, Gyorgy, 67, 72
Administrative guidance, 168
Agency for International
  Development (AID), 164–65,
  172, 253n63
Agricultural reform, 12–13,
  200–203; in Hungary, 12, 48f,
  55f, 200, 202, 227nn11–14;
  in ROC, 12, 147–55, 200ff,
  246nn11–14, 247nn15–18, 20–
  22; in Soviet Union, 12, 95–104
  passim, 200ff, 235n16, 237n29;
  in PRC, 13, 19, 55–56, 80, 95–
  102, 147–55 *passim*, 201ff,
  227nn13–14
Akhmatova, Anna, 86
Alliance policy, 50–51
Anti–Bourgeois Liberalization
  Movement, 28, 52, 94, 235nn14–
  15
Anti-Communist uprising, in
  Hungary, 53, 200
Anti–Spiritual Pollution
  Campaign, 52, 160, 235n14
Authoritarianism, political, 11,
  222n18

Bai Hua, 52
Bankruptcy, in PRC, 62, 77
"Beijing University school" (Beida
  Xuepai), 25, 255n69
"Bird cage economy," 187
Borodin, Mikhail, 245n4
Brezhnev, Leonid, 184
Brus, Wlodzimierz, 225n4
Budget constraint: soft, 23, 29, 33f,
  69, 73, 181–82; hard, 100, 164,
  181, 236n24
Bukharin, Nikolay, 85f, 91f, 112,
  221n14, 232n3, 237n29, 239n39;
  Bukharinism, 2, 237n29
Bulgaria, 226n10

Capitalism, 4, 7, 8, 220n8. *See also*
  Special Economic Zones (SEZs);
  State capitalism
Case studies, 12–15, 200ff
Chao, T. C., 167
Ch'en Ch'eng, 148, 157, 172, 186,
  246n11, 254n67
Chen Yun, 30, 94, 128, 187
Chiang Kai-shek, 12, 141–46
  passim, 172, 186, 245n6

Library of Congress Cataloging-in-Publication Data

Wu, Yu-Shan.
  Comparative economic transformations : mainland China, Hungary,
the Soviet Union, and Taiwan / Yu-Shan Wu.
      p.   cm.
  ISBN 0-8047-2388-5
    1. China—Economic policy—1976–   2. China—Economic
conditions—1976–   3. Right of property—China.   4. Mixed economy—
China.   5. Hungary—Economic policy.   6. Soviet Union—Economic
policy—1917–1928.   7. Taiwan—Economic policy—1945–1975.
8. Comparative economics.   I. Title.
  HC427.92.W853   1994
  338.9—dc20   94-20504
                                                          CIP

⊗ This book is printed on acid-free paper.